Financial Acronyms

Financial Education Is Your Best Investment

I0480404

Published March 06, 2019

Revision 2.1

Financial Terms Dictionary

Copyright And Trademark Notices

Limits of Liability and Disclaimer of Warranties

The materials in this book are provided "as is" and without warranties of any kind either express or implied. The Author disclaims all warranties, express or implied, including, but not limited to, implied warranties of merchantability and fitness for a particular purpose.

The Author does not warrant that defects will be corrected, or that that the site or the server that makes this eBook available are free of viruses or other harmful components. The Author does not warrant or make any representations regarding the use or the results of the use of the materials in this book in terms of their correctness, accuracy, reliability, or otherwise. Applicable law may not allow the exclusion of implied warranties, so the above exclusion may not apply to you.

Under no circumstances, including, but not limited to, negligence, shall the Author be liable for any special or consequential damages that result from the use of, or the inability to use this eBook, even if the Author or his authorized representative has been advised of the possibility of such damages.

Applicable law may not allow the limitation or exclusion of liability or incidental or consequential damages, so the above limitation or exclusion may not apply to you. In no event shall the Author's total liability to you for all damages, losses, and causes of action (whether in contract, tort, including but not limited to, negligence or otherwise) exceed the amount paid by you, if any, for this eBook.

Facts and information are believed to be accurate at the time they were placed in this book. All data provided in this book is to be used for information purposes only. The information contained within is not intended to provide specific legal, financial or tax advice, or any other advice whatsoever, for any individual or company and should not be relied upon in that regard. The services described are only offered in jurisdictions where they may be legally offered. Information provided is not all-inclusive and is limited to information that is made available and such information should not be relied upon as all-inclusive or accurate.

You are advised to do your own due diligence when it comes to making business decisions and should use caution and seek the advice of qualified professionals. You should check with your accountant, lawyer, or professional advisor, before acting on this or any information. You may not consider any examples, documents, or other content in this eBook or otherwise provided by the Author to be the equivalent of professional advice.

The Author assumes no responsibility for any losses or damages resulting from your use of any link, information, or opportunity contained in this book or within any other information disclosed by the author in any form whatsoever.

About the Author

Thomas Herold is a successful entrepreneur, mediator, author, and personal development coach. He published over 20 books with over 200,000 copies distributed worldwide and the founder of seven online businesses.

For over ten years Thomas Herold has studied the monetary system and has experienced some profound insights on how money and wealth are related. After three years of successful investing in silver, he released 'Building Wealth with Silver - How to Profit From The Biggest Wealth Transfer in History' in 2012. One of the first books that illustrate in a remarkable, simple way the monetary system and its consequences.

He is the founder and CEO of the 'Financial Terms Dictionary' book series and website, which explains in detail and comprehensive form over 1000 financial terms. In his financial book series, he informs in detail and with practical examples all aspects of the financial sector. His educational materials are designed to help people get started with financial education.

In his 2018 released book 'The Money Deception', Mr. Herold provides the most sophisticated insight and shocking details about the current monetary system. Never before has the massive manipulation of money caused so much economic inequality in the world. In spite of these frightening facts, 'The Money Deception' also provides remarkable and simple solutions to create abundance for all people, and it's a must read if you want to survive the global monetary transformation that's underway right now.

For more information please visit:

Financial Terms Dictionary

Financial Dictionary Series

There are 12 books in this financial terms series available. Click the link below to see an overview and available formats on Amazon.

Thomas Herold Author page on Amazon

Please leave your review on Amazon:

This book is self-published and the author does not have a contract with one of the five largest publishers, which are able to support the author's work with advertising. If you like this book, please consider leaving a solid 5-star review on Amazon.

Table Of Contents

401(k) Plan

401k retirement plans are specific kinds of accounts that the government established to help individuals to plan and save for retirement. Individuals fund these accounts using pre-taxed dollars from payrolls.

People invest money in these accounts into several different types of investments. These include stocks, mutual funds, and bonds. Gains earned in the account include dividends, capital gains, and interest. These gains do not get taxed until the owners withdraw the funds.

The name of the 401k comes from the portion of Internal Revenue Service Code which pertains to it. This vehicle for saving for retirement began in 1981 when an act of Congress created it.

There are a number of benefits to 401k accounts that recommend them to individuals. Five of these include tax benefits, flexibility of investments, employer matching programs, loan abilities, and portability.

The advantageous tax benefits are one of the main reasons that 401k plans are so popular. Money contributed does not become taxable until individuals withdraw it. Similarly gains accrued in the account are also tax-deferred. Over several decades, this makes a significant difference in the amount of money that people can save.

Investments that the IRS allows in these 401k retirement plans provide some flexibility. Those who do not want to take on much risk can choose to put more of their funds into shorter term bonds which are lower risk. Others who are more concerned with developing wealth over the long term can put a larger percentage of the money into equities like stocks and mutual funds. Company stock can also be acquired at a discount with many employers.

A tremendous edge that these 401k retirement plans provide their owners is the employer match feature. A great number of employers match their employees' contributions as a company benefit. This is done on a percentage basis. Newer employees may receive a 25% of contributions match, while employees who have been at a company longer may receive 50% or even 100% matches. Matches are only made on a certain maximum percentage of income that an employee contributes. This is the closest thing to free money a person can obtain at work.

Loan abilities from 401k retirements are a helpful feature for individuals in times of need. When people find themselves needing money with no other place to turn, the government permits them to obtain 401k loans from the plan. The plan administrator has to approve it as well. Loans from 401k plans are not taxed or penalized so long as they are repaid according to the repayment schedule and terms.

There are no restrictions on the uses of such loans. Some employers have minimum amounts that can be borrowed of $1,000 and a maximum number of loans an employee can take at a time. Sometimes employees will have to get their spouse's written consent before the company will issue the loan.

There are limits on the amount of a balance that can be borrowed. This is typically as much as 50% of the vested balance to no more than $50,000. When an employer will not allow an employee to take out a loan against the plan, hardship withdrawals can be requested. These are taxed and also penalized at a 10% rate.

Portability means the 401k retirement plan can go with the employees as they change jobs. Investors have four different choices for their 401k plan when they move to another company. They can choose to leave the plan with the old employer and pay any administration fees for the account staying there. They might instead do a rollover of their account to the new employer's 401k retirement plan.

A third option is to convert the 401k retirement plan into an Individual Retirement Account. Finally they might decide to close the 401k and receive the proceeds in cash. This would mean all money would be subject to taxes and the 10% penalty fee.

403(b) Plan

403(b) plans were created for employees of schools, churches, and tax exempt organizations. Individuals who are eligible may establish and maintain their own 403(b) accounts. Their employers can and often do make contributions to the employees' accounts. Individuals are able to open one of three different types of 403(b)s.

The first is an annuity plan that an insurance company establishes. These types of plans are sometimes called TDAs tax deferred annuities or TSAs tax sheltered annuities. A second plan type is an account which a retirement custodian offers and manages. With these 403(b)s, the account holders may only choose from mutual funds and regulated investment companies that the custodian allows. The final type is a retirement income account. These accounts accept a combination of mutual funds or annuities for the investment choices.

Employers have some control over these accounts. They are able to decide which financial institution will hold the employees' 403(b) accounts. This determines the kind of plan that the employees are able to set up and fund. Employers receive several advantages from choosing to offer a 403(b).

The benefits which they get to offer their employees are worthwhile. This helps to ensure valuable employees stay with the organization. They also enjoy sharing the funding costs between themselves and their employees. Employers may also choose for the 403(b) to only accept employee contributions if they do not wish to participate financially in the account.

Employees also experience several benefits from these types of retirement vehicles. They may contribute tax deferred dollars from their income. They may also contribute taxed dollars to the accounts. In these Roth 403(b)s, all of their earnings accrue tax free for the entire life of the account. Deferred tax payments until retirement typically allow for the employees to pay fewer taxes as they are often in a more advantageous tax bracket at retirement point. Employees may also obtain loans from their 403(b) accounts as they need them.

A variety of non profit organizations may choose to establish such a 403(b) plan for their employees. This includes any 501(c)(3) tax exempt organization, co-op hospital service organizations, public school systems, ministers at churches, Native American public school systems, and (USUHS) Uniformed Services for the University of the Health Sciences.

Such 403(b) plans can obtain a variety of contribution types. Employees may have elective deferral contributions taken out of each paycheck. These are taken out in a pretax dollars arrangement. Employees also have the ability to contribute taxed dollars to the accounts. They have these deducted from their payrolls as well.

Employers may also choose to make contributions which are either discretionary or fixed amounts as they desire. Employees and employers may make contributions to Roth 403(b) accounts. These 403(b) accounts may also receive any combination of the previously mentioned contribution types, which demonstrates their flexibility.

Employees have generous annual contribution limits with these plans. In 2016, they may contribute up to $18,000 (or $24,000 if they are over 50 years old and catching up on contributions for retirement). For 2016, employers may also deposit as much as $53,000 (up to 100% of the employee compensation) as an annual contribution.

Regarding distributions, the rules are comparable to the other types of retirement savings vehicles. Distributions of deferred taxed dollars become taxable like regular income when the employee receives them. If these are taken before the employee turns 59 ½, then the withdrawn dollars are assessed the standard 10% penalty for early withdrawals. There are some exceptions to this penalty for which an employee may qualify. One of these exceptions is if the employee terminates the job even before reaching the age of retirement.

Adjustable Rate Mortgage (ARM)

Adjustable Rate Mortgages, also known by their acronym ARM's, are those mortgages whose interest rates change from time to time. These changes commonly occur based on an index. As a result of changing interest rates, payments will rise and fall along with them.

Adjustable Rate Mortgages involve a number of different elements. These include margins, indexes, discounts, negative amortization, caps on payments and rates, recalculating of your loan, and payment options. When considering an adjustable rate mortgage, you should always understand both the most that your monthly payments might go up, as well as your ability to make these higher payments in the future.

Initial payments and rates are important to understand with these ARM's. They stay in effect for only certain time frames that run from merely a month to as long as five years or longer. With some of these ARM's, these initial payments and rates will vary tremendously from those that are in effect later in the life of the loan. Your payments and rates can change significantly even when interest rates remain level. A way to determine how much this will vary on a particular ARM loan is to compare the annual percentage rate and the initial rate. Should this APR prove to be much greater than the initial rate, then likely the payments and rates will similarly turn out to be significantly greater when the loan adjusts.

It is important to understand that the majority of Adjustable Rate Mortgages' monthly payments and interest rates will vary by the month, the quarter, the year, the three year period, and the five year time frame. The time between these changes in rate is referred to as the adjustment period. Loans that feature one year periods are called one year ARM's, as an example.

These Adjustable Rate Mortgages' interest rates are comprised of two portions of index and margin. The index actually follows interest rates themselves. Your payments are impacted by limits on how far the rate can rise or fall. As the index rises, so will your interest rates and payments generally. As the index declines, your monthly payments could similarly fall, assuming that your ARM is one that adjusts down. ARM rates can be based on a number of different indexes, including LIBOR the London Interbank Offered rate, COFI the Cost of Funds Index, and a CMT one year constant maturity Treasury security. Other lenders use their own proprietary model.

Margin proves to be the premium to the rate that a lender itself adds. This is commonly a couple of percentage points that are added directly to the index rate amount. These amounts vary from one lender to the next, and are commonly fixed during the loan term. The fully indexed rate is comprised of index plus margin. When the loan's initial rate turns out to be lower than the fully indexed rate, this is referred to as a discounted index rate. So an index that sat at five percent and had a three percent margin tacked on would be a fully indexed rate of eight percent.

Adjusted Gross Income (AGI)

Adjusted Gross Income (AGI) refers to a means of calculating income off of an individual's actual gross income. People use this figure in order to determine the amount of their income which the Internal Revenue Service will subject to tax assessment. It is ultimately the United States tax code which creates this AGI figure. This number should never be confused with the actual gross income. Gross income is merely the total amount of all money individuals realize and earn over a year long period.

The Adjusted Gross Income considers a range of deductions which it subtracts from the individuals in question's actual gross incomes. The result is the basis off of which the person's individual income taxes become calculated at the end of the tax year. Where tax activities and the Internal Revenue Service are concerned, this figure generally proves to be more useful than gross income alone.

All relevant deductions that apply to gross income and turn it into Adjusted Gross Income come from above the line deductions. This simply signifies that they must be reflected on the tax calculations ahead of dependents, military service, and other exemptions. There are a number of such deductions which count in the compiling of this AGI. Among the best known and most common are the following: contributions to retirement plans, business expenses which are not reimbursed, medical expenses, losses from property sales, and alimony or child support.

To calculate up individuals' Adjusted Gross Income, it is first necessary to figure up all reported income in the year being considered. Additional taxable income sources also have to be added in to the total. This includes any compensation for unemployment, property sales' profits, Social Security payments, pensions, and other sources of income that did not become reported on the tax return. Once this complete earnings' total has been figured up, it is necessary to subtract out all relevant deductions to come up with the appropriate AGI.

The Internal Revenue Service makes it easier to come up with all of the potential deductions pertaining to gross income by going to their IRS website. Here they provide a rules list for all potential deductions' requirements. Some of these prove to be extremely specific. This is why people have to carefully study the tax code in order to be certain of their eligibility for any and all deductions that they take.

Once individuals have figured out their AGI, they are able to then add in the government's normal federal tax deductions to finish calculating their taxable income. For some tax payers, this will mean itemizing out their various expenses to come up with the itemized deductions alternatively. Sometimes this works out better for taxpayers. One thing that a tax payer must be careful to never do is to not confuse their Adjusted Gross Income with their MAGI modified adjusted gross income.

In fact the modified adjusted gross income is supposed to be totally separate from the AGI. It is utilized to figure out the deductible dollar amount from the person's IRA individual retirement account. It will also be employed to decide if the private parties are eligible for specific tax deductions. In order to figure up this MAGI, tax payers have to add back in some items like foreign housing deductions, foreign earned income, IRA contribution deductions, higher education cost deductions, and student loan deductions.

In many cases, the MAGI is often much the same as the AGI for a given individual. Yet it is important to be aware that even tiny differences can significantly impact the overall tax return for an individual. In particular, such variances will impact a person's eligibility to receive particular benefits allowed under the ACA Affordable Care Act.

American Bankers Association (ABA)

The American Bankers Association, or ABA, is a trade association of the U.S. banks large and small conveniently located in Washington, D.C. This powerful lobbying organization hails back to 1875 when it was established by several bankers.

Today, the ABA has grown to represent banks of all stripes and sizes and encompasses more than 95% of all bank assets in the nation. This means that money center banks, regional banks, community thrift banks, mutual savings banks, savings and loans associations, trust companies, and large commercial banks all count the ABA as their voice before the federal government. The typical sized member bank boasts around $250 million in assets.

This trade and industry group proves to be the biggest banking trade association by far within the U.S. today. It is also known as the biggest financial trade group anywhere in the United States. The American Bankers Association thrives and prospers because of its impressive range of both services and products it delivers to member institutions. This includes help in such diverse industry segments as insurance, staff training and education, asset management, capital management, consulting, and risk-compliance endeavors.

Probably the most famous creation of the American Bankers Association remains the all important nine digit routing numbers which designate all banks everywhere within the U.S. These routing numbers are pictured on every single check and are also necessary identification for wire transfer transactions. The ABA can truthfully boast that it created this system over a hundred years ago, way back in 1910.

Today's American Bankers Association keeps extremely busy lobbying with Congress for its banking members and their common interests. The group has concentrated its efforts in the last several years on banning the so-called unfair tax exempt status enjoyed by credit unions. Credit unions originally catered to selective and tiny targeted memberships, as with a particular company's own employees. This did not threaten commercial banks and other similar financial institutions.

More recently though, to bank's undying enmity and impotency in the face of this real and rising threat, credit unions found the means to vastly expand their roles of membership and possible pools of customers. It is no exaggeration to state that numerous credit unions can boast over $1 billion in assets nowadays. This makes them as big as some of the larger and even too big to fail banks.

The ABA strenuously maintains that such credit unions have morphed into a structure and operations which are so similar to the traditional commercial banks that they no longer deserve this special favor of tax exempt status. It was actually the infamous Panic of 1873 that gave rise to the initial founding of the American Bankers Association. A banker James Howenstein of St. Louis, Missouri, one day discovered that he was up against a proverbial wall in his bank. He only possessed several hundred dollars in cash against his millions of deposits he needed to return back to panicking depositors.

By falling back on assistance and knowledge willingly provided by his peers in the banking business via rapid and frequent correspondence, Mr. Howenstein escaped from his business-threatening dilemma to survive. He then knew that he had been saved by this informal network and fraternal organization of fellow bankers and wanted to expand on this successful construct.

To this effect, Mr. Hownestein convened his first meeting of 17 different bankers on May 24, 1875 in New York City. Together they made plans for an initial American Bankers Association convention that did successfully take place on July 20, 1875 in Saratoga Springs, New York. Fully 349 different bankers who hailed from 31 states as well as the nation's capital attended.

Chief among the first endeavors of the ABA proved to be setting up the American Institute of Banking. They founded this in 1903 in order to offer certificates and examinations as professional banking education in their local branch chapters. This AIB offered interested participants a different way to pursue a banking career than by going to university for a degree in law and finance.

American Institute of Banking (AIB)

The American Institute of Banking (AIB) is a venerable educational and training institution for the United States based banking industry which was established by the American Bankers Association (ABA) back in 1907.

This AIB offers continuing training and a full range of banking career education for parties who are interested in the banking field or who are already participants within it. Over 150,000 existing bankers take part in their extensive range of continuing educational programs every year. As such, the AIB is the definitive and universally recognized continuing education curriculum for those within the fields of financial services.

American Institute of Banking programs were created to boost, refresh, and improve the job skills and knowledge base of those working in or seeking to work within the financial services industry. Completing some of these degreed programs can provide a path to AIB certificates and even diplomas which are universally recognized within the banking realm. They can also help with obtaining required professional licenses.

These programs encompass more than the traditional open enrollment programs provided throughout all of the various states. The AIB of today also offers convenient digital format purchase of its services and products, training provided in-house and Internet-based provision of online classes and coursework, tests, and study teams classes. These are only a few of the many options for its in-depth and extensive industry-wide programs.

The American Institute of Banking falls under the umbrella of the founder American Bankers Association. This means that all AIB programs and courses are provided through the local area branches of the ABA and its providers. Among its many classes and programs are core courses in such fields as business fundamentals; general banking; consumer, commercial, and mortgage lending; retail banking; asset management; compliance issues; and marketing.

In-bank branch training utilizes instructions and resources to offer specifically tailored delivery of the various ABA training regimens within a banker's own branch. It might also be offered off site in the immediate area, depending on demand.

In recent years, the American Institute of Banking has moved aggressively into the digital age with its instructional offerings. Thanks to this decision, they now offer Internet-based online versions of their best selling, traditional instructor-driven AIB courses. They provide extensive information, schedules, and enrollment forms for this mode of education on their website.

The American Institute of Banking offers certificate programs which it tailored to help participants boost their knowledge of and performance in banking utilizing course curriculum which has been bank tested for a specific bank focus. These courses run the gamut across a variety of skill sets and content and each complement the other. Certificate-driven courses are shorter in length and typically run from one to three weeks in total duration.

The American Institute of Banking also provides full-scale banking diplomas. These are awarded for successfully completing both required and elective option courses. Courses which provide at least two hours of credit award traditional grade levels of A, B, C, or D. In order for courses to count towards one of the AIB diplomas, students must receive a C or higher overall average. One course can be utilized towards one or multiple certificates or diplomas.

The ABA has recently decided to roll up the separately branded AIB into its own proprietary programs. All American Institute of Banking courses are now provided as a division of ABA Training. These courses, whether offered in person or online, generally meet the requirements mandated by the ICB Institute of Certified Bankers for continuing education credits and appropriate exams. The ABA online training was designed specifically to be cost affordable and flexible. This is why they aim to constantly update the information and learning experienced which is now able to be accessed at any time, from any place.

American International Group (AIG)

American International Group is one of the largest insurance companies in the world. It boasts over 90 million customers living in over 100 countries around the globe. The company has provided risk management and insurance services for customers for almost a hundred years.

Today the company is changing to try to meet their clients' needs better. They are simplifying the corporate structure to be able to work more directly with their customers, to provide value and help quicker and with greater efficiency, and to offer better transparency. They are striving for greater focus, leaner operations, and higher profits.

AIG proves to be the largest commercial insurance company for both the United States and Canada. They rank as biggest nonlife insurance operation in the world based on market capitalization. Fully 98% of Fortune 500 companies, 90% of Fortune Global 500 corporations, and 96% of Fortune 1000 Companies carry their insurance products or services.

American International Group began life as the brain child and insurance project of American Cornelius Vander Starr in 1919. He established it as the AAU American Asiatic Underwriters general insurance company in Shanghai at this time. This outfit expanded throughout China and then around the world.

Each new culture and market they encountered helped them to broaden their concept of risk and the means of helping to manage it for their customers. As World War II was breaking out, the company wisely relocated its headquarters from Shanghai in China to New York City. The company continued to expand successfully throughout Latin America, Asia, Africa, and Europe through 2008.

When the financial crisis erupted in the United States in 2008, the U.S. government had to bail out the company to save it from collapse. Edward M. Liddy was appointed as Chairman of AIG in order to navigate it through the chaotic and troubled operating environment and company era. By 2012, AIG had succeeded in restructuring the company. They also repaid all of the aid and loans from the U.S. government with profits that year, re-launched their damaged brand, and restored their reputation.

AIG boasts a number of impressive accomplishments in the intervening years since emerging from the financial crisis. They have once again become a market leader for aiding families in safeguarding their financial futures. They are the number one ranked fixed rate deferred annuity providers. AIG is among the biggest sellers of group retirement plans as well. In a number of countries throughout the globe, the outfit is a personal insurance policy leader. Nearly half of the wealthiest Americans (as measured by the Forbes 400 Richest Americans) choose AIG for their nonlife insurance needs.

AIG has won and continues to win numerous awards for their performance, service, and products. In 2016 they were honored with the top spot at the Business Insurance Innovation Awards. This is a position that they or one of their companies have successfully held for 7 years in a row. They won three honors at the Travvy Awards in 2016. They also earned a third year in a row place on the Diversity Inc. 25 Noteworthy Companies for Diversity.

AIG is also pioneering technology and data science techniques for helping to ensure their clients are better informed and safer. They have an unrivaled amount of information and expertise that they utilize to provide insights into a wide variety of sectors around the globe. These enable them to help stop losses and reap better results for the company and its customers. AIG routinely shares the exploration results of this information with governments, researchers, non government organizations, and experts in various fields.

American Stock Exchange (AMEX)

The AMEX is the acronym for the American Stock Exchange. This exchange proves to be the third biggest such stock market in all of the United States when trading volume is considered, after the NYSE and the NASDAQ national exchanges. Located in the American financial center of New York, the AMEX carries around ten percent of every security that is listed within the United States. In the past, it had a much larger market share of traded securities.

The origins of the AMEX lie before it was called the American Stock Exchange. In 1953, the New York Curb Exchange became known as the AMEX. This exchange proved to be a mutual organization that the members owned. In decades past, the American Stock Exchange had an important position as a major competitor for the New York Stock Exchange. This role gradually fell to the rising NASDAQ stock exchange.

Back on the seventeenth of January in 2008, the NYSE Euronext exchange announced its intentions to buy out the American Stock Exchange in consideration of $260 million in NYSE stock. They completed the transaction on the first of October in 2008. NYSE originally intended to integrate the AMEX exchange into its Alternext European small cap exchange. They first renamed it the NYSE Alternext U.S. By March of 2009, NYSE had scrapped this plan and renamed it the NYSE Amex Equities exchange.

The overwhelming majority of AMEX trading these days is done in small cap company stocks, derivatives, and exchange traded funds. These are niches that the AMEX exchange carved out and maintained for itself despite the rising allure of the newer NASDAQ in the 1990's. The AMEX observes regular trading session hours running from 9:30 in the morning to 4:00 in the afternoon on Monday through Friday. The exchange is closed on Saturdays, Sundays, and all holidays that the exchange announces in advance.

Annual Percentage Rate (APR)

The annual percentage rate, or APR, is the actual interest rate that a loan charges each year. This single percentage number is truthfully used to represent the literal annual expense of using money over the life span of a given loan. Annual percentage rate not only covers interest charged, but can also be comprised of extra costs or fees that are attached to a given loan transaction.

Credit cards and loans commonly offer differing explanations for transaction fees, the structure of their interest rates, and any late fees that are assessed. The annual percentage rate provides an easy to understand formula for expressing to borrowers the real and actual percentage number of fees and interest so that they can measure these up against the rates that other possible lenders will charge them.

Annual percentage rate can include many different elements besides interest. With a nominal APR, it simply involves the rate of a given payment period multiplied out to the exact numbers of payment periods existing in a year. The effective APR is often referred to as the mathematically true rate of interest for a given year. Effective APR's are commonly the fees charged plus the rate of compound interest.

On a home mortgage, effective annual percentage rates could factor in Private Mortgage Insurance, discount points, and even processing costs. Some hidden fees do not make their ways into an effective APR number. Because of this, you should always read the fine print surrounding an APR and the costs associated with a mortgage or loan. As an example of how an effective APR can be deceptive with mortgages, the one time fees that are charged in the front of a mortgage are commonly assumed to be divided over a loan's long repayment period. If you only utilize the loan for a short time frame, then the APR number will be thrown off by this. An effective APR on a mortgage might look lower than it actually is when the loan will be paid off significantly earlier than the term of the loan.

The government created the concept of annual percentage rate to stop loan companies and credit cards issuers from deceiving consumers with fancy expressions of interest charges and fees. The law requires that all loan issuers and credit card companies have to demonstrate this annual percentage rate to all customers. This is so the consumers will obtain a fair comprehension of the true rates that are associated with their particular transactions. While credit card companies are in fact permitted to promote their monthly basis of interest rates, they still have to clearly show the actual annual percentage rate to their customers in advance of a contract or agreement being signed by the consumer.

Annual percentage rate is sometimes confused with annual percentage yield. This can be vastly different from the APR. Annual percentage yield includes calculations of compounded interest in its numbers.

Annual Percentage Yield (APY)

APY describes the amount of compound interest which individuals or businesses will earn in a given year (or longer time period). Investments in money market accounts, savings accounts, and CD Certificates of Deposit all pay out such interest. It is the annual percentage yield that demonstrates precisely the amount in interest individuals will receive. This is helpful for people or businesses trying to ascertain which investments and banks offer superior returns by comparing and contrasting their real yields. In general, higher Annual Percentage Yields are better to have (unless one is comparing interest on credit card debts).

This APY is practical to understand and measure simply because it considers compound interest and the miracle of compounding within any account. Simple interest rates do not do this. Compounding is simply earning interest on interest that has already accrued and been paid. It signifies that individuals are gaining a greater amount in interest than the corresponding interest rate literally indicates.

It is always a good idea to consider a real world example for clarification purposes. If Fred deposits $10,000 into a particular savings account that provides a two percent yearly interest rate, then at the end of that first year Fred will have $10,200. This assumes that the interest is paid one time per year. If the bank were to figure up and pay out the interest on a daily basis, it would increase the amount to $10,202. The extra $2 may seem small, but given a longer time frame of from 10 to 30 years, this amount can add up, particularly if larger deposits are involved.

APY should never be confused with APR. They have some similarities, but APR does not consider compounding. It is once again a simpler means of computing interest. Credit card loans are an area where it is important to understand the differences between annual percentage rate and annual percentage yield. When people carry a balance, they will be paying higher APY's then the APR the firm actually quotes. This is because interest is assessed monthly, which means that interest on the interest will be computed on each following month.

The key to obtaining a better APY on investments and savings accounts lies in getting as frequent a compounding period as possible. Quarterly compounding is better than annually, yet daily is the most superior form of compounding possible. This means that as individuals are looking to increase their APY's personally, it is important to have the money compounding as frequently as they can practically achieve.

When two CD Certificates of Deposit pay out the same rate, it is best to select that one which actually pays out both more frequently and also boasts the greater APY. With CD's, the interest payments become automatically reinvested. More frequent reinvestment is always better. This will help any individual or business to earn a greater amount of interest on the interest payments already earned and paid out.

Calculating the annual percentage yield is not an easy task. Business calculators as well as computer algorithms mostly do it for people nowadays. The simplest way to find the APY for a given account is to plug in the information including the initial deposit, compounding frequency period, interest rate, and amount of overall time for the period considered. These smart calculators will then tell you both the effective annual percentage yield as well as the ending balance on the hypothetical account at the end of the given time period.

Asset Backed Security (ABS)

An Asset Backed Security is also known by its acronym ABS. This refers to a type of financial security. These are commonly backed up using either a lease, a loan, or receivables against company assets (which would not include either mortgage backed securities or real estate). With the world of investing, such ABS provide other choices for those who wish to invest in something other than common corporate debt issues.

It is interesting to note that these Asset Backed Securities are more or less identical to MBS Mortgage Backed Securities. The primary difference lies in the securities which back the two financial instruments. With the ABS, they can include credit card debt, leases, loans, royalties, and even the receivables of the company issuing the debt. Yet these mortgage based securities may never underlie the ABS.

Such an Asset Backed Security delivers to the issuer of the security a means of creating more cash for the business. It allows yield hungry investors the chance to sink their money into a great range of assets which generate income. It is worth noting that most of these underlying assets will not be liquid. This means that they can not be readily sold as stand alone assets. Yet in pooling such assets into a single conglomeration, a financial security may be created. This is done in the process referred to as securitization. This permits the asset owner to employ them in a marketable fashion.

Among the assets of such pools could be car loans, home equity loans, student loans, credit card receivables, or other anticipated cash flow items. The capacity of Asset Backed Security issuers to be creative should never be underestimated. There have even been ABS which were established utilizing the cash flow generated by movie release revenues, aircraft leases, creative works and other forms of royalty payments, and even solar energy photovoltaic revenue streams. Practically any scenario where cash is produced can be packaged up via securitization into an ABS.

It is often helpful to consider an example of this somewhat complicated Asset Backed Security topic. Consider the case of a fictitious firm Car Loans For Everybody. When individuals wish to borrow funds to purchase a car, Car Loans For Everybody will issue them the cash in a check. The individual will have to pay back the loan along with a specified interest amount at a certain time in monthly installments. It could be that Car Loans is so successful at making automobile loans that they deplete their cash reserves and can no longer issue additional loans. They have the ability to sell off their present book of loans to the fictitious investment firm Imperial Legends. Imperial Legends will then provide them with the cash they need to continue issuing new loans.

This is only where the securitization process begins. Imperial Legends investment firm would then arrange the bought out loans into a collection of parcels known in the business as tranches. A tranche effectively is a batch of loans that posses similar features. This would include interest rates, maturity dates, and anticipated rates of delinquency. After this, the Imperial Legends firm would offer new securities with features much like bonds in every tranche they created.

Finally, investors will buy such securities. They obtain the underlying cash flow out of the pool of car loans, less the administration fee, which Imperial Legends will keep to cover their costs and towards their profit.

There are three typical types of tranches in an Asset Backed Security. These are commonly referred to as Class A, Class B, and Class C. Senior most tranches belong to Class A. They are generally the biggest tranche. They will be structured in such a way as to obtain a decent investment rating so that they are easily marketable to investors.

With the Class B tranche, the credit quality will necessarily be lower. This inversely means that the yield will be higher than that of the senior tranche. Since the risk is greater, investors need to be compensated for their appropriate risk of defaults.

Class C tranche has the lowest credit rating of all. It could be the credit quality is so poor that investors will refuse to consider it altogether. In such cases, the ABS issuer then holds the Class C tranche, collects the incoming revenues every month, and absorbs any losses themselves.

Assets Under Management (AUM)

Assets under management (AUM) refer to the aggregate market value of all assets which an investment management firm or other financial institution (such as a bank) manages for its investor clients. The exact definition of AUM varies from one company to another. Each of them has their own distinctive proprietary formula for figuring up this all important statistic.

There are financial institutions, management companies, hedge funds, and banks that include the client bank deposits, cash, and mutual funds within their calculations. Still others choose to limit this figure to the funds which are under actual discretionary management using the sole choices of the fund manager. In this case, the investor gives over total investment responsibility and control to the management firm and fund manager in question.

Assets under management describe the amount of investment money which such an investment management firm actually controls. These investments are kept within a hedge fund or mutual fund. They are usually actively managed by a brokerage company, venture capital firm, or portfolio manager.

Assets under management express the amount of cash in the fund. It can also reveal the total amount of assets which they manage for their total client base. Alternatively it can be used to refer to the complete amount of assets the company manages for only one particular client. This would include all of the money which the manager is able to utilize in making transactions. As an example, if investors have placed $50,000 within their investment portfolios, the manager of the fund is allowed to purchase and sell whichever shares he so chooses by applying the funds of the investors without having to obtain their consent in advance.

The actual AUM fluctuates daily on every given market trading day. This depends on the investor money flow from one asset fund to another. The performance of assets also changes the Assets under management figure as well. The change in fund value or company investments will therefore alter the total AUM.

Every regulatory regime makes its own rules regarding how large a company must be to be closely regulated. Within the United States, after a given investment management firm possesses in excess of $30 million under management, they are required by law to register their company with the supreme oversight agency the SEC Securities and Exchange Commission. A given investor's AUM total will decide on what level of service they will receive from their brokerage firm or financial advisor. A great number of companies maintain minimum AUM amounts for certain kinds of investments. This has much to do with qualification levels of the investor in question. Some forms of investments also involve minimum purchase agreement requirements.

Figuring up the total Assets under management requires one of several calculations. With superior investment performance, the figure will rise in every case. As new customers join a firm or additional assets are obtained, this will also increase the AUM. The figure will drop as performance of the investments diminishes, with clients leaving the firm, redemptions, withdrawals, and fund closures. Because AUM includes all investor capital, it may also be comprised of the executives' assets with the firm.

The total currency amount of Assets under management matters immensely to a management company because of the management fees which they derive from these figures. It is true that an investment company garners a certain percentage in management fees based upon these assets. They are also able to employ their AUM numbers as a type of marketing tool to bring in still more investors and assets to the fund. Investors get a true feel for the size of the financial management company and its operations compared to the various competitors within the industry when they consider the figure. This still does not reveal full details about the potential of the investment company and its various investment choices and strategies.

Bank for International Settlements (BIS)

The Bank for International Settlements proves to be the oldest entity in the world for international financial organization. Central banks of the world established this bank on May 17 of 1930. Today 60 different central banks are members of this bank of central banks. Their economies represent 95% of all the combined Gross Domestic Product of the globe.

This Bank for International Settlements is also known by its acronym the BIS. It has an elegant mission. The goals of this organization are to help out the member central banks as they seek out financial and monetary stability, to serve as the bank for central banks, and to promote international financial cooperation in achieving stability. World headquarters for the BIS are located in Basel, Switzerland. The group also maintains two other important representative regional offices. These are in Hong Kong the Special Administrative Region of China for Asia-Pacific and in Mexico City for the Americas.

The two regional representative offices are hubs for the various BIS activities. They work to encourage cooperation between the region's central banks, supervisory authorities, and the BIS itself. This is why these offices promote data and information exchange, help to set up seminars and meetings, and provide information on the economic and financial research for the Americas and Asia.

Another important role of the Bank for International Settlements lies in its banking services. These two regional offices assist with delivering such services to the Americas and Asia-Pacific regions. Officers routinely visit the member central banks' reserve managers as part of this mission. In its Asian office it maintains a treasury dealing room for the region that offers daily trading functions for regional central banks.

The BIS set up its regional Representative Office of the Americas back in November of 2002 in Mexico City. The goal was to increase the Americas regional activities of the bank in better coordination with the headquarters office in Switzerland. They also established the Consultative Council for the Americas back in May of 2008. This advising committee helps the board of directors for the BIS to better understand the issues in the Americas region.

Members of this council include central bank governors from the Americas' region member central banks. This includes the U.S., Peru, Mexico, Colombia, Chile, Canada, Brazil, and Argentina.

The bank founded its increasingly important regional Asian office on July 11 of 1998 in Hong Kong as the Representative Office for Asia and the Pacific. It acts as an area forum for economic and monetary research that is useful for the central banks and provides the regional central banks with the settlement and exchange banking services.

Improving cooperation among the various member central banks in the Asian region is another important function. This office also maintains the Asian Consultative Council. The group is comprised of central bank governors from the Asia-Pacific region member central banks. Its members include Thailand, Singapore, the Philippines, New Zealand, Malaysia, Korea, Japan, Indonesia, India, Hong Kong, China, and Australia.

The Bank for International Settlements is different from other banks in the world in several important aspects. All of its customers are either international organizations or central banks. They do not open accounts for international companies or private individuals. The BIS does not offer any financial or advisory services to any investors or corporations. It also does not take in deposits from or make loans to parties that are not central banks or international organizations. The bank does make some of its research available at no cost to companies and members of the public.

Bitcoin Currency (BTC)

Bitcoin is the name of a new electronic currency. An unknown individual who called himself Satoshi Nakamoto created this currency in 2009. This world's first widespread virtual currency appeals to many individuals because there are no banks or governments involved in issuing, trading, spending, or processing the transactions. There are also no transaction fees involved. Owners do not have to provide their actual identity to use them.

Bitcoin users like that they are able to purchase goods and services completely anonymously. They also enjoy the inexpensive and simple to use international payment system. This exists because this currency is not heavily regulated nor tied to any single bank or nation. Small businesses tend to like Bitcoin since they do not have to pay any credit card usage fees.

Many speculators have purchased Bitcoins for investment. Booms and busts in this currency are all too common. Those who bought in to the crypto currency early made spectacular returns as the value skyrocketed with growing demand. Others lost fortunes as the price of the Bitcoins subsequently crashed in value.

There are several ways to obtain these Bitcoins. Users buy them on open marketplaces known as Bitcoin exchanges. Those who wish to have them can buy and sell it with a variety of different currencies. Mt. Gox was the largest Bitcoin marketplace until it spectacularly collapsed and went bankrupt. Many clients who held their Bitcoins at Mt. Gox lost most of their money there at the time.

Individuals also buy and sell Bitcoins by transferring them to each other and by paying with them. They can do this with their computers or mobile apps. This is much like sending cash with a digital service like PayPal.

A last way to obtain Bitcoins is by mining them. Mining is the way that individuals create new Bitcoins. They do this by utilizing computers to solve complicated math problems or puzzles. When such a puzzle is solved, 25 Bitcoins are awarded to the group which solves them.

Owners keep their Bitcoins in a digital wallet. This can be stored on a personal computer or in the cloud. A virtual wallet is much like an electronic bank account which permits owners to receive or send Bitcoins, to save their money, or to pay for their goods and services. These wallets do not receive the protection of FDIC insurance as do traditional bank accounts.

To users, Bitcoins are simply computer programs or mobile apps which give the owners the Bitcoin wallet. The payment system is easier to utilize than is a credit card or debit card purchase. An individual does not require a merchant account in order to receive the currency. All an individual has to do to make a payment is to put the payment amount and address of the recipient then click send.

An important fact about Bitcoin is that no one owns the actual network. Bitcoin users control the Bitcoin currency. Various developers work on the software to improve it. Users are able to decide which version or software they use it on, which prohibits developers from forcefully changing the operation. For the software to work properly, all Bitcoin users have to work with programs that abide by the same rules.

As with most new currencies Bitcoin is not without problems. When digital wallets are left in the cloud, some servers have been hacked and coins stolen. Bitcoin exchanges like Mt. Gox have failed. Other companies have disappeared with their clients' Bitcoins. When the wallets stay on a person's computer, they can be destroyed by viruses or accidentally deleted.

Increasing government regulation appears to be in the future of Bitcoin and other crypto currencies. Because of the anonymous nature of the currency, they have evolved into the preferred payment method for illegal activities such as drugs and smuggling. Governments are concerned about being able to trace these types of activities back to the users. They are also worried about not being able to tax transactions made in Bitcoin currency.

BNP Paribas

BNP Paribas is the largest French-based bank in the world. It has strong roots in the banking history of Europe. Today it remains one of the leading banks on the continent and Euro zone as well as an important international banking group. The group claims 189,000 employees around the world, of which the overwhelming majority of 146,610 are based in Europe.

It also has an extensive international network of branches and employees. The bank maintains 19,845 employees in America; 12,180 workers in Asia; 9,860 staff members in Africa; and 580 employees in the Middle East, as of 2015. BNP Paribas locations can be found in 75 different countries and territories around the world. For 2015, it boasted 42.9 billion euros of revenue and 6.7 billion euros of net profit.

The bank organizes itself along two main business lines. These are Retail Banking and Services (RBS) and the Corporate Institutional Banking (CIB) divisions. The Retail Banking & Services division covers its retail banking activities and specialized financial products and services in both France and the rest of the world. The company subdivides this into Domestic Markets and International Financial Services.

The group's Domestic Markets is comprised of the company's four retail banking networks found in the euro zone, as well as three specific lines of business. The retail bank networks are FRB French Retail Banking located in France, BNP Paribas Fortis in Belgium, BNL in Italy, and BGL BNP Paribas found in Luxembourg. Its three specific business lines are Arval the long term corporate leasing program, its Leasing Solutions that provide financing and rental services, and its Personal Investors that offer online brokerage services and savings vehicles.

Corporate clients also can access the business of Cash Management and Factoring. High Net Worth Individuals have the company's Wealth Management business as their private banking franchise within the domestic markets of the group. As of 2015, the Domestic Markets subdivision boasts over 15 million individual customers located in 27 countries. The bank also counts almost 1 million clients comprised of professional individuals, small businesses, and corporate entities. To service these numerous accounts, they devote the efforts of 68,000 employees in these over two dozen countries.

International Financial Services of the group handles the company's diversified business activities operating in over 60 countries. The group's Personal Finance provides credit to people residing in 30 countries. They deliver products and services via such major brands as Findomestic, Cofinoga, and Cetelem.

The IFS division also operates several other businesses. International Retail Banking covers the retail bank operations in another 15 non-euro zone nations like TEB in Turkey and Bank of the West in the U.S. BNP Paribas Cardif offers savings and insurance for assets, projects, and individuals living in 36 countries.

IFS rounds out its business lines with three specific asset management and private banking operations. These include the group's Wealth Management for private banking, their Investment Partners for asset management, and their BNP Paribas Real Estate for international real estate services. All of the International Financial Services businesses and lines together employ over 80,000 staff residing in over 60 countries.

The group's Corporate & Institutional Banking (CIB) prides itself on being a leading worldwide provider of financial products and services to its institutional and corporate clients around the globe. They group counts 13,000 of these clients in 57 countries throughout Europe/Middle East/Africa, the America, and Asia Pacific. To support them it maintains nearly 30,000 staff.

The company delivers specialized services that help their clients through treasury, financing, securities services, capital markets, and financial advisory offerings. It proves to be a world-renowned leader throughout numerous disciplines. As such, CIB has vast expertise in derivatives, risk management, structured financing, and other areas. The CIB division serves as a bridge between the two types of clients it counts by helping its corporate clients to obtain financing while offering investment possibilities to its institutional investors.

British Bankers Association (BBA)

The British Bankers Association turns out to be the members' representative for the biggest international banking cluster in the world. This main trade association for the British banking sector boasts over 200 member banks headquartered in both the U.K. and more than 50 other countries that run operations in over 180 jurisdictions around the globe. As such fully 80% of all the systemically critical banks on earth carry membership with the BBA. This is the voice of UK banking.

The BBA claims the greatest and most comprehensive policy resources for those banks operating in the UK. They represent membership not only to the government of the U.K., but also throughout Europe and globally. Besides this impressive membership roster, their network also is comprised of more than 80 of the foremost professional and financial services organizations in the world.

The BBA's members collectively manage over £7 trillion (British pounds) of British bank assets. The members employ almost half a million people throughout the country. Their contributions to the British economy every year are more than £60 billion. Members loan in excess of £150 billion out to business based in the U.K.

The British Bankers Association works to encourage both initiatives and policies that promote the interests of not only banks but also the overall public. They have three principal priorities in their work. The first is to help out customers. This includes both businesses and consumers. The second is to encourage growth. By this they intend to support Britain as the world's global financial center. Finally they are interested in improving standards in the industry on both an ethical and professional level.

The BBA works with two strategic aims in mind. The first is to encourage a superior and improving banking sector for the overall U.K. They do this by working alongside banks and other beneficiaries to increase trust in the banking industry, by raising standards, by encouraging growth, and by assisting customers. They promise to facilitate public approval and overall awareness of the important position banks play in the economy. They are also aspiring to build appreciation for the advantages of hosting an internationally critical banking sector.

Chief among their public relations tasks are to encourage acknowledgement of the substantial improvements the sector has gone through since the global financial crisis. The BBA's goal is to be understood as an agent of positive change that makes a better banking industry by its non members and members alike. They strive to be a trusted partner of both banking regulators and the government. They also take the initiative to impact international and national debates on banking issues.

Their second strategic aim is to be the banking industry's trade association that is world class. They are the principal trade association for the foremost sector of the British economy as well as the main trade group for the foremost banking cluster in the world. This is why they aim to be best in class in their operations.

Before September in 2012, the BBA both compiled and published the LIBOR London Interbank Offered Rate, the most important interest rate in the world. They lost their role in managing the rate after the Barclays scandal erupted that showed the bank had been consistently manipulating the rate for a number of years. As lobby organization for the rate submitting banks, the Bank of England decided the BBA's conflict of interest was too great.

Nowadays the BBA puts on training and events throughout Britain. These include training classes, briefings, and forums besides their annual industry dinners and conferences. They also publish a monthly report that covers figures on high street banking. This is used in their Annual Abstract of Banking Statistics that they produce every August. BBA furthermore runs the GOLD Global Operational Loss Database for members. This serves as a helpful tool in helping to manage risk from operations.

Bureau of Economic Analysis (BEA)

The Bureau of Economic Analysis is also known by its acronym the BEA. It is a bureau within the United States Department of Commerce. This BEA develops and publishes statistics for economic accounts that help a variety of groups to make decisions and to understand the economic performance of the U.S. Among the parties that follow their publications and statistics are business and government leaders, researchers, and members of the American public.

The publications which the Bureau of Economic Analysis produces prove to be among the most critical statistics of economics in the country. This includes such national benchmark economic indicators as the GDP Gross Domestic Product along with the balance of payments. The PCE Personal Consumption Expenditures Index is also compiled and released as part of their national economic data.

These and other statistics which the Bureau of Economic Analysis publishes have significant impact on important decisions in the U.S. Public policymakers, consumer households, individual people, and business heads use these numbers. They impact such important business, personal, and economic fundamentals as exchange rates, interest rates, budget and tax forecasts, investment plans for businesses, and the distribution of federal funds. These federal government grant monies total in excess of $390 billion. Numerous agencies distribute them to local and state organizations and communities.

Besides the two national bell weather statistics of GDP and balance of payments, the Bureau of Economic Analysis also puts together and publishes a variety of regional, national, international, and industry specific economic accounts. These deliver crucial information on a range of issues. Among these are relationships between various industries, economic development on a regional basis, and the position of the United States in the global economy as a whole.

Chief among the important statistics the Bureau of Economic Analysis keeps and uses are the NIPAs National Income and Product Accounts. They serve as a cornerstone for all of the agencies' other national and regional statistics. They include the country's gross domestic product numbers and other relevant measurements.

Many individuals are not aware of the depth of the international statistics which the Bureau of Economic Analysis keeps and provides on its website. Their international trade and investment country facts cover all of the nations in the world. These statistics are essentially complete reports on each nation's trade and direct foreign investment with the United States.

They provide information on the exports from and imports to the U.S. from each country. They also showcase the dollar amount of direct foreign investment to and from America for each nation selected. Included in this information is a detailed breakdown of the different types of imports, exports, and trade goods exchanged between each country selected and the United States.

Regional reports which the BEA provides cover GDP on a state by state and metropolitan area basis. They also deliver information on each state's and local area personal income throughout the country. The PCE Personal Consumption Expenditures is provided on a state wide level under this category of information as well.

For industry reports, the BEA offers a GDP by industry report and statistics. They also offer an annual industry accounts section which includes a 50 year survey of current business input-output and GDP figures.

Bureau of Engraving and Printing (BEP)

The Bureau of Engraving and Printing is the Treasury Department entity that actually makes the United States' currency. Their mission centers on creating and producing American currency notes which are trusted around the world. They have a vision to be considered the world standard for securities printing. This is so that they can deliver the public and their customers with the best products that are exceptionally well designed and manufactured.

The main activities of the BEP are to print up billions of Federal Reserve notes (or dollars) every single year. They then deliver these to the Federal Reserve System for distribution into the economy. It is the Federal Reserve that exists to be the American central bank. They bear the responsibility to be certain that sufficient coins and bills currency are in active circulation. The BEP handles all of the U.S. printed bills but does not make any coins. United States coins are always minted at the U.S. Mint.

When various federal agencies have concerns or questions about document security, they turn to the BEP for help and advice. The BEP also engages in research and development for improving their utilization of automation processes in production. They are always seeking out technologies to deter counterfeiters of U.S. currency and security documents as well.

It is no understatement to say that currency creation at the BEP offices has changed drastically from its origins in 1862. In those early years, they used the basement in the Treasury building. Here a handful of individuals worked with hand cranked machines to print and separate notes. Today's BEP does not engage in an easy process or job.

Nowadays making the currency bills takes greatly skilled and expertly trained craftspeople who work with specially designed equipment. They utilize both sophisticated and world leading technology alongside the time tested old world printing methods. Producing the currency takes numerous specific steps. This starts with designing, engraving, and making the plates. The specially sourced paper is then plate printed and inspected. Bills are numbered and re-inspected again before being packaged and shipped to their customer the Federal Reserve Bank.

The Bureau of Engraving and Printing also offers redemption of mutilated currency services and the sale of shredded currency. BEP will redeem such mutilated currency for free for the public. If the bills are so damaged that the value can not be conclusively determined, they can be sent on to the BEP so that their trained experts can examine them. After their determination is made, they will redeem the currency for full face value.

They accept currency that has been mutilated by water, fire, chemicals, or explosives; deterioration or petrification from burying; or insect, animal, or rodent damage. Bills missing security features are also treated as mutilated. For them to consider these bills without supporting documentation and explanations for what happened, at least half of the note has to be identifiable as American currency and remain.

If less than 50% is present, Treasury will require proof that the rest of the currency has been destroyed. Each year the department examines 30,000 mutilated currency claims and redeems them for more than $30 million.

The BEP also sells bags of shredded currency as novelty souvenir items. The Fort Worth and Washington, D.C. BEP visitor centers offer them in pre-packed small amounts for those who just want to have some. The D.C. visitor center and online store of the BEP also sell larger five pound bags of such shredded currency. In order to obtain larger quantities, individuals must get permission from the Treasury department and obtain them from one of the Federal Reserve Banks.

Capital Expenditures

Capital expenditure refers to money that a firm employs to purchase physical assets. This can also be used to upgrade existing assets. These can include items such as equipment, industrial buildings, and property. It is also known as CapEx. Companies often use this CapEx to make new investments or to begin a new project.

Other corporations utilize capital expenditures to build up their operations' size and scale. Such expenditures can cover many different items like buying a new piece of equipment, fixing the roof on a company building, or constructing a new factory for the company.

Accounting procedures utilize this capital expenditure concept regularly. Expenses will be labeled as CapEx if the item the company buys is a new purchase of a capital asset. They also fall under this category when the purchase is some type of investment that extends the practical life of an already owned capital asset.

When a purchase falls under the capital expenditure's category, the accounting department will be required to capitalize it. They do this when the fixed cost of the purchase is spread out over the asset's useful life. In other cases, the money they spend will only keep the capital item in its present condition. For these scenarios the company and accountants may simply deduct the entire expense for the year in which they spend the money.

Different industries will employ varying levels of capital expenditures. Some use very little, while others are more capital intensive. Among the most intensive capital industries in the world are the exploration and production of energy such as oil or natural gas, manufacturing businesses, telecommunications, and electricity, gas, and water utilities.

It is important to not confuse capital expenditures with other ideas like operating expenses, known as OPEX, or revenue expenditures. Operating and revenue expenses are money that companies pay to cover the daily cost of running the business. Revenue expenses are different from CapEx in another significant way. The former can be completely deducted from taxes in the year in which the company spends them.

Capital expenditures can be used to help come up with the relative value of a company also. Cash flow to capital expenditure ratio is one such measure. It is commonly referred to as CF/CapEx. This explains the ability of a company to purchase assets for long term use by utilizing its free cash flow. This ratio commonly goes up and down for businesses as they engage in cycles of small capital versus large capital expenses.

Ideally a business wants to have a higher multiple in this ratio. Higher numbers signify that the company is in a position of solid financial health and strength. This is because firms that possess the financial capabilities to invest in their future with capital expenditures can expand with greater ease and flexibility.

Cash flows to capital expenditures are ratios that are specific to every industry. Each segment's ratio will be different. This means that the ratio of one company in one business should not be compared to a second company in another industry. Instead, the ratio is only useful for comparison when two companies that possess comparable CapEx requirements are examined. Comparing various CapEx ratios from two oil firms or utility companies makes sense. Holding up the CapEx ratios of an oil company or telecom firm against a consulting business or advertising agency does not.

The higher a company's capital expenditure is, the lower its other measures of financial health may be. As an example, firms with high CapEx will often show less free cash flow to equity.

Cash Flow Statement (CFS)

The Cash Flow Statement (CFS) proves to be one of three critical components in any corporation's financial reports. The other two are income statements and balance sheets. From 1987, the SEC Securities Exchange Commission has mandated that such cash flow statements be included with all corporate financial reports. This statement details the quantities of cash and cash equivalents that come into and flow out of a firm. Such a CFS permits the stake holders and potential investors alike to comprehend the way corporations' operations are functioning, how they are effectively spending the money, and from where their money originates in the first place.

There are differences that separate these Cash Flow Statements from the balance sheets and income statements. The principal one is that CFSs do not cover the future anticipated outgoing and incoming cash amounts which have already been recorded under the credit sales category. It explains why the component cash is never identical to net income. Both balance sheets and income statements cover not only cash sales, but also sales that happen on credit. In the end, a firm's cash flow is derived from three separate means of money coming in and leaving a corporation. These are cash from operations, cash from financing, and cash from investing.

Cash from Operations comprise both the cash inflow and outflow which result from the mainstay operation of the business. This means that they show the quantity of cash that the firms' services and products actually accrue to the business. Cash from operations would usually include changes to cash, depreciation, accounts receivable, accounts payable, and inventory.

The Cash from Financing component includes loans, changes in debt, and dividends. As capital becomes raised, this is a cash-in accounting item. As dividends pay out, it becomes marked as a cash-out event. As an example, when firms sell bonds on the markets, the firm obtains cash financing. As the corporation pays the associated interest out to the holders of the bonds, then the firm reduces its cash by the corresponding amount.

The final category of Cash from Investing covers all changes in assets, equipment, or company investments. These are commonly considered to be cash out events. This is because cash will be utilized to purchase new buildings, buy factory or other production equipment, and acquire other types of assets which are short term (like securities which are easily marketable). It is not always the case that these are cash negative events though. As any firms choose to sell off one or more of their assets, this creates a cash-in transaction. It would then be notated as a positive accounting item under the cash from investing category. When companies sell shares they hold in another firm, the revenue this generates becomes accounted for under the Cash from Investing.

Cash flow becomes calculated by adjustments that accountants make to net income. They simply add in (or alternatively subtract out) any differences in expenses, revenue, and credit types of transactions that appear on the income statements and balance sheets since the last accounting period. Such transactions happen every accounting period. These adjustments will be reviewed and amended as non-cash items go into the income statement under net income while liabilities and total assets go on to the balance sheet. Since not every type of financial transaction of a firm relates to real cash items, a great number of items must be reconsidered when the accountants are figuring up the cash flow from operations.

Company accountants deduce the cash flow statement calculations and compile them into official corporate report documents every reportable quarter. The SEC requires that they make this a part of every quarterly report and also each annual report which they must divulge to analysts and members of the investing public by law.

Cash On Cash Return (CCR)

Cash on cash return, also known by its acronym CCR, is an investing term. It describes a ratio of the yearly cash flow before taxes against the total sum of cash invested. This cash on cash return is expressed as a percentage.

Cash on cash return is mostly utilized to analyze any income generating asset's actual cash flow situation. This percentage is commonly applied as a simple and quick test to decide if an asset under consideration is worthy of additional study and analysis. An investor who believed that cash flow is the greatest goal would be most interested in an analysis based on cash on cash return. Others employ it to discover if a particular property or asset turns out to be under priced. This would mean that equity in a property would exist immediately upon purchase.

Cash on cash return formulas do not figure in any deprecation or appreciation of an income producing asset. This means that the cash on cash return number may be skewed to the high side if some of the cash flow produced turns out to be a return on capital. This is because return on capital is not income.

Another limitation to cash on cash returns as a measurement lies in the fact that the calculation is more or less one of simple interest. This means that it does not take into consideration the compounding of interest. As a result of this, investments that provide a lower compound interest rate might be better over time than those that provide greater cash on cash returns, which is only a simple interest calculation.

A last downside to using cash on cash returns as a means of evaluating an investment centers around the fact that they are only pre tax cash flow evaluations. This means that your tax situation as a unique investor will not be considered in the formula. Varying tax situations can determine if an investment is a good match for you or not.

Consider an example of figuring up out a cash on cash return. You could buy an apartment complex for $1,200,000 using a down payment of $300,000. Every month, the resulting rental cash flow after expenses for this property is $5,000. This means that in a year, the income before tax would amount to $60,000, as $5,000 was multiplied by twelve months. This would make the cash on cash return the cash flow for the year before taxes of $60,000 over the entire amount of money invested in the asset of $300,000. This results in an actual twenty percent cash on cash return.

CBOE Volatility Index (VIX)

The CBOE Volatility Index (VIX) refers to the VIX ticker symbol on the CBOE Chicago Board Options Exchange. This is the famed volatility index that displays the expectations of the market for future volatility in the markets over the coming 30 days. This number comes from utilizing the implied volatilities from a huge selection of the index options on the S&P 500. The volatility measurement is intended to be looking forward, comes from the results of volatilities on both puts and calls, and has become the most popular measure for assessing market risk. This is why investors often refer to it as the gold standard of "investor fear gauge."

This crucial measurement of market participants' expectations for shorter-term volatility is revealed by the stock index options prices set for the S&P 500. It was unveiled back in 1993 and has since grown into the leading bell weather for market volatility and investors' sentiment in the globe. Since a number of larger and important investors wanted to have tradable instruments based on the market expectation for future volatility, VX based futures arose in 2004. In 2006, the exchange introduced the VIX options.

Originally, the Chicago Board of Options Exchange created the CBOE Volatility Index (VIX) to develop a range of volatility based products. After the CBOE led the way in innovation, a few other measures of volatility indices were also created. The VXN tracks volatility on the NASDAQ 100 while the VXD tracks volatility on the DJIA Dow Jones Industrial Average.

Yet it is the CBOE Volatility Index (VIX) that remains the original attempt at developing and instituting a form of volatility index. Originally this was intended as a weighted measure for the implied volatility for eight S&P 100 calls and puts with strike prices that were then at the money. After ten years of wild success in 2004, the options expanded to a broader index the S&P 500 that permits a more representative portrayal of the expectations of investors for future market volatility.

When the CBOE Volatility Index (VIX) values rise to over 30, then huge amounts of volatility are on display because of the uncertainty and fear of investors. Values under 20 reveal a complacent and less stressed epoch in the stock markets. For much of 2017, these levels at been at record lows below 12.

Computers actually figure up the VIX as they compile the S&P 500 index. It is different in that it is not based upon underlying stock prices. Rather it relies on the options prices from the S&P 500 to estimate the volatility levels of such options and how they will change from that date to the expiration date of the underlying options. The CBOE then compiles the prices of multiple options to derive their number of aggregate volatility that the index actually tracks.

Thanks to the options based upon the VIX, investors are able to trade them. The CBOE also offers another 24 volatility based ETP exchange traded products that bring the VIX indices up to a total 25.

Actual movements in the CBOE Volatility Index (VIX) mostly come down to the market reactions. Consider an example to better grasp this somewhat challenging concept. On June 13th of 2016, the VIX itself roared higher by over 23 percent. It reached a daily high of 20.97, its best level in more than three months. This spike occurred as a result of a worldwide U.S. equities hard sell off.

Global investors feared the uncertainty in the markets and opted to cash out of all gains and to realize some losses. This led to a greater supply of equities. According to the well-proven law of greater supply and decreasing demand, this led to higher market volatility and a greater VIX number as a direct result.

Certificate of Deposit (CD)

A Certificate of Deposit refers to a kind of savings vehicle which generally provides greater returns for money invested than the typical savings accounts do. There is very little risk in such an account. They also come without monthly fees. Besides this, these CDs prove to be significantly different from the age old savings accounts for several reasons.

Such a Certificate of Deposit stands for a time deposit. While an individual who has a savings account is freely able to make additional deposits or withdraw available funds relatively at will, this is not the case with CDs. Holders of CDs consent to tying up their money for a minimum length of time. Banks calls this the term length. Such term lengths might be only a few days. They could also extend up to ten years out. Standard CD's run from typically three months to five years.

In general, the longer the term length proves to be, the better the rate of interest the Certificate of Deposit will pay. The longer the term length is, the greater amount of time an individual ties up the money in the account at the bank too. It makes sense that the bank rewards customers for committing to a longer amount of time with a larger CD rate than they pay on comparable savings accounts.

Banks generally quote these CD rates using the APY annual percentage yield. This rate takes into account the compounding periods on how often the CD pays interest which can then earn still more interest on it. The banks have the choice of compounding periods based on annually, quarterly, monthly, and daily compounding. The closer a CD compounds to a daily rate, the higher the APY will actually prove to be.

There are penalties involved with drawing the money out of the certificate of deposit before its final maturity date. While every bank is different, most banks will levy a penalty of from three to six months in accrued interest for breaking the time deposit early. This is why financial professionals will counsel against taking money out of a CD early unless it is desperately important to access the funds.

The U.S. FDIC Federal Deposit Insurance Corporation backs the CDs at the overwhelming majority of commercial banks in the country. These Certificates of Deposit are government guaranteed in amounts of up to $250,000. With the credit union CDs, these certificates become insured by the NCUA National Credit Union Administration for the same maximum amounts. Credit unions which are state-chartered will often utilize private insurance for their CDs. Not any of these forms of insurance cover the penalties for taking out the funds ahead of maturity. Such coverage comes automatically and does not have to be applied for in order for the time deposit to be insured.

There are several different varieties of Certificates of Deposit available. Variable rate CDs are those whose interest rate is connected to the prime interest rate, market indices, Treasury bills rates, or another underlying benchmark. They help depositors to gain from any future point interest rate increases. Callable CDs often include a better rate of interest than a traditional CD. The bank can unilaterally reduce the maturity term period on demand though.

No or low penalty CDs pay lower interest rates but allow investors to more easily obtain their money back from the time deposit without expensive penalties. They often require holders to keep a certain minimum balance in the CD. IRA CDs are traditional certificates of deposit which are contained within an IRA Individual Retirement Account. There are tax advantages and deferrals on taxes of interest payments with these. Finally, Jumbo CDs pay greater rates of interest in exchange for extremely high minimum balances of typically $100,000 and higher.

Certified Public Accountant (CPA)

CPA's, or certified public accountants, are accountants who have taken and successfully completed a series of demanding exams that are given by the American Institute of Certified Public Accountants. Many states also have their own state level exams that have to be passed along with the national one.

CPA'a are accountants in every sense of the word, but not every accountant is qualified as a CPA. Because of the difficulties in becoming a CPA, there are many accountants who either never attempt or never succeed in successfully passing the Certified Public Accountant exam. This does not mean such an accountant is not qualified to practice accounting tasks, only that he or she will not be allowed to do tasks that require specific CPA credentials.

Such Certified Public Accountants do a number of varying tasks and jobs. Many will provide advice and simple income tax preparing for various clients who might be comprised of corporations, small companies, or individuals. Besides this, Certified Public Accountants practice many other tasks that include auditing, keeping the records of businesses, and consulting for business entities.

Keeping a CPA license is not accomplished through automatic renewal. Certified Public Accountants are required to engage in a full one hundred and twenty hours of courses on continuing education in every three year period. This is so that they will be on top of any and all changes going on in the field of their chosen profession.

The opportunities for Certified Public Accountants are many and varied. The FBI seeks to hire them routinely, preferring applicant candidates with either such a CPA background or alternatively an attorney background. Numerous state and Federal government agencies offer CPA's opportunities by providing CPA positions. Businesses ranging from small companies to large corporations also seek them out. With these firms, CPA's can occupy positions ranging from controllers, to CFO or Chief Financial Officers, to CEO's or Chief Executive Officers.

Among the most significant parts that CPA's can play proves to be one of a consultant. As a consultant, Certified Public Accountants can be looking into possible means of saving small businesses or even enormous corporations money on expenses or putting together specific financial plans that permit a corporation or business to appear more appealing to investors or possible buyers. Certified Public Accountants are sworn to a particular code of ethical conduct. They are required to provide their clients with honest and reliable advice that is also ethical.

Certified Public Accountants who do not stay within the bounds of their ethical code can lead to the total financial failure of a firm. This turned out to be the case in recent years at Enron, the energy trading and producing giant. Not only were Enron corporate executives charged for illegal accounting activities, but also a number of CPA's from nationally renowned accounting firm Arthur Anderson were charged with unethical practices of accounting.

Chicago Board of Options Exchange (CBOE)

CBOE is the acronym for the Chicago Board of Options Exchange. The exchange arose in 1973. Since then it has grown to become the biggest options' market on the planet. As a market leader in technological innovation and creative financial products that are new and ground breaking, it has pushed the envelope on electronic forms of trading over the years. The Chicago Board concentrates its efforts on options contracts pertaining to indices, single stock equities, and interest rates. This exchange has such a broad and deep reach in options that it can claim to host a majority of the options traded around the globe. Industry insiders refer to this largest option exchange in the world as the "See-bo."

The CBOE has come an enormous distance since its very first trading day back in 1973. On that first day, the exchange offered 16 individual stocks and actually traded 911 contracts. The daily average volume nowadays is well in excess of a million contracts every market day. They trade these massive numbers of options primarily on single equity options, indices options, and options on ETF exchange traded funds and ETN exchange traded notes.

The market is the home for the volatility index options, which trade on this index investors affectionately call the VIX. This VIX is universally held to be the leading equity market volatility barometer in the globe. Besides this index, investors can also trade options on such internationally known and popular indices as the SPX S&P 500, the DJX Dow Jones 30 Industrials, the London FTSE, the MSCI, the NDX NASDAQ 100, and the RUT Russell 200 Index.

The exchange has counted itself a global leader and even pioneer in the purveying of stock indices options which are cash settled. Investors are able to take advantage of these tools in order to hedge their portfolio exposure and manage their risk. They can also gather regular premium income to help increase or stabilize the returns on their various portfolios. Every single trading day, literally billions of dollars in value of options transact through these ranges of popular and beloved indices.

The CBOE boasts creating the single stock options market all by itself, as well as the universe of ETF and ETN options. Investors throughout the world can utilize these exchange traded product and single stock options to hedge the positions they have in the stocks, manage their risk, and create additional income through writing covered calls.

Today's exchange provides the vast range of literally thousands of different publically exchange traded stocks, ETNs and ETFs with option tradability. By selling cash secured puts and covered calls, investors are able to boost their portfolio income and hedge their various literal stock positions. It is important to keep in mind that these particular financial products come with physical settlement when expiration occurs. This means that any options on single stock securities still held at expiration would be delivered. With the options on the various indices, the expiration settlement is cash-based.

CBOE worked to ensure that investors of all sizes could participate in these contracts. To that effect, they pioneered the concept of mini options. The exchange's website offers a full range of product details and contract specifications on the various mini options contracts, such as the ever popular Mini S&P 500 contract.

In other ground breaking product firsts, CBOE led the world with such innovative options ideas as weekly options that offer end of week expiration for precisely targeted strategies, quarterly and end of month options on the S&P 500, FLEX Options that permit investors to customize their options contract terms (including styles of exercise, exercise prices and dates), strategy benchmark indices like the PUT and BXM indices, and social media indices. With the Social Media Indexes, the Chicago Board of Options Exchange is partnering up with SMA Social Market Analytics to create a range of interesting indices based on such SMA data which allows for the CBOE-SMA Index Suite of products based on social media.

CME Group

The CME Group is the Chicago Mercantile Exchange group of futures market companies. It calls itself the most diverse and global leading marketplace for futures and derivatives. The group itself is made up of four different DCM Designated Contract Markets. These include the Chicago Mercantile Exchange (CME), Chicago Board of Trade (CBOT), New York Mercantile Exchange (NYMEX), and the Commodity Exchange (COMEX). All four exchanges have their own commodities which they trade as well as different historical beginnings.

The world comes to the CME Group to manage its risk. The group provides the greatest variety of worldwide benchmark products in every significant class of assets. Through these offerings they assist businesses around the globe in compensating for the many risks they face in the uncertain global economy of today. Chicago Mercantile Exchange received the honors of Exchange of the Year and Risk Awards Winner for 2016.

Beyond their various trading products they offer an educational Futures Institute with a Futures Challenge competition to try to help potential investors learn how to trade these markets. This program takes six days and allows participants to learn interactively and simulate their own trading while they compete against others for cash awards. First place offers $1,000, second place $500, and third place a $250 reward. In order to compete, participants must complete six training modules, lay out their trade plan, and pass a quiz. This gives them a good understanding of the basic operations of futures trading.

The Chicago Mercantile Exchange represents the largest futures and options on futures exchange in the United States and the second largest one in the world. The commodities available to trade on this exchange center on currencies, interest rates, stock indices, equities, and a few agricultural products. CME was established in 1898 as a non profit company. In its early days investors knew the exchange as the Chicago Butter and Egg Board all the way till 1919. CME proved to be the first financial exchange in the U.S. to demutualize so that it could become a company owned by stockholders in November of 2000.

The CBOT's roots go back to 1848. In its initial days it allowed for trading of agricultural products like soybeans, corn, and wheat. Today it offers trading in agricultural as well as financial contracts. Futures contracts and options today are available on a number of additional products such as energy, U.S. Treasury bonds, gold, and silver.

For many decades the exchange functioned solely as an open auction market. Traders would get together in a trading pit and utilize hand signals to buy and sell. Now the CBOT also offers futures contracts that are electronically traded. The entity became a for profit company via an IPO on the New York Stock Exchange in October of 2005.

NYMEX is the largest futures exchange for physical commodities in the world. The trading done here occurs through the two divisions of NYMEX and COMEX. On NYMEX, traders can participate with platinum, palladium, and energy markets. In COMEX they are able to trade precious and industrial metals such as silver, gold, and copper. COMEX also offers index options on the FTSE 100 exchange in London.

During the day, NYMEX and COMEX utilize a system of open outcry on the floor. After regular trading hours, all trading is done on an electronic trading system. Dairy merchants originally founded the NYMEX as the Butter and Cheese Exchange of New York. NYMEX and COMEX merged together in 1994. Today the exchanges specialize in precious metals and energy products.

Collateralized Debt Obligations (CDO)

Collateralized Debt Obligations are one of the financial weapons of mass destruction that helped to derail the global financial system in the financial crisis of 2007-2010. They are literally securities that are supposed to be of investment grade. The backing of collateralized debt obligations proves to be pools of loans, bonds, and similar assets. These investments are rated by the main ratings agencies of Moody's, Standard and Poors, and Fitch rating companies.

The actual value of collateralized debt obligations comes from their asset backing. These asset backed securities' payments and values both derive from their portfolios of associated assets that are fixed income types of instruments. CDO's securities are divided into different classes of risk that are called tranches.

The senior most tranches are deemed to be the most secure forms of securities. Since principal and interest payments are given out according to the most senior securities first, the junior level tranches pay the higher coupon payments and interest rates to help reward investors who are willing to take on the greater levels of default risk that they assume.

The original CDO was only offered in 1987 by bankers for Imperial Savings Association that failed and became folded in to the Resolution Trust Corporation in 1990. This should have been a warning about collateralized debt obligations, but their popularity only grew apace during the following ten years. CDO's rapidly became the fastest expanding part of the synthetic asset backed securities market. There are several reasons for why this proved to be the case. The main one revolved around the returns of two to three percentage points greater than corporate bonds that possessed identical credit ratings.

CDO's also appealed to a larger number of investors and asset managers from investment trusts, unit trusts, and mutual funds, to insurance companies, investment banks, and private banks. Structured investment vehicles also made use of them to defray risk. CDO's popularity also had to do with the high profit margins that they made for their creators and sellers.

A number of different investors and economists have raised their voices against collateralized debt obligations, derivatives in general, and other asset backed securities. This includes both former IMF Head Economist Raghuram Rajan and legendary billionaire investor Warren Buffet. They have claimed that such instruments only increase and spread around the uncertainty and risk that surrounds these underlying assets' values to a larger and wider pool of owners instead of lessening the risk via diversification.

Though the majority of the investment world remained skeptical of their criticism, the credit crisis in 2007 and 2008 proved that these dissenters had merit to their views. It is now understood that the major credit rating agencies did not sufficiently take into account the massive risks that were associated with the CDO's and ABS's, such as a nationwide housing value collapse.

Because the value of collateralized debt obligations are forced to be valued according to mark to market accounting, where their values are immediately updated to the market value, they have declined dramatically in value on the banks' and others owners' balance sheets as their actual value on the market has plummeted.

Collateralized Mortgage Obligation (CMO)

Collateralized mortgage obligations are investments that contain home mortgages. These mortgages underlie the securities themselves. These CMO yields and results derive from the home mortgage loans' performance on which they are based. This is true with other mortgage backed securities as well.

Lenders sell these loans to an intermediary firm. Such an intermediary pools these loans together and issues certificates based on them. Investors are able to buy these certificates to earn the principal and interest payments from the mortgages. The payments these homeowners make go through the intermediary firm before finally reaching the investors who bought them.

The performance of collateralized mortgage obligations depends on the track record of the mortgage payers. What makes them different from other types of mortgage backed securities is that it is not only a single loan on which they are based. Rather they are categorized by groups of loans according to the payment period for the mortgages within the pool itself.

Issuers set up CMOs this way to try to reduce the effects of a mortgage being prepaid. This can often be a problem for investments based on only a single mortgage as owners refinance their loans and pay off the initial one on which the investment was based. With the CMOs, the risk of home owners defaulting is spread across a number of different mortgages and shared by many investors.

Tranches are the different categories within the mortgage pools on which the collateralized mortgage obligations are based. The tranches are often divided according to the mortgage repayment schedules of the loans. For each tranche, the issuer creates bonds with different interest rates and maturity dates. These CMO bonds can come with maturity dates of twenty, ten, five, and two years. The bondholders of each individual tranche receive the coupon or interest payments out of the mortgage pool. Principal payments accrue initially to those bonds in the first tranche which mature soonest.

The bonds on collateralized mortgage obligations turn out to be highly rated. This is especially the case when they are backed by GSE government mortgages and similar types of high grade loans. This means that the risk of default is low compared with other mortgage backed securities.

There are three types of groups who issue these CMOs. The FHLMC Federal Home Loan Mortgage Corporation issues many of them. Other GSE Government Sponsored Enterprises like Ginnie Mae provide them as well. There are also private companies which issue these CMOs. Many investors consider the ones issued by the government agencies to be less risky, but this is not necessarily the case. The government is not required to bail out the GSEs and their CMOs.

There are investors who choose to hold their CMO bonds until they mature. Others will re-sell or buy them using the secondary market. The prices for these investments on this market go up and down based on any changes in the interest rates.

The other most common type of mortgage backed securities besides these CMOs are pass through securities. Pass throughs are usually based on a single or few mortgages set up like a trust that collects and passes through the interest and principal repayments.

Collective Investment Fund (CIF)

A collective investment fund is a vehicles that manages a combined group of trust accounts. They are sometimes called collective investment trusts. Trust companies or banks operate these funds. The idea behind them is to pool together the funds and assets of organizations and individuals so that the managers can create bigger and better diversified portfolios.

Two types of these CIFs exist. A1 funds are combined together so that their operators can effectively reinvest or initially invest them. With A2 funds, trusts contribute assets that are not subject to any federal income taxes.

The main goal with a collective investment fund lies in utilizing superior economy of scale in order to reduce costs. The operators are able to combine together pensions and profit sharing funds to come up with a greater amount of assets. Banks then put these funds which are pooled together in a master trust account. The bank that controls the account then serves as executor or trustee of the CIF.

Banks that serve collective investment funds are the fiduciaries. This means that keep the legal title for the fund and all assets within it. The individuals or groups that participate in the CIF still own the results of the invested fund' assets. This makes them the beneficial owners of the relevant assets. Those who are participating within the fund do not actually own any individual assets that the CIF holds. They do maintain an interest in the aggregated assets of the fund.

Banks designed these collective investment funds so that they could improve their investment management tactics. They do this when they pull together a number of accounts' assets and merge them into a single fund with a common investment strategy. Pooling these assets into only one account allows the banks to dramatically reduce their administrative and operating costs for the fund. The investment strategy they come up with is structured to optimize the performance of the investments.

There are a number of different collective investment funds operating. Invesco Trust Company operates several of them. Examples of their funds are the Invesco Balanced Risk Commodity Trust and the Invesco Global

Opportunities Trust.

Though comptrollers use the name collective investment funds, other names sometimes refer to these vehicles. Generally applied names for them include common funds, common trust funds, comingled trusts, and collective trusts. An important characteristic of CIFs is that they are not regulated by the Investment Act of 1940 (as with mutual funds) or the SEC Securities Exchange Commission. Instead the OCC Office of the Comptroller of the Currency regulates and oversees them.

Mutual funds and collective investment funds are both pooled funds with an important distinction. These CIFs are not registered investment vehicles. Instead they exist in a class that is similar to hedge funds.

In 1927, the world's first collective fund began. Thanks to the stock market crash that occurred only two years later, CIFs became a scapegoat. They were believed to have contributed to the severe crash. This caused regulators to heavily restrict them. Banks could only provide them to trust clients or by utilizing employee benefit plans. They received a significant boost in the Pension Protection Act of 2006. This act chose them to be the standard option in defined contribution plans. Now 401(k) plans often feature them as an option for stable value.

Commodities Futures Trading Commission (CFTC)

The CFTC is the regulatory agency whose acronym stands for the Commodities Futures Trading Commission. This group arose as a direct result of the Congressionally enacted Commodity Futures Trading Commission Act of 1974. Since that time, the group has carried the responsibility of regulating both the commodity options and futures markets. Their goals range from protecting investors from manipulative endeavors of firms to promoting fair, efficient, and competitive futures markets to stopping fraud and other abusive trading practices.

This regulatory group with vast powers is a fully independent agency under the umbrella of the United States' government. Besides their core objectives listed above, they seek to use their considerable powers to safeguard against systemic risk and to encourage transparent and financially viable markets. Following the Global Financial Crisis of 2007-2009 they have been working towards greater transparency and more stringent regulation of the swaps market, a multiple trillion dollar enterprise. The Dodd Frank Wall Street Reform and Consumer Protection Act of 2010 gives them this authority and ability to transition into this additional role as safe guardian of the swaps markets.

Five different committees comprise the CFTC. Each of these governing groups reports to a commissioner. The President of the United States appoints these commissioners directly which the Senate must then approve. The areas of concentration for the five committees include global markets, technology, agriculture, energy and environmental markets, and cooperation with the SEC Securities Exchange Commission. Each committee is made up of people with backgrounds in and connections to various industries and their interests. This includes the commodities exchanges, the futures exchanges, traders, the environment, and consumers.

The history of regulation of these futures and commodities markets stretches back nearly a century. While these contracts have been trading in the United States for longer than 150 years, they have only been Federally regulated from the 1920s. The original Congressional act that gave the government the authority to regulate and monitor these high stakes and leveraged markets was the Grain Futures Act of 1922. This authority was expanded by the Commodity Exchange Act of 1936.

With the advent of technological advances in the 1970s, the futures and commodity contracts trading has rapidly grown well beyond the original agricultural and other physical types of commodities. It now spans a dizzying range of financial instruments. Among these are the securities of foreign (and American) governments, foreign currencies, and foreign and American stock indices, and even individual company shares. Because of this rapid and spiraling expansion into countless other arenas, Congress decided to act to ensure that the oversight functions of these markets were adequate to handle the vast array of new activity.

They passed the Commodity Futures Trading Commission Act of 1974 in order to establish the CFTC. This new agency took the place of the U.S. Department of Agriculture and its Commodity Exchange Authority with regards to regulating both commodity futures and options exchanges and markets throughout the U.S. This new Act enabled vast changes to the old simple powers which the Commodity Exchange Act of 1936 had granted.

When their original mandate expired around the year 2000, Congress updated it with the Commodity Futures Modernization Act of 2000. This act mandated that the CFTC and the SEC begin to establish a combined regulatory authority for the relatively new single stock futures. These financial instruments had started trading in November of 2002. By 2003, such swaps had massively and exponentially expanded from the time when they had been originally introduced in the latter years of the 1970s.

As with the SEC, the CFTC does not exercise direct regulatory control for individual companies in the commodity and futures markets and their corporate financial soundness. The exception to this general rule pertains to huge swap participants and the now-regulated swap dealers. For these organizations, the CFTC actually sets the minimum capital standards as mandated by the Dodd-Frank Act.

Since 2014, the Commodities Futures Trading Commission has also gained oversight over the DCM designated contract markets. This includes the derivatives clearing organizations, swap execution facilities, swap dealers, swap data repository, commodity pool operators, and futures commission merchants, as well as other intermediary groups. This regulatory body also coordinates its efforts with major international counterparts, such as the British regulatory group the Financial Conduct Authority that oversees the London Metal Exchange.

Commodity Exchange (COMEX)

The COMEX Commodity Exchange is the wholly owned subsidiary of the Chicago Mercantile Group that is responsible for both precious metals and base metals futures and options on futures trading. This once independent exchange is where the speculators, hedging companies, and traders all come to participate in trading FTSE 100 London exchange index options, along with precious metals silver and gold futures and options on futures, and industrial metals futures such as copper, aluminum, lead, and zinc futures.

For the first more than half a century of its existence, the Commodity Exchange proved to be an individually owned and run commodities futures exchange. COMEX arose in New York back in 1933 in the depths of the Great Depression. Through ups and downs in the markets, this exchange endured.

On December 31st of 1974, the Commodity Exchange launched its gold futures contract. This was the date when Americans regained the right to own gold again after a more than 40 year hiatus. This made it the biggest and most important center around the globe for gold futures and options. COMEX next launched options trading based on their gold futures in 1982 to cement their place in the world futures market and history. Silver has also been traded on the exchange since the 1970s.

COMEX merged with rival exchange NYMEX in 1994 to form the two still separately run exchanges under the listing of NYMEX Holdings, Inc. They did not obtain their publicly traded listing on the New York Stock Exchange until November 17th of 2006 when it began to trade under the ticker symbol of NMX. This new entity did not maintain its independence for long.

By March of 2008 the Chicago Mercantile Exchange Group of Chicago had conclusively committed to an agreement to purchase all of NYMEX holdings at a combined stock and cash offering that totaled $11.2 billion. The deal successfully completed in August of 2008.

From this point forward, the once independent and then jointly held NYMEX and COMEX exchanges continued their existence as Designated Contract

Markets of the CME Group. As such, they joined the two sister exchanges of the organization, the Chicago Mercantile Exchange and the Chicago Board of Trade. All four of these exchanges together make up the DCMs of the CME Group.

COMEX still maintains its separate identity under the CME Group. The precious metals trade is what it is best known for today. This precious metals complex volume that it transacts both monthly and annually is so large that it is greater than the volume of all competing futures exchanges in the world combined.

Commodities Exchange brings in participation from around the globe. A substantial number of the traders from East Asia, Europe, and the Middle East remain at their offices until the daily closure of COMEX.

This fact provides the Commodities Exchange with unparalleled liquidity almost around the clock. This more or less explains why it has been so very successful for the past near century despite intense competition in a constantly changing global trading environment. The hours that it trades continue to reflect the global participation. This is why the Commodities Exchange has opened ever earlier in order to meet the needs of the Asian, Middle Eastern, and European overseas trading clientele base.

Electronic trading on COMEX starts from the night previously from 4pm until the following morning at 7am. The regular trading session occurs from 8:20am through to 2:30pm. This means that COMEX is open for 21 hours per trading day from Monday to Thursday. Sunday electronic hours begin from 7pm EST. The group publishes both exchange open interest and volume every trading day.

Commodity Futures Modernization Act (CFMA)

In the year 2000, the U.S. Government passed the Commodity Futures Modernization Act. The act did several things. First it reaffirmed the regulatory authority of the Commodity Futures Trading Commission over all American futures markets. This authority became extended for a period of five years with this act.

A second and more significant result of the act came about as the government allowed Single Stock Futures to be traded for the first time in the United States. Other countries already allowed their investors to trade these particular types of futures when Congress passed this act. In America up to this point where the CFMA passed, it was illegal for investors to participate. Yet investors were eager to gain the leverage that these futures delivered.

Single Stock Futures are popular precisely because they do allow significant exposure to equity markets. A single stock future is a special kind of futures contract. The instrument allows a buyer to trade a certain number of shares in a single company at a price that they agree on now for a particular date in the future. The price is known as the strike price or futures price. The future date that the two parties set is the delivery date.

Buyers of these contracts are long the future in the stock. Sellers of the contract are short the stock in question. The buyer makes money if the price of the underlying stock increases, while the seller makes money if the value of the underlying stock declines. There is no cost to open the contract besides commissions and fees.

Single Stock Futures trade typically in contracts of 100 shares. Buying the contract does not cause any dividend or voting rights to transfer from the seller to the buyer. Futures trade using margin and provide tremendous leverage. There are no short selling rules applied to them as there are to stocks themselves.

Other countries adopted the Single Stock Futures trading ahead of the United States. The American market was not allowed to trade them before the passage of the Commodity Futures Modernization Act of 2000. This was because there was conflict between the two regulatory agencies the U.S. Securities and Exchange Commission and the Commodity Futures Trading Commission. The two could not work out which agency would regulate these new Single Stock Futures products and trading.

When the government passed the CFMA of 2000 into law, they agreed to a compromise. Both of these agencies decided to share the jurisdiction under a plan that allowed the Single Stock Futures to finally start trading on November 8 of 2002. This allowed the United States based traders to catch up with other countries who were already trading these instruments.

The Commodity Futures Modernization Act brought the United States into a global market of the Single Stock Futures that included Great Britain, Spain, South Africa, India, and other countries. The South African market has traditionally been the largest of the single stock futures marketplaces. Their average numbers of contracts amount to 700,000 each day.

Though the CFMA allowed single stock futures to be traded, this did not establish a marketplace for them on which they could be traded in the U.S. Two different companies began trading them initially. One of these closed. The remaining company trading these types of futures in the U.S. is now known as the One Chicago. This is a joint venture of the main Chicago commodities and futures exchanges the Chicago Mercantile Exchange, the Chicago Board Options Exchange, and the Chicago Board of Trade.

Common Securitization Platform (CSP)

During the financial crisis that started back in 2008, the federal government took control of both Fannie Mae and Freddie Mac the government sponsored enterprises because they became insolvent. One of the ideas that the since-then managing agency the FHFA Federal Housing Finance Agency came up with is the Common Securitization Platform. This strategic goal resulted from the FHFAs *2014 Strategic Plan for the Conservatorships of Fannie Mae and Freddie Mac* report.

The hope with this Common Securitization Platform is to create a new and greatly improved securitization infrastructure for both Freddie Mac and Fannie Mae. These two groups are collectively known as the Enterprises. Their new platform is to be for American mortgage loans which are backed up by single family kinds of properties.

In order to put this vision into reality, the two GSEs have established a joint venture called CSS Common Securitization Solutions. It is actually designing the Common Securitization Platform under the leadership and direction of the FHFA. The CSS fills the role of agent for both enterprises to help with issuing the single family mortgage securities. It also is handling disclosures when the securities are issued and in the future. Besides this, CSS is administering such securities after they are issued.

Among the more important tasks the Common Securitization Solutions is carrying out with regards to the program surrounds the operational capabilities of the Common Securitization Platform. CSS is responsible for creating these so that the CSP will run. The CSP will eventually support the securitizing activities of the GSEs and their single family mortgage program. This will culminate in the two Enterprises issuing one Single Security, which will actually be a single mortgage backed security.

Issuing this Single Security is important for several reasons. The FHFA along with Fannie Mae and Freddie Mac all want to see their securities' all around liquidity improve. This will also aid in the mission of the two GSEs to ensure the country's housing finance markets remain liquid too.

Common Securitization Platform is both a technology and operating platform then. In the future, it will handle a great number of the critical back office functions and operations of the Single Security. It will also take over the majority of the two GSEs present securitization operations in the single family mortgages for them. Without the CSP, it would be practically impossible to actually launch and integrate the Single Security.

Single Security is the future of Freddie Mac and Fannie Mae. It will help to ensure that adequate financing for fixed rate mortgages and loans continues for the one unit to four unit single family properties. The way that it will actually do this is by taking elements from both of the GSEs and combining the best of each.

There are three areas where these different procedures have to be aligned for the Single Security to function properly. The key features of the Fannie Mae mortgage backed securities and the Freddie Mac participation certificates will be taken mostly from Fannie's mortgage backed securities model. Investor disclosures will be modeled after Freddie's participation certificates. A final area to be aligned concerns the practices and policies that will be utilized to take loans out of securities.

The Single Security endeavor also promises to allow for some exchanges of old for new securities. This pertains particularly to the 45 day Participation Certificates of Freddie Mac. These will be exchangeable for 55 day time frame Single Securities that Freddie Mac will issue.

Compound Annual Growth Rate (CAGR)

Compound Annual Growth Rate refers to the measurement which attempts to reduce the volatility of annual gains in growth during a set out number of years. The growth gains it considers include income, profits, customers, and more. The idea is to reduce the volatility over the years as if the growth had occurred evenly each year in the time frame under consideration. It can also be defined more technically as the average annual rate of growth for a given investment throughout a defined time period that exceeds a single year.

This means that the Compound Annual Growth Rate is not actually the real rate of return. Instead it is more like a representative figure. In other words, it is a fictitious percentage that spells out the investment return rate assuming that growth in said investment had been even and consistent over the years. In the real world, this almost never occurs. The reason to use such an artificial construct as this CAGR is to make the returns on a given investment more understandable.

Determining this Compound Annual Growth Rate is complex. It involves taking the investment value at the conclusion of the period under consideration. This must be divided by the value from the start of the period. The result has to be raised to a power of one divided by the total period length. This number that results must then be subtracted from the whole number one to get the final result for CAGR. It is a complicated formula that is difficult for most people to grasp if they are not mathematicians.

This is why looking at a tangible example makes it simpler to follow. Assume a certain corporation had three years of sales that were $300 million in the first year, $450 million in the second year, and $800 million in the third year. The growth rate was different every year. Its second year it increased by 50 percent while its third year the growth rate was almost 78 percent. Using the Compound Annual Growth Rate would smooth this out to provide a picture as if the company's rate of growth per year had been steady over the three years considered. It is the compounding part that makes the formula so complex. This also explains why investors and analysts who figure this value will use a business calculator or a program that figures out the equation for them once they plug in the appropriate numbers of starting value, end value, and number of years.

Yet the Compound Annual Growth Rate is useful to businesses, investors, and analysts in particular. It helps investors who are interested in comparing and contrasting the rates of growth (over a predetermined amount of time) for two or more funds or firms. This would not be a simple task if they instead utilized the volatile and changing year over year growth rates.

Thanks to the simplicity of this measurement, it has utility in several other cases. In its simplest form, investors or analysts can employ the CAGR to figure out the average annual growth for one investment. As an example, investments might gain in relative value each year at the varying rates of plus seven percent the first year, minus one percent the second year, then plus six percent the third year. Using this CAGR will help the investor or analyst to get a bigger picture of the three year progress made by the investment in question.

Congressional Budget Office (CBO)

The Congressional Budget Office was created by Congress in 1975. Since that time, it has continuously developed and published its own independent analyses for economic and budget related issues. Its goal is to support the process of making Congressional budgets. Ever year the agency puts together literally hundreds of estimates for costs of proposed legislation as well as dozens of routine reports.

The CBO is religiously non partisan so that it can engage in unbiased and objective analysis. It only hires staff based on their professional abilities and does not consider their political affiliations. CBO never engages in recommending policies. It is concerned with all of its reports and price estimates explaining its analytical methodology.

The CBO produces Baseline Budget and Economic Projections. It does this regularly to come up with predictions for economic and budget outcomes. These estimates assume that the present conditions for revenues and spending will continue. Such baseline projections extend for 10 year time frames as utilized in the process of Congressional budget making.

Long Term Budget Projections are another item that the Congressional Budget Office offers Congress. These extend well beyond the usual 10 year budget forecasts to cover the next 30 years. They reveal the impacts of economic developments, demographic trends, and increasing health care expenses for federal deficits, spending, and revenues.

With the Cost Estimate analyses, the Congressional Budget Office delivers estimates in writing for the expenses created by every bill which the committees in Congress approve. They reveal the ways the bill will impact revenues or spending for the coming five to 10 years.

The CBO also develops Analytic Reports which consider specific elements of the tax code, programs of federal spending, and economic and budget constraints. Such reports pertain to a number of elements of federal policy. This includes economic growth, health care, social insurance, taxes, income security, the environment, energy, national security, education, financial issues, infrastructure, and other areas.

Once the President submits his Presidential Budget, CBO get involved. It re-estimates the impacts of it. The office does this by using its particular methods for economic estimating and forecasting.

From time to time, the CBO comes up with a volume on Budget Options. This reference work provides a number of ways that the government could reduce its budget deficits. The options are varied and come from a number of sources. They include raising additional revenues and lowering spending.

The Congressional Budget Office also produces Sequestration Reports. They must put out estimates of funding caps on discretionary programs in every fiscal year that goes through 2021. They consider these numbers to determine if cancelling the pre-allocation of budgeted resources is necessary.

The CBO knows what it should study because of its mandates. It's responsibilities are to assist the Senate and House Budget Committees in their jurisdictional affairs. They also are directed to support various other committees of the Congress. This includes especially the Finance, Ways and Means, and Appropriations Committees as well as the leadership of Congress. They are required by law to produce many of the annual reports which they create. The best known of these remains the Budget and Economic Outlook.

Consumer Financial Protection Bureau (CFPB)

The CFPB is the Consumer Financial Protection Bureau. Congress created this government agency in 2008 as one of the reactions it took to the devastating financial crisis and Great Recession, the worst financial shocks to the system since the end of the 1930s era Great Depression.

The idea was to erect an organization that would protect consumers from risks and predatory practices of Wall Street and the mega banks which already had been determined as "too big to fail." The Dodd-Frank Wall Street Reform and Consumer Protection Act actually set up this new entity the CFPB.

The role of this new twenty-first century organization is to assist consumers in the financial markets through creating rules that are more efficient and fair, by continuously and equitably enforcing the rules, and by helping consumers to be able to gain additional command over their own economic futures and affairs.

The Consumer Financial Protection Bureau's goal is to ensure that the various financial markets function fairly and appropriately for providers, consumers, and the all around national economy. To this effect they strive to safeguard consumers from deceptive, predatory, abusive, and unfair activities in the marketplaces. They enforce action on any companies which break the laws. The CFPB provides people with the tools and information they require to make decisions that are smart for their own situations.

The Consumer Financial Protection Bureau believes in and labors towards a financial market that works fairly. This means that the terms, risks, and prices of any deals must be transparent and obvious in advance so that all consumers are able to know their choices and fairly and effectively comparison shop. They work to see that all corporations abide by the identical consumer protection rules. Each company must fairly compete to provide high quality goods and services.

To see this vision become reality, the Consumer Financial Protection Bureau strives to empower, enforce, and educate. Empowering means that they develop tools, answer commonly posed queries, and offer helpful tips for consumers who are interested in making their way through the various financial options to shop around for the deal that best meets their needs. They pride themselves on their effective enforcement of the rules against predatory operations and actions that break the law.

The CFPB has obtained and returned literally billions of dollars in damages to customers who were wronged. Education means that the CFPB fosters consumer abilities and educational opportunities from a young age extending on to retirement. They inform financial companies of their legal and ethical responsibilities and publish research to help out consumers.

The Consumer Financial Protection Bureau operates in several core functions. They acknowledge that the government created them to offer one accountability agency to enforce the laws for federal consumer finance and to safeguard consumers in the financial arena. This used to be the purview of a number of different agencies. Among the CFPB's core functions are receiving complaints from consumers, enforcing the discrimination laws in consumer finance, and creating and enforcing rules to rid the market of abusive, deceptive, and predatory actions by companies.

They also foster financial education among consumers, regulate and oversee the financial markets for upcoming risks for consumers, and do research on consumer's experiences in utilizing financial services and products. They do this to try to locate problems lurking in the financial marketplace so that more fair ultimate outcomes can be achieved for American consumers everywhere.

As of 2016, Richard Cordray is the Consumer Financial Protection Bureau's first director. Before he assumed this important responsibility, he served in the role as head of the Bureau's Office of Enforcement.

Consumer Price Index (CPI)

The Consumer Price Index, also known by its acronym of CPI, actually measures changes that take place over time in the level of the pricing of various consumer goods and services that American households buy. The Bureau of Labor Statistics in the U.S. says that the Consumer Price Index is a measurement of the over time change in the prices that urban consumers actually pay for a certain grouping of consumer goods and services.

This consumer price index is not literal in the sense of what inflation really turns out to be. Instead, it is a statistical estimate that is built utilizing the costs of a basket of sample items that are supposed to be representative for the entire economy. These goods and services' prices are ascertained from time to time. In actual practice, both sub indices such as clothing, and even sub-sub indices, such as men's dress shirts, are calculated for varying sub-categories of services and goods. These are then taken and added together to create the total index. The different goods are assigned varying weights as shares of the total amount of the expenditures of consumers that the index covers.

Two essential pieces of information are necessary to build the consumer price index. These are the weighting data and the pricing data. Weighting data comes from estimates of differing kinds of expenditure shares as a percentage of the entire expenditure that the index covers. Sample household expenditure surveys are sourced to figure what the weightings should be. Otherwise, the National Income and Product Accounts estimates of expenditures on consumption are utilized. Pricing data is gathered from a sampling of goods and services taken from a sample range of sales outlets in varying locations and at a sampling of times.

The consumer price index is figured up monthly in the United States. Some other countries determine their CPI's on a quarterly basis. The different components of the consumer price index include food, clothing, and housing, all of which are weighted averages of the sub-sub indices. The CPI index literally compares the prices of one month with the prices in the reference month.

Consumer Price Index is only one of a few different pricing indices that the majority of national statistical agencies calculate. Inflation is figured up using the yearly percentage changes in the underlying consume price index. Uses of this CPI can include adjusting real values of pensions, salaries, and wages for inflation's effects, as well as for monitoring costs, and showing alterations in actual values through deflating the monetary magnitudes. The CPI and US National Income and Product Accounts prove to be among the most carefully followed of economic indicators.

Cost of living index is another measurement that is generated based on the consumer price index. It demonstrates how much consumer expenditures need to adjust to compensate for changes in prices. This details how much consumers need to keep up a constant standard of living.

Cost of Goods Sold (COGS)

The Cost of Goods Sold refers to those costs which directly arise from the creation of a firm's goods or services. The phrase also sometimes is summarized by its acronym COGS or by an alternative name the "cost of sales." It will cover many expenses. Among these are all of the materials the company utilizes to physically produce the goods.

It also considers the labor expenses employed to create the items. It will not include expenses that are considered to be indirect. This means that sales force and distribution expenses will not be taken into account. COGS shows up on income statements. Accountants and economists can utilize it to subtract it out from the given company's revenues in order to establish the firm's gross margin.

Every business has the ultimate goal to earn profits at the heart of what it is doing. This is why a less expensive goods production for their product or service will lead to higher profits, all else being equal. A fuller explanation of what the Cost of Goods Sold includes involves inventory, materials, labor, factory equipment for production, and even overhead. All of these factors of production directly pertain to the goods or services the company produces. The calculation also takes into consideration the freight or shipping of inputs utilized. It would never include associated costs like rent for a facility or general payrolls of a company.

Looking at an example helps to clarify the Cost of Goods Sold concept. Where an automobile manufacturer is concerned, there will be a number of material costs. Chief among these would be those parts that actually combine to produce the car, as well as the cost of labor for assembling the car. The COGS would not include the cost of the sales force personnel which actually sell the car nor the price for getting the cars out to the dealership. Both of these last ideas are post-production costs, so they are not a part of the primary COGS.

There are a number of different ways for calculating the Cost of Goods Sold. It also varies from one certain kind of business to those in another industry. Among the most simple means of figuring this number out is to start with the costs of inventory over the production period. Next they would add in the aggregate purchase amounts in the same time frame. They would likely then subtract out the inventory at the end of production point. Such a calculation will provide the literal cost of the inventory which the company produced in a given time frame.

Another example helps to make the explanation clearer. Assume that a firm begins its production phase with $15 million worth of inventory. If they make $3 million in additional purchase in this time and end the production period with $14 million of inventory, then the firm's Cost of Goods Sold is calculated by taking the $15 million and adding in the $3 million in purchases and subtracting out the final $14 million in remaining inventory. This gives a final COGS of $15M plus $3M minus $14M for a final result of $4M.

The significance to this formula and Cost of Goods Sold figure is important. The COGS reveals how effectively the firm is able to convert its inventory into revenues and profits. This is why it is critical to compare the COGS against the revenue of the period under consideration. When the company above had a revenue exceeding $4 million, then it would boast a gross profit that was positive. If the revenue of the firm in question was less than the $4 million COGS, then there would be a negative gross profit. In other words, understanding and knowing the COGS figure for a company tells investors which companies are ultimately successful and which are in financial trouble, assuming that state of (negative profit) affairs continues for long.

Council of Economic Advisers (CEA)

The President's Council of Economic Advisors proves to be an agency of the President's Executive Office. They give the President unbiased and non partisan economic advice for coming up with both international and national economic policies. This council is made up of three people of whom one is the chair. They use analysis of empirical evidence based on economic research to come up with their regular recommendations to the President. They gather the most esteemed information they can to help the President in putting together the critical national economic policy and annual report.

In 2016 the Chairman of this CEA was Jason Furman. The two members of the group were Jay Shambaugh and Sandra Black. Distinguished one time chairs of the group include former Chairmen of the Federal Reserve Alan Greenspan and Ben Bernanke and 2016 Federal Reserve Chairperson Janet Yellen. This council receives significant support from a number of staff members. Among their support personnel are staff economists and senior economists, research assistants, and a statistical back office.

Congress established this Council of Economic Advisors for the President with its 1946 Employment Act. In this act, the legislation called for three members whom the President would appoint. The Senate was to advise on selection and give consent on the final selection of these members. Members chosen for the CEA are to be recognized for their experience, training, and accomplishments in the field of economics.

Their purpose in greater detail is to consider and explain the economic developments to the President and to review the activities and programs the government establishes for economic appropriateness. They are also expected to create and recommend policies to encourage production, better employment, and higher purchasing power in a freely competitive economy. One of the three members the President is to appoint as Chairman for the council.

The council specifically has five different duties in the performance of their role. They have to help with and give advice for the Economic Report that the President's office prepares annually. They are instructed to collect information that is timely and accepted on the economic trends and developments in the U.S. They can then analyze and understand if the trends are interfering with attaining the stated Presidential policy. The group has to put all of this information together and turn it in to the President.

A third role is to consider the activities and programs of the government. The CEA is supposed to ascertain which of these activities and programs are helping to advance the policy and which are hurting it so they can let the President know.

They must also create and recommend policies for the President that help to develop and encourage competitive free enterprise. These policies should help to reduce and stop economic fluctuations and to improve national production, employment, and purchasing power.

Finally, the Council of Economic Advisors was set up to create and provide a range of reports and studies that have bearing on national economic legislation and policies. These are to be drawn up as the President requests them.

Every month the CEA prepares a report for the Joint Economic Committee of Congress. This is known as the *Economic Indicators*. In this publication there is information on income, gross domestic product, business activity, production, employment, prices, credit, money, security markets, international statistics, and the finances of the Federal government.

They also produce reports and fact sheets on a nearly every month basis that address a wide variety of economic issues. These reports and the speeches and testimony of the members of the Council of Economic Advisors are all available to the public on their official website.

Debt Coverage Ratio (DCR)

Debt coverage ratio has different meanings dependent on what entity is using it. In the world of corporate finance, it is the amount of cash flow that a company has to service its current debts. This ratio utilizes the net operating income divided by the debt payments due in a year or less. This includes principal, interest, lease payments, and the sinking fund.

It has a different meaning with governments and individuals. For finances of a national government, debt coverage ratio refers to the export earnings required for the country to make its yearly principal and interest payments with the external debts of the nation. With individual finance, banks and their loan officers utilize this ratio to decide on income property loans.

Debt coverage ratios must be higher than one in order for the government, company, or individual to prove enough income to satisfy its present debt obligations. With a DCR under 1, it lacks the means to do so. This ratio is determined by dividing Net Operating Income by the Total Debt Service.

The net operating income turns out to be the revenue of a company less its operating expenses. This does not cover interest payments or taxes. The NOI can also equate to the EBIT Earnings Before Interest and Tax. Investors and lenders which are evaluating the creditworthiness of corporations and companies should use criteria that is consistent when they figure out the DCR.

Total debt service is the term that concerns the present debt obligations. This will include principal, interest, lease payments, and sinking fund all owed in the next year. Balance sheets also include both the long term debt current portion and the short term debt.

When a debt coverage ratio is lower than one, it says that the entity cash flow is negative. With a DCR of .90, the company would only possess sufficient NOI to handle 90% of their yearly debt payments. With personal finance this would mean that the borrower had to access some outside funds each month in order to cover the payments. Lenders usually discourage loans with negative cash flow. They may permit them when the borrower can show a strong outside income.

Lenders almost always consider the debt coverage ratio of borrowers before they extend loans to them. They do not want to loan money to entities with lower than one. Such groups will have to draw on sources outside of their traditional income or borrow more in order to make their debt payments. When the DCR is dangerously close to one, then the borrower is considered to be vulnerable to a slowdown in income. Only a minor setback to its cash flow would mean it would not be able to service the debts. Some lenders will actually insist that the borrowers keep minimum levels of debt coverage ratios while they have a loan balance. In these cases, borrowers whose ratios decline below this minimum level are in technical default.

Lenders can be more lenient on debt coverage ratios when the economy is booming. An expanding economy means that credit is available more easily. This often causes lenders to work with companies and individuals on their lower ratios. The problem is that borrowers which are under qualified can impact the stability of the economy.

In the 2008 financial crisis, subprime borrowers received credit in the form of mortgages without proper consideration of their finances. As such borrowers defaulted in large numbers, the lenders that had made loans to them failed. The largest savings and loan institution Washington Mutual turned out to be the most egregious example of this scenario.

Debt Relief Order

A Debt Relief Order (also known by their acronym DRO) refers to a British legal system type of insolvency method which is relatively new. It was Chapter 4 from the Tribunals, Courts, and Enforcement Act 2007 that actually created these new orders. The advantage that such DROs offer is a less expensive, faster, and simpler means of receiving bankruptcy styled relief in Great Britain.

The DRO works well for those indebted individuals who possess no or very few assets (under 1,000 British pounds without owning a home), and who count tiny disposable income levels (which have to be under 50 pounds sterling each month). Individuals who meet these criteria and several others may pay only a 90 pounds one time fee and then make application for the Debt Relief Order without a court appearance. Participants can even pay this fairly reasonable fee in a period of installments before they file the application for the order. Such DROs took the full force of law for both England and Wales on April 6th of 2009.

There are a range of specific requirements that individuals must meet in order to qualify for such a Debt Relief Order. It must be clear the persons can not pay their debts. They must not owe more than 20,000 pounds in total unsecured bills. Homeowners do not qualify, nor do those who have over 1,000 pounds in total gross assets. They can only keep their car if its value is under 1,000 pounds. The debt holder has to live in Wales or England or at least have been resident or engaged in business in either place within the past three years. They also may not have been issued a DRO in the prior six years.

Besides this the indebted individuals may not be part of any other kind of insolvency proceedings. These include bankruptcies which are not yet discharged, voluntary individual arrangements, present debt relief restrictions, present bankruptcy restrictions, a bankruptcy petition, or an interim order. It is true that these Debt Relief Orders are still insolvency forms that will be publicly listed in the insolvency services website.

In order for Debt Relief Orders to be successfully implemented, there must be a government approved intermediary who handles the event with the relevant authorities. For intermediaries to be approved, they generally have to be debt advice organization personnel which have experience as debt advisors. Some of these approved organizations include the Consumer Credit Counseling Service, one of the Citizens Advice Bureaus, Baines and Ernst National Debtline, Think Money, Payplan, the Institute of Money Advisers, and members of the entity Advice UK. Any of these approved intermediaries are able to consider the information of the persons applying, discern if they are DRO eligible, and finally make an online application on their behalf. These intermediaries who are approved do not charge fees to submit such applications.

The Official Receivers are able to issue the Debt Relief Orders after they obtain both the fee and the application. No court involvement is necessary if the applicant is eligible. Otherwise they will reject the application out of hand. These Official Receivers also have the authority to rescind these DROs if more relevant information on the debtors' financial conditions appears after the order has been granted. There are also criminal charges and penalties allowed by the British law if the applicants knowingly perjure themselves or provide deliberately misleading information on their financial conditions, assets, debts, and other personal financial costs.

Back in November of 2014, the New Policy Institute released data (research funded by the Trust for London) on the quantities of debt relief orders throughout different parts of the United Kingdom. Unsurprisingly, the total numbers of these DROs for London in the years of 2009 to 2013 proved to be vastly less than the rest of England's average.

Dividend Reinvestment Plans

Dividend Reinvestment Plans are also known by their acronyms as DRIPs or even DRPs. These plans come from corporations and companies which permit their investors to take their cash dividends in the form of reinvesting options. Generally this amounts to the investors acquiring extra fractional shares or additional whole shares. It occurs on the payment date of the dividend. DRIPs are intelligent means of growing the actual value in an investment holding.

The majority of these Dividend Reinvestment Plans allow their own investors to purchase these shares directly from the company. This provides them with a commission-free buy in usually offered at a substantial price discount to the present price of the shares on the stock market exchange. The majority of them will not accept reinvestments for under $10.

These Dividend Reinvestment Plans allow their shareholders to continuously invest in differing amounts over the span of longer-term timeframe investments in publically traded companies. Stake holders are able to buy either whole shares or even fractional shares through such dividend reinvestments in the best-known, most-famous public companies for only $10 or more at a single time.

Choosing this option means that investors forego their quarterly dividend payment check. The DRIP operating entity could be a transfer agent, company itself, or brokerage company. They will utilize the money from the dividend check to buy extra shares on behalf of the investor in question in the relevant company.

When the corporations directly operate their own Dividend Reinvestment Plans, they will appoint particular times throughout the year when they will permit the DRIP program buy in of additional shares from the company stakeholders. This is generally on a quarterly basis. The corporations in question never wade into secondary markets on exchanges to buy the shares then resell them to their investors. Instead the shares proffered through the DRIP come out of the companies' treasury reserve shares.

It is also important to note that such Dividend Reinvestment Plans shares issued directly by the company in question may not ever be resold on the stock market exchanges. Investors who wish to cash out of them will be forced to resell them back to the corporation which originally issued these for the present price on the stock market. When DRIPs run by brokerage companies are involved, the firm will just buy the shares for the investors who are acquiring them out of the secondary markets then tally such share into the brokerage account. In this case, these shares may be finally resold in the secondary market where they were originally acquired.

For those companies which do not directly offer their own share holders Dividend Reinvestment Plans, these can simply be established via a brokerage company. This is because a great number of the stock brokers permit their customers to reinvest such dividend payments directly into the stock shares which they already hold within their accounts. It is important that though such dividends do not come directly to the shareholders bank accounts, the IRS still requires that they be reported on a tax return like taxable income.

Many companies actually provide some significant incentives to take dividends from their DRIPs. They might provide a substantial discount of anywhere from one to ten percent from the present market share price. This can amount to a major savings when it is added to the lack of commissions on the trade.

Longer term advantages center on the miracle of compounded reinvestments on the returns. As the dividends become higher, the stake holders will receive an ever higher amount for every share they possess. This will then allow them to buy a still greater quantity of additional shares at each dividend payment. In a longer time frame, this will significantly boost the aggregate returns of the stock investment. This can really work to the advantage of the investors if the share price goes down and they gain the ability to cost average down with their DRIP share purchases. It offers them the possibility of significant gains from their reduced cost basis.

Companies like these DRIPs because they do not have to pay out as much capital when they are able to simply issue reserve shares from their treasury in lieu of cash dividend payouts. It also increases the loyalty of the shareholders, who will more likely hold on to the shares even when there are declines in the price of the share or the overall stock market.

Dow Jones Industrial Average (DJIA)

The Dow Jones Industrial Average, commonly referred to by its acronym DJIA, is also many times called the Dow 30, the Dow Jones, the Dow, or even just the Industrial Average. It proves to be the second oldest stock market index in the Untied States after the Dow Jones Transportation Average. The Dow Jones Industrial Average came into being when Charles Dow, the co founder of Dow Jones and Company worked with a business colleague Edward Jones, a statistician, to come up with an index that monitors the industrial sector. This index demonstrates the daily stock market trading session progress of thirty of the largest companies that are publicly traded within the U.S.

Ironically, most of the present day thirty companies listed in this index no longer have much or even anything to do with the historical definition of heavy industry. The components in the average are weighted by price and scaled in order to adjust for the impacts of stock splits and varying other forms of adjustments. This means that the total value that you see in the daily representation of the Dow Jones does not prove to be the true average of the different company stock prices.

Instead, it is the total of such company prices that are added up and then divided by a special divisor. This divisor is a number that is adjusted any time one of the company stocks underlying it pays a dividend or engages in a stock split. In this way, the index presents a constant value that is not altered by the external factors of the component stocks.

The Dow Jones Industrial Average remains one of the most heavily followed and carefully watched indices in the American stock market, along with peers the S&P 500 Index, the NASDAQ composite, and the Russell 2000 Index. The founder Dow intended for the index to monitor the American industrial sector's actual performance. Even so, the index is constantly affected by much more than simply the economic and corporate reports issued. It responds to both foreign and domestic incidents and political episodes like terrorism and war, as well as any natural disasters that might cause economic damage.

The Dow Jones Industrial Average's thirty components simultaneously trade on either the New York Stock Exchange Euronext or the NASDAQ OMX, which are the two largest American stock market outfits. Derivatives based on Dow components trade via the Chicago Board Options Exchange, as well as with the Chicago Mercantile Exchange Group. The latter is the largest futures exchange outfit on earth, and it presently owns fully ninety percent of the Dow Jones founded indexing business, along with this Industrial Average.

Investors who are interested in gaining the ability to track the progress of the Dow Jones Industrial average have several choices. There are index funds that buy the components of the index so that you do not have to own all thirty companies yourself. You might also invest in the Dow 30 by purchasing shares of the Exchange Traded Fund known as the Diamonds ETF. This trades under the AMEX exchange via the symbol DIA. Finally, you could by options and futures contracts based on the performance of the Dow Jones Average on the Chicago Board of Trade.

Due Process Oversight Committee (DPOC)

Within the structure and organization of the IFRS International Financial Reporting Standards, the trustees have various bodies that help them to perform their duties. The Due Process Oversight Committee is the one that carries the responsibility to monitor the procedures for effective due process. They also do this for the IASB International Accounting Standards Board and its Interpretations Committee.

This Due Process Oversight Committee generally holds meetings four times per year on the sidelines of the usually quarterly IFRS Foundation trustees meeting. When they require additional meetings, the DPOC usually handles them via conference call. Each year, they select different international locations for their meeting places. One of their quarterly meetings is usually held in London. In May and June of 2016, the IFRC Trustees and DPOC met in Jakarta and London, respectively. The Trustees and committee met in Beijing in October of 2015, London in June of 2015, Toronto in of April 2015, and Zurich in February of 2015.

There are a number of different responsibilities that the Due Process Oversight Committee carries out for the IFRS and the IASB. These are all spelled out within the Interpretations Committee Due Process Handbook of both the IFRS and the IASB. The first of these is to review the standard setting activities in which the IASB and staff of the IFRS Foundation engage. They do this review of due process activities routinely and with expediency as their mandate requires.

The Due Process Oversight Committee is also responsible for reviewing the Due Process Handbook that governs the committee among other things. They are to suggest updates to it that are in order. These updates would pertain to developing new and reviewing old standards, their various interpretations, and the Taxonomy of the IFRS itself. They do this to make sure that the procedures of the IASB are the best practice possible.

Besides this the Due Process Committee is tasked with reviewing the consultative groups of the IASB. They check who makes up the groups to ensure that the perspectives included are well balanced. They wish to have representation from the various relevant sub-disciplines. It is the committee's aim to ensure that these consultative groups are effective in their duties.

When outside parties request information on any due process issues, this Due Process Committee is the one that has to respond to them. They work with the technical staff of the Director for Trustee Activities to cohesively do so.

The IFRS Foundation bodies are also monitored for effectiveness by the Due Process Oversight Committee. They check up on the activities that involve standard setting at both the Interpretations Committee and the IFRS Advisory Council. Other groups within the IFRS Foundation which address the setting of standards are also followed up on by this Due Process Committee.

Finally, this important oversight committee is responsible for coming up with and issuing its recommendations to the IFRS Trustees about changing the committees. When the Due Process Oversight Committee determines that the makeup of these various committees that deal with due process needs to be changed, they let the Trustees know so that the committees can be appropriately re-balanced.

The Due Process Oversight Committee issues summaries of all of its meetings. These and any other papers and reports which they author are all found on their websites which are sub-pages of the International Financial Reporting Standards and the International Accounting Standards Board.

Earned Income Tax Credit (EITC)

The Earned Income Tax Credit, also known by its acronym EITC or EIC (for Earned Income Credit), is a benefit offered by the Internal Revenue Service to working people who only have lower to moderate levels of income. In order to qualify for it, prospective taxpayers have to measure up to specific requirements in a year in which they file their tax return.

The IRS requires that they file even when they do not owe any taxes, or if they otherwise do not have to file a tax return. A key benefit of the EITC is that it not only lowers the amount in tax receipts these families owe the government, but it can also create a negative tax liability that translates into a personal income tax refund.

Among the requirements necessary to qualify for this Earned Income Tax Credit, individuals have to receive at least some income while working as an employee for a person or business. Alternatively, they are able to qualify by owning or running either a farm or a business. There are also basic additional rules that involve having a qualifying child or children who meet each of the qualifying rules as set out by the IRS.

The Earned Income Tax Credit is intended primarily to help those families who have children, though it can also apply to other couples and individuals who receive lower to moderate levels of income. The actual amount of the benefits from the EITC is based upon the specific income of the filers as well as the actual number of children they have.

For those couples and individuals who claim children which qualify, they must be able to prove age, parental relationship, and shared residency. For the tax year 2013, the income levels that met IRS requirements had to be under $37,870 on up to under $51,567, which varied based on the numbers of children considered to be dependent in the family. Those workers who have no children yet who earn under $14,340 for an individual or $19,680 for married couples were eligible to get a tiny EITC amount in benefits. Those who do not have children which qualify are able to utilize U.S. tax forms including 1040, 1040A, or 1040EZ to apply. When qualifying children are involved, the head of household filer must utilize either the 1040 or 1040A forms alongside an attached Schedule EITC.

In the tax year of 2013, the IRS had established maximum benefit levels which individuals, couple, and families with qualifying children could obtain. For those who had no children which qualified, the maximum was $487. With a single child who qualified, the maximum benefit rose to $3,250. Where there were two children, this amount grew to $5,372. Finally, with three or even more children who were qualified, the maximum amount increased to $6,044. Each year, these numbers are raised according to the inflation index. In tax year 2015, this reduced tax revenues owed to the U.S. federal government by a not-insignificant around $70 billion.

It should not come as a surprise that these Earned Income Tax Credits have been and still remain a significant item for discussion in the ongoing political conversations within the United States. The debate has centered on the question of which approach would help the poor and lower middle class most. One idea is to raise the minimum wage significantly. The other is to boost the maximum amounts of the EITC. Back in the year 2000, The American Economic Association took a random survey of 1,000 of their members to learn their perspective. Over 75 percent of American economists agreed that it made sense to increase the program of the Earned Income Tax Credit.

Earnings Per Share (EPS)

Earnings per share refer to the given total of earnings that a company has for every share of the firm's stock that is outstanding. There are several formulas for calculating earnings per share. These depend on which segment of earnings are being considered. The FASB, or Financial Accounting Standards Board, makes corporations report such earnings per share on their income statement for all of the major components of such statements including discontinued operations, continuing operations, extraordinary items, and net income.

To figure up the basic net earnings per share formula, you only have to divide the profit for the year by the average number of common shares of stock. With discontinued operations, it is only a matter of taking the discontinued operations income and dividing it by the average number of common stock shares outstanding. Continuing operations earnings per share equal the continuing operations income over the average number of common shares. Extraordinary items works with the income from extraordinary items and divides it by the weighted average number of common shares.

Besides the basic earnings per share numbers, there are three different types of earnings per share. Last year's earning per share are the Trailing EPS. These are the only completely known earnings for a company. The Current earnings per share are the ones for this year. These are partially projections in the end until the last quarterly numbers are released. Finally, Forward earnings per share are earnings numbers for the future. These are entirely based on predictions.

Earnings per share calculations do not take into account preferred dividends on categories besides net income and continued operations. Such continuing operations and even net income earnings per share calculations turn out to be more complex as preferred share dividends are taken off of the top of net income before the earnings per share is actually calculated. Since preferred stock shares have the right to income payments ahead of common stock payments, any money that is given out as preferred dividends is cash which can not be considered to be potentially available for giving out to every share of the commonly held stock.

Preferred dividends for the present year are generally the only ones that are taken off of such income. There is a prevalent exception to this. If preferred shares prove to be cumulative then this means that dividends for the entire year are taken off, regardless of if they have been declared yet or not. Dividends that the company is behind on paying are not contemplated when the earnings per share is calculated.

Earnings per share as a financial measuring stick for a company are extremely important. In theory, this forms the underlying basis for the value of the stock in question. Another critical measurement of stock price is price to earnings value, also known as the PE ratio. This PE ratio is determined by taking the earnings per share and dividing them into the price of the stock. Earnings per share are useful in measuring up one corporation against another one, if they are involved in the same business segment or industry. They do not tell you if the stock is a good buy or not. They also do not reveal what the overall market thinks about the company. This is where the PE ratio is more useful.

Efficient Market Hypothesis (EMH)

The efficient market hypothesis is also known by its acronym EMH. It refers to an investment theory which claims that investors can not outperform the stock markets practically on a consistent basis. This is because the efficiencies created by the inner workings of the stock market mean present day share prices will always reflect and incorporate all relevant and practical information.

The idea states that stocks will practically always sell for their true fair value on the various stock exchanges. This infers that the typical investor can not efficiently buy undervalued shares or sell them at overly high prices. This is why it is theoretically impossible for investors to better the ultimate return of the stock markets no matter how expertly they select stocks or how well they time the markets. Efficient market hypothesis claims that the only means of outperforming the markets is through buying investments with higher risk and therefore coming with accompanying better returns.

Despite the fact that this efficient market hypothesis remains a foundation of modern day financial theories, it is still regarded with suspicion and controversy. Many investors and especially stock picking fund managers consistently defy it and try to select their own stocks. Those who concur with the EMH theory state that stock pickers are wasting their time in an effort to track down undervalued shares, or in predicting market trends, using either technical or fundamental analysis.

Clearly the economists and other scholarly individuals can hold up a significant amount of evidence that supports the efficient market hypothesis. Despite this, a broad range and variety of arguments against it still exist. Legendary investing stock pickers like Warren Buffet have managed to outperform the markets year in and year out over many decades. This should not be consistently possible at all by the arguments and logic of the EMH.

Other critics of the efficient market hypothesis hold up such Black Swan Events as the Black Monday 1987 crash in the stock markets. On this particular occasion, the DJIA Dow Jones Industrial Average plunged by in excess of 20 percent in only one day. This does raise a valid point about stock prices and how efficiently they are always valued when they can suddenly fall by a fifth of their value in only hours.

Believers in this efficient market hypothesis argue that markets are both efficient and random. This means that investors should be able to make their best consistent returns by choosing to invest in low fee, unmanaged, broadly representative portfolios. Morningstar Inc., the famous market research firm has compiled a great amount of data to support this assertion. They compiled the returns of active fund managers in every category. Then they held these up versus an index of relevant funds or ETF exchange traded funds. The study concluded that for any year to year period, there were merely two different groups of active fund managers who managed to consistently outperform the passively held funds over half the time. The two that outperformed were the diversified emerging markets funds and the small growth funds.

As far as all of the remaining categories such as U.S. large value, U.S. large blend, and U.S large growth (and most others), those who invested in either ETFs or lower cost index funds would have made higher returns. It is true that a small percentage of the active fund managers do manage to realize superior performances versus the passively managed funds at times and points. The problem that this presents for individual investors lies in predicting which fund managers will do this. Fewer than a quarter of the best performing active fund managers can outperform their passive manager benchmark funds consistently. Certainly Warren Buffet counts as one of those most successful few. It helps to explain his enduring popularity and success with investors for decades now.

Election Stock Market (ESM)

Election stock markets refer to financial markets whose contracts track the predicted and actual outcome of national elections. They are also called election prediction markets. Investors who participate in such futures contract forms of exchanges invest real money, purchase and sell contracts which are listed, take on the risk of losing their invested funds, and make profits on their positions. Such ESMs work much like traditional futures exchanges and commodity exchanges that cover future time deliveries of livestock, grains, and precious metals.

The real function and mission of such Election stock markets lies in correctly predicting the outcome of a national or provincial election. It might aim to forecast the popular vote shares or numbers of seats which the political parties obtain in legislative or alternatively parliamentary elections. Those markets that are effective prove to be highly reliable at contemplating information even before it becomes available in opinion polls. Such polls often require a few days to do and compile. The various traders in such an exchange tend to put aside their personal bias politically as they have real financial incentive to correctly share their honest opinion.

There are two other purposes for these Election stock markets. Naturally they are intended as a means of teaching people about elections and futures markets. Besides this though, the professors and universities that run them also rely on them for useful research surrounding election forecasting and the behavior of the electorate.

There are two such universities which have run these Election stock markets for more than a decade in North America. The main one in the United States is the Iowa Electronic Markets, founded and run by the Tippie College of Business of the University of Iowa. This market focuses its efforts on tracking mainly the congressional and presidential elections.

The University of British Columbia and its Sauder School of Business runs the Canadian-based UBC Election Stock Market. UBC concentrates on both provincial and federal elections for Canada. Both operate as not for profit enterprises for the purpose of research. Because of this, neither of them charges trading fees or commissions for trades. They generally limit the investment amounts to a range of between five hundred U.S. dollars and one thousand Canadian dollars.

In the last few years, new prediction markets which are privately operated have appeared. These markets do assess commissions and fees to pay for their costs of operation and for profit. Some charge net profits' commissions while others levy a per transaction fee. Among the commercial markets are The Washington Stock Exchange and Irish-based Intrade Prediction Markets. Each of these follows predictions for a wide-ranging series of geopolitical events. The commercially operated markets bring in significantly more volume and investment since they do not place arbitrary limits on an investors' participation.

Two main payout concepts exist with these Election stock markets. In the first model, the system proves to be a winner takes all type of market. One winning contract will pay the promised full face value amount (commonly one dollar) while all others will be worth zero. A party winning a full majority or plurality or a yes or no referendum are examples of this structured scenario.

In the other model, there are partial payouts on a few contracts which result from the percentage proportions on a given result. This percentage will commonly be multiplied by the standard dollar to determine the proportional payout. Two typical examples of this are a popular vote market share and a percentage of seats result for a given political party. The payouts would be figured according to the popular vote percentage share for the party in question. Traders often make money by purchasing those contracts which they feel are undervalued or by selling others which they believe to be overvalued.

Employee Stock Option (ESO)

Employee stock options are call options that are awarded privately rather than publicly. They turn out to be the most common form of equity compensation provided to employees of a business. Companies give out these options to their employees to provide them with an incentive to build up the market value of the company. These options may not be sold on the open markets.

An ESO provides the receiving employees with the right but not obligation to buy a preset quantity of shares of the company. The contract specifies a time frame within which these must be acquired before they expire worthless. The price they employees can buy them at is the current price which becomes the strike price. These time limits for using them are generally ten years. Companies spell all of these terms out in the options agreement.

These options are only valuable to the employee if the price of the company stock increases during the exercise time-frame. This is because the employees then are able to purchase the discounted shares at the same time as they sell them for the greater price on the market. The difference between the two prices represents their profit.

If the share price of the company declines, they are unable to use them and will see them eventually expire worthless. This is why companies utilize employee stock options instead of large salaries to encourage their employees. This provides the companies with great incentive to build up the value of the company. Three principle types of ESO exist in the form of non statutory, incentive, and reload employee stock options.

Non statutory employee stock options are also called non-qualified. These prove to be the normal kinds of ESOs. In such a contract, employees are not permitted to use these options during the vesting period. This vesting timeframe ranges from one to three years. When they are sold, the employee makes the spread between current price and strike price times the number of shares he or she sells. These types of ESOs become taxable at the employee's regular income tax level.

Graduated vesting in these options allows the employees to sell a percentage of the options such as maybe 10% in the first year. Each year another 10% would become available until the full 100% level is achieved by year ten. Incentive stock options are set up to lower taxes as much as possible. Employees can not exercise the option to buy the stock until after a year. They can not actually sell the stock until another year after buying it.

This type of option creates a risk that the stock price may decline over the year long holding time frame. The advantage to the employee is that these ISOs receive far better tax treatment. The tax rate defaults to the long term capital gains rate instead of the traditional full income tax rate. Upper level management are usually the ones who receive such tax advantageous ISOs from their companies.

The third type of employee stock options are called Reload ESOs. These begin their contract lives as non-statutory ESOs. The employees engage in their first exercise of the contract where they make money on the transaction. At this point, the employees who exercise are given a special reload of the employee stock option. In this process the company issues new options to the employee. The present market price at time of issue becomes the new strike price for the reloaded options. This way the employee is constantly re-incentivized to perform for the company.

Employee Stock Ownership Plan (ESOP)

An Employee Stock Ownership Plan refers to a type of retirement plan. They are also called by their acronym ESOP. These plans permit employing companies to either provide cash or stock shares directly to the employee benefits plan. These plans hold one account for every employee who participates in them. The stock shares that the employers contribute become vested over a pre-determined period of years.

Once they are partially or fully vested, employees are able to access them. It is important to note that with these ESOPs, employees never actually hold or purchase the shares of the stock directly when they are employees of the firm. Once the employee becomes retired, fired, disabled, or deceased, the stock shares become distributed.

One should never confuse an Employee Ownership Stock Plan with an employee stock option plan. These stock option plans are not really retirement plans. Rather they only provide the right to purchase the company stock for a given, pre-determined price in a certain time period.

One benefit that makes these Employee Stock Ownership Plans popular with providers and participants alike is their tax advantaged status. The reason they are considered to be qualified is because the company participating, the shareholder who sells, and the participants are each able to enjoy varying tax benefits. This is why these ESOPs are typically utilized by companies as part of their corporate financial strategy at the same time they are employed to encourage the employees to be sympathetic to the company stakeholders and their interests.

Without a doubt, the Employee Stock Ownership Plan is part and parcel of the compensation that employees enjoy from their company. This is why they are utilized to keep the employees working for the overall good of the company as a whole. They have a stake in the stock share price rising over time since they are part owners in the company stock.

These benefits from the Employee Stock Ownership Plan accrue to the employees at no upfront cost. The shares are kept for the receiving employees in a trust to ensure they grow safely to the point where the employee resigns or retires (or is fired).

These companies are actually employee-owned to some degree. Employee-owned corporations are those that have a majority of their shares in the hands of the company employees. This makes them cooperatives but for the fact that the firm's capital is unevenly distributed. Much of the time, such employee-owned corporations do not provide voting rights to all of the shareholders. Besides this, the senior-most employees and management will always have the distinct advantage of receiving a greater number of shares than the newer employees.

There are several other competing forms of employee ownership benefits. Among these are stock options, direct purchase plans, phantom stock, restricted stock, and stock appreciation rights. Stock options give their employees the chance to purchase shares of company stock for a set price in a fixed amount of time. A direct purchase plan permits employees to buy their shares in the company using their own after tax dollars.

Phantom stock delivers special cash bonuses in reward for superior employee results. The bonus amounts equal to the sale price of a certain quantity of stock shares. Restricted stock provides employees the ability to obtain shares either in the form of gift or by buying them, once they have met certain minimum employment period benchmarks. Stock appreciation rights provide employees with the ability to increase the value of a pre-assigned quantity of shares. Such shares typically become actually payable in the form of cash.

Environmental Impact Statement (EIS)

The Environmental Impact Statement (EIS) analyzes and succinctly describes any potential proposed actions and the substantial effects these may cause for the environment where they will take place. Such an EIS is always made available to members of the public who wish to learn more about or comment on them. There are five components that every EIS has to contain per the rules.

The opening element to an Environmental Impact Statement is the description of the intended action. This portion will detail why it is needed and what are the benefits it offers. As a second item, they must also contain detailed information describing the setting of the environment and any areas that will be impacted by the action the document proposes.

The third part and substance of the Environmental Impact Statement surrounds a detailed analysis. This analysis has to consider all of the effects on the environment that the action will cause. As a fourth part of the EIS, it must also contain another analysis. This must suggest any practical alternatives to the intended action in question. Each of these alternate actions must be addressed for why they are not superior.

Finally, the EIS has to contain an outline of the means for lessoning the negative impacts on the environment. If possible, it should spell out a way to avoid these harmful effects altogether.

The reason that companies, organizations, or federal agencies prepare an Environmental Impact Statement is to learn what the consequences of their actions will be for the environment and how they can mitigate them. In this case, the word environment refers to the physical and natural environment. It also pertains to the mutual relationship between the environment and individuals. EIS definitions for the word environment involve many different components. These include water, land, air, life forms, structures, site environmental values. They also cover the aspects of culture, social concerns, and the economy.

Impacts from a proposed action are not always negative. They can be positive or sometimes both positive and negative. The idea is to find ways to lesson the impacts, especially the harmful ones. Sometimes the effects can not be effectively lessened. This is why the EIS will also go into detail on any alternatives to the proposed action which might involve fewer negative effects on the environment.

There are a variety of national regulations and federal laws that the American federal government has passed so that impacts on the environment can be calculated. These also mandate that alternative actions must be considered. The statute that stipulates when such an Environmental Impact Statement has to be created is known as NEPA the National Environmental Policy Act of 1969.

This centerpiece legislation was established primarily to govern federal agencies in their actions on the environment. It also relates to company or organizational efforts that will impact the environment. It means that these agencies or parties have to not only detail what the potential action will do. They must also outline what they might reasonably do as an alternative to the suggested course of action.

These laws also require that enough information has to be included so that the Environmental Protection Agency or other reviewing group is able to adequately consider the pros and cons of every alternative action. The group that bears responsibility for the content and format of these Environmental Impact Statements is the CEQ Council for Environmental Quality. It is usually the Federal Environmental Protection Agency or a state's Department of Environmental Conservation that will require such a statement to be put together on a project.

Environmental Protection Agency (EPA)

The Environmental Protection Agency is the United States' environmental enforcement group. It is not a cabinet level department, though its Administrator typically receives cabinet status and rank. The president appoints the administrator after the individual is approved by the Congress. The EPA is headquartered in Washington, D.C. It also operates ten regional offices and 27 laboratories throughout the U.S.

President Richard Nixon originally proposed the EPA and created it by signing an executive order. It started operating December 2nd of 1970. President Nixon's order received ratification from Congress via committee hearings in the Senate and the House of Representatives.

The mission of the Environmental Protection Agency lies in protecting human health and the environment. To do this, it engages in research and environmental assessments. The group also promotes education. It carries the responsibility for enforcing environmental standards as provided in the national laws. The EPA does this by consulting with the federal, state, local, and tribal governments. Some of this enforcement, monitoring, and permitting it delegates out to the fifty states and the recognized Indian tribes.

The powers of the EPA allow it to issue sanctions and levy fines. Whenever possible it works with the government and industries to prevent pollution voluntarily. It also promotes efforts to conserve energy throughout the country.

The Environmental Protection Agency has a number of priorities in its mission. First and foremost it is interested in protecting Americans from substantial risks to their health as well as the environment in which they work, live, and learn. To do this, they carry out the best scientific research so that environmental risk can be effectively reduced on a national level. They also work to enforce the federal laws which safeguard the environment and health fairly and efficiently.

The EPA feels that every individual and group in society should be able to access correct information for taking care of environmental risks and health.

This includes businesses, people, communities, and local, state, and tribal governments. They want to see environmental protection treated as a critical priority in all American policies. Energy, economic growth, natural resources, transportation, health, industry, agriculture, and foreign trade should all be taken into consideration when making environmental policy.

Making the protection of the environment help with sustainable and economically productive development is another concern of the Environmental Protection Agency. They make it their business to ensure that the U.S. is leading other nations in protecting the world's environment as well.

The EPA carries out a number of activities in order to see through their mission and goals. The primary one is to develop and enforce the environmental regulations. Congress passes laws that the EPA puts into effect by writing regulations. They set national standards for state and tribal governments to enforce on their own. They also help these groups if they can not achieve the national standards. Enforcing such regulations becomes necessary if they are not able to convince offenders voluntarily.

The EPA gives many grants out to educational groups, state programs, not for profits, and others. Almost half of their budget is devoted to this. These finance everything from cleaning up communities to paying for scientific studies. They also sponsor dozens of partnerships as part of this. Some of these help to recycle solid waste, lower greenhouse emissions, and conserve energy and water.

The group spends a lot of time and effort studying environmental issues. In their over two dozen labs around the country, they find and attempt to solve these problems. They also share the findings with academic circles, the private sector, other government agencies, and foreign countries. The Environmental Protection Agency publishes online and written materials regarding what they learn and their various activities.

Equal Credit Opportunity Act (ECOA)

The Equal Credit Opportunity Act is also known as the ECOA. Congress created this regulation in order to provide all legal American residents with a fair and reasonable opportunity to obtain loans from banks or other financial institutions that make loans.

The act clearly states that such organizations may not discriminate against individual people for any reason that does not directly pertain to their credit history and file. It makes it illegal for lenders and creditors alike to take into consideration such factors as the consumer's color, race, ethnicity, nation of origin, religion, sex, or marital status when they are determining whether or not they will accept the credit or loan application.

Besides this, the law prohibits denying any credit application because of the age of the applicant. This assumes that the person applying has attained the legal minimum age and demonstrates the mental abilities necessary to execute such a contract. Finally, companies making loans may not reject an applicant because he or she receives public assistance funds from the government.

The governmental agency responsible for enforcing this Equal Credit Opportunity Act turns out to be the FTC Federal Trade Commission. As the consumer protection agency for the country, the FTC monitors lending organizations to make sure that they are not in violation of any of these discriminatory rules. Creditors are allowed to ask applicants for such information as their color, race, religion, sex, ethnicity, nation of origin, age, or marital status.

They are not allowed to consider any of these factors when determining whether or not to extend credit or even when deciding the terms of the credit which they are offering. The fact remains that not all people applying for credit will receive it or will obtain it on equal terms. Many factors are taken into consideration by lenders in ascertaining a person's creditworthiness, such as expenses, income, credit history, and levels of debts.

This Equal Credit Opportunity Act specifically protects consumers when they transact with investors or organizations that routinely offer credit. This includes loan and finance companies, banks, department or retail stores, credit unions, and credit card companies. Every party who is a part of the credit granting or terms setting decisions has to abide by the rules of the ECOA. This includes even the finance arrangers such as real estate brokers.

As a person applies for a mortgage, lenders will routinely inquire about some of the elements of information that are forbidden to be considered in the ultimate application decision. Because of this, applicants do not have to respond to these questions. The only considerations which they are allowed to employ in judging the merits of the individual must be information that is financially relevant, like the person's income, credit score, and present debt levels.

The Equal Credit Opportunity Act will not allow lenders to make approval decisions because of an individual's present or past marital status. They will require that applicants inform them of any child support or alimony payments which they are making. Persons receiving such substantial payments as part of their income should also disclose this so that they can obtain the loan. Companies may refuse to provide a loan because the individual's financial obligations along with child support payments are too high to pay back the loan under the required terms. This does not mean that a person can be turned down for a loan because he or she is or has been divorced.

The penalties for violating the Equal Credit Opportunity Act are severe. Class action lawsuits can be brought against them. Organizations found guilty of ignoring this act can be made to pay damages that amount to either $500,000 or a percent of the applicant's net worth, whichever is less.

European Central Bank (ECB)

The European Central Bank is responsible for the European Union's monetary system and for maintaining the euro currency. The EU created this central bank of European central banks in June of 1998. It works alongside the various national banks of the EU member states to come up with unified monetary policy. This policy is intended to help achieve price stability throughout the countries in the EU.

The ECB became responsible for the EU's monetary police on January 1 of 1999. This was the point in time when the euro currency became adopted by the various EU nations. This landmark event was the culmination of 20 years of steps towards a currency union.

In 1979, eight of the EU nations created the EMS European Monetary System. It effectively fixed the exchange rates between the eight participating nations. By 2002, the ECB had become more entrenched. Twelve EU nations signed on to a common monetary policy and formed the European Economic and Monetary Union that year.

The European Central Bank is independent of political groups in the various institutions of the EU such as the European Commission, European Parliament, and European Council. It handles all EU monetary issues and policies. Maintaining price stability is the first goal of the central bank. It also sets the important interest rates for the Eurozone and area.

Besides creating monetary policy for the Eurozone block, the ECB also engages in foreign exchange, holds reserve currencies, and authorizes euro bank note issues. Euro currency is actually created, printed, and maintained by the European System of Central Banks, also known as the ESCB.

The ECB has become involved in some controversial activities which were beyond the scope of its original role. It has further expanded its mandate in recent years by buying up bonds of financial companies like banks and also sovereign countries whose bonds are not finding enough interested subscribers at competitive low rates.

They have been practicing this quantitative easing and injecting money into euro area economies in an effort to encourage growth and to increase financial liquidity in the banking system. Keeping the interest rates down on sovereign national bonds also improves the budgets and balance sheets of the euro area countries which are struggling. The result of these activities has led to negative real interest rates in Europe.

Individual EU countries collect their own taxes. They also determine their own national budgets. The ECB has nothing to do with these activities. National governments work together at the EU level to come up with uniform rules on public finances. This helps them to cooperate better on policies for employment, growth, and financial stability.

The financial crisis that broke out around the globe in 2008 hit some European countries especially hard. It created a need for the ECB to work closely with the European Commission and the national governments of the EU and Eurozone members in a series of coordinated, sustained actions.

These groups are continuing to strive together to promote employment and growth, keep credit flowing to consumers and businesses at affordable prices, safeguard savings, and to guarantee inter-European financial stability. This has led to the accusation of critics of the European institutions that they only work effective when there are crises, as in a management by crisis style.

Despite these ongoing and best efforts of the ECB and other European institutions, severe imbalances and problems remain in several Eurozone countries. As of 2016, unemployment in Spain still sat at over 25% and Greece teetered on the brink of yet another recession and potential insolvency.

European Investment Bank (EIB)

The European Investment Bank proves to be the bank of the European Union. As such it is the one and only bank which is both representing the EU member states' interests and also owned by the same member countries. This EIB works hand in glove with the other institutions of the European Union in order to carry out the common EU policies.

This European Investment Bank turns out to be the biggest multilateral lender and borrower on the planet. It delivers finance via loans and joint ventures as well as expertise to support projects of sustainable investments. While over 90 percent of the bank's projects remain in Europe, they are still a substantially large investor throughout the globe.

The European Investment Bank betters the quality of life for individuals within and without the continent of Europe by offering expertise and finance on projects which encourage SME's (small to medium enterprises), infrastructure, innovation, and climate action. Their enormous and far flung enterprises in areas of lending, blending, and advisory services work for the good of EU residents and citizens, along with residents of numerous countries which are not a part of the European Union.

Lending is the overwhelming center of activity for the European Investment Bank. By far the greatest share of the bank's financing occurs via loans. They do also provide microfinance, guarantees, and equity investment, among other types of financing. The bank is able to harness their vast financial resources in order to borrow money on the world markets at extremely competitive rates. They then deliver these cost savings to those projects which they deem to be economically practical and which foster the objectives of EU policy.

Lending accounts for nearly 90 percent of all their financial commitments. The European Investment Bank actually lends money to clients of all sizes and purposes in order to encourage jobs and sustainable growth. The support of this well-regarded institution tends to attract other investors to the projects. Such projects must be over 25 million Euros in order to qualify for a loan. They also facilitate intermediated loans through local area banks.

With their venture capital program, they assist fund managers to invest capital in growth area SME's and high technology companies. Microfinance they offer for both fund and equity investments as well.

Blending is the tool whereby the European Investment Bank helps to release funding from other financial sources by collaborating on a project. This support especially comes out of the EU budget. When blended along with loans, it helps to ensure a fully financed package of investment in a given project.

The EIB offers structured finance to give support to high priority projects. Guarantees ensure that a good project will be able to bring in sufficient new investment from other partners. Project bonds help to unlock funding for infrastructure projects. The InnovFin initiative delivers innovators EU based finance. The bank also partners with donors in trust funds. They support transport infrastructure and the JEREMIE project which delivers financial engineering and flexible finance to SME enterprises.

Other blending programs include ESIF Financial Instruments, the JESSICA program which supports urban development, the Private Finance for Energy Efficiency (PF4EE) program, and the Mutual Reliance Initiative offering efficient partnerships for development and growth.
Blending programs also include the Natural Capital Financing Facility to combine the bank's financing with that of the European Commission as part of the LIFE Program to assist climate and environmental actions. An interesting last blending program proves to be the Risk Capital Facility for the Southern Neighborhood. This gives access to debt and equity financing for SMEs found throughout the Mediterranean regions. Its goal is to foster growth which is inclusive, job creation in the private sector, and development in the private sector.

Advising services provide technical assistance and expertise in the form of project and administrative management capabilities. This helps to bring in other investment. Both pubic authorities and private companies are able to rely on the technical and financial experience of the European Investment Advisory Hub to make sure the entity obtains the best people needed for a given project.

European Monetary System (EMS)

In 1979 a few European nations linked their currencies together in an arrangement and system to stabilize exchange rates called the European Monetary System. This system endured until the EMU European Economic and Monetary Union succeeded it.

As an important institution within the European Union, the EMU established the euro. The origin of the EMS lay in an effort to reduce significant changes in exchange rates between the European nations and to reign in inflation. It led to the creation of the European Central Bank in June of 1998 and the euro in January of 1999.

After the failure of the defunct Bretton Woods Agreement in 1972, the Europeans wanted to create a new exchange rate system of their own to help encourage political and economic unity throughout the EU. They came up with the EMS in 1979 as a means of moving towards the common currency of the future.

The EMS eventually formed its successor the European Currency Unit. With the ECU, exchange rates could be formulated by methods that were official. In the first year of the EMS, currency values proved to be uneven. Adjustments had to be made to lower weaker currencies while increasing the stronger currency values. In 1986 they came up with a more stable system of altering national interest rates instead.

Crisis broke out in the EMS in the early years of the 1990s. Germany's reunification created political and economic conditions that made the exchange rate bands less workable. Britain withdrew permanently from EMS in 1992. They became more independent from the central EU this way and banded together with Denmark and Sweden in refusing to become members of the eurozone.

This did not stop other nations within the EU from continuing to push for closer economic integration and a common currency. They formed the European Monetary Institute in 1994 to set up an orderly transition to the ECB that arose in 1998. The main tasks of the new ECB were to come up with one interest rate and monetary policy by laboring alongside the national central banks.

The ECB was not given the role originally of lending money to governments in financial crises or increasing employment rates like the majority of central banks. This would later cause delays and problems in bailing out struggling countries in the financial crisis that began in earnest in 2008.

The end of 1998 saw the majority of nations in the EU cut their interest rates at the same time to encourage economic growth while preparing to implement the Euro currency. This is when they established the EMU to succeed the EMS as the primary economic policy mechanism in the European Union. The adoption and subsequent circulation of the euro by the eurozone countries proved to be a significant step towards the aimed for European political unity. The EMU has helped member nations attempt to work toward lower inflation, less public spending, and lesser government debts.

Hidden weaknesses in the European Monetary System became obvious during the global financial crisis of 2008 and the following years. Member nations like Greece, Portugal, Spain, Ireland, and Cyprus ran up high deficits that later erupted in the European sovereign debt crisis.

Because these countries did not have national currencies to devalue, they could not increase their exports. The EMU forbade them from spending additional money and running higher deficits to help increase employment. EMS policies had expressly forbidden eurozone bailouts to any countries whose economies were in trouble.

After months of arguments from the larger economy members such as Germany and France, the EMU at last came up with bailout policies that allowed aid to be dispensed to peripheral members who were struggling. They set up the European Stability Mechanism as a permanent pool of money to help out economies of struggling EU member states in 2012. This allowed a few of the countries in trouble like Spain, Portugal, and Ireland to make some progress on recoveries.

European Monetary Union (EMU)

The European Monetary Union is also known by its long-time acronym of EMU. The full name of this is the European Economic and Monetary Union. This refers to the succeeding protocol to the original EMS European Monetary System. It means the combining of European Union member nations into a frame work for a centralized economic policy set and system. The most visible and greatest representation of this union is the euro currency, which has become the national currency for more than half the EU member states.

It was via a three-staged process that the EMU succeeded the EMS. The final third phase included the adopting of the euro currency which replaced the long-time national currencies such as the franc, peso, and mark. It was successfully concluded by all of the original EU members besides Denmark and the United Kingdom. Both of these countries received opts-outs from taking on the euro in place of their beloved sovereign national currencies.

The real history of such an economic and monetary union began with the French Foreign Minister Robert Schuman's speech, which became known as the Schuman Declaration on May 9th of 1950. He reasoned that the one sure way to ensure the peace lasted in Europe that had suffered from devastating world wars two times in only thirty years was to craft Europe into one single economic polity. It was his landmark speech that gave rise to the Treaty of Paris in 1951. This actually forged the ECSC European Coal and Steel Community betwixt signatories Germany, Italy, France, Belgium. Luxembourg, and the Netherlands.

This original treaty strengthened through the subsequent Treaties of Rome that led to the creation of the EEC European Economic Community. Next came the Treaty of Paris that lasted through 2002. In the 1960s and 1970s, the politicians across Europe adopted the Werner Plan, yet later economic disruptions including the Saudi oil embargo and break down of the Bretton Woods agreement meant that they could not merge economically any further at this point.

The Maastrict Treaty of 1992 created a literal timeline to establish the European Monetary Union. By 1998, they had successfully formed the ECB

European Central Bank which established conversion rates that were fixed between all of the member state currencies. This led to the rise of the euro single currency that started physically circulating in 2002.

Yet there were hidden flaw in the EMU design. Greece became the first severe example of these. It was revealed by 2009 that Greece had been intentionally under reporting the amount of its severe budget deficits it ran since they started using the Euro in 2001. As a result, the nation experienced what amounts to the most serious economic crisis in modern history. The proud country had no choice but to agree to two painful bailout and austerity packages from the EU and ECB in only five years. Continued bailouts remained essential to Greece being able to repay its massive debts to its many creditors.

The unemployment rate in Greece rose to as high as 25 percent (in general) and 50 percent (for people less than 25 years old). The county's government was forced to instill capital controls to prevent monetary flight and also launch a bank holiday to limit the amounts of euros which depositors could withdraw from the banking system in any given day. The only way out of their still ongoing crisis would be to leave the EMU and return to their ancient currency the Drachma. This would allow them to severely devalue their currency and increase the competitiveness of their exports abroad.

European Stability Mechanism (ESM)

The European Stability Mechanism is a significant part of the financial stability and safeguard mechanisms in the Euro Zone area. It replaced the EFSF European Financial Stability Facility in 2013. This original EFSF was never intended to be permanent. Instead it was designed as a temporary solution to financial problems within the EU.

The European Stability Mechanism that took over for it was better established to deliver financial help to those Eurozone member countries that found themselves either threatened by or actually experiencing financial difficulties.

These two financial facilities ran concurrently from October of 2012 through June of 2013. Beginning in July of 2013 the EFSF could no longer begin new programs for financial support or help. The program still exists to manage and collect repayments of debts that are outstanding.

Once all of the existing loans that the EFSF program made have been repaid and all funding instruments and guarantors have received full payment for their contributions, then the EFSF will cease to exist entirely. This makes the replacing ESM the only and ongoing internal means for delivering aid in response to new calls for financial assistance from Eurozone member nations.

The European Stability Mechanism proves to be the principal means of resolving crises for nations which participate in the Euro. It obtains its money by issuing debt obligations. This permits it to fund financial aid and loans to the member countries of the Euro area. The European Council actually created the ESM in December of 2010. Participating Euro member states came together and signed a treaty between the governments on February 2 of 2012. October 8 of 2012 was the day they inaugurated the new ESM.

This ESM has great flexibility in funding its distressed member states. As various conditions are met, it is able to deliver loans as part of a program for macroeconomic adjustment. The mechanism is also able to buy member countries' debt in either the secondary or primary markets.

It can help to recapitalize banks of member states by loaning the governments money for this purpose. It can also deliver credit lines as a means of providing financial help as a precaution. In worst case and last resort conditions, the facility is allowed to recapitalize banks and other financial institutions directly. This is limited to times when resolution funds and bail ins are not enough to make the bank financially viable again.

The resources of the ESM are considerable. It has a capital base that has been subscribed in the amount of 704.8 billion. Of this amount, 80.5 billion has been paid in to the facility. The remaining 624.3 billion is classified as callable capital when it is needed. The fund is able to loan out a maximum total of 500 billion.

The ESM is based in Luxembourg. It is governed by public international law as an intergovernmental organization. It has only government shareholders making up its ownership. These are the 19 member countries that make up the Euro area. In 2016, 153 staff members worked under the direction of Klaus Regling the managing director.

European countries which are in trouble have other outside recourses for help besides the ESM. The principal other provider of assistance is the International Monetary Fund. The EU has supported having its own ESM, along with the predecessors the EFSF and the European Financial Stabilization Mechanism because it feared the consequences of some of its member states' problems with debt. Not all of the EZ countries suffered from debt issues. One EZ country failing could have contagious effects and widespread repercussions on the other national economies' health.

Exchange Rate Mechanism (ERM)

Exchange Rate Mechanisms are systems that were established to maintain a certain range of exchange for currencies as measured against other currencies. These ERMs can be run in three different ways. On one extreme they can float freely. This permits the systems to trade without the central banks and governments intervening.

The fixed Exchange rate mechanisms will do whatever it takes to maintain rates pegged at a specific value. In between these two extremes are the managed ERMs. The best known example of one of these is the European Exchange Rate Mechanism known as ERM II. It is in use today for those countries who wish to become a part of the EU monetary union.

The European Economic Community formally introduced the European ERM system to the world on March 13, 1979. It was a part of the EMS European Monetary System. The goal of this new system centered on attaining monetary stability throughout Europe by reducing the variable exchange rates. This was set up to prepare the way for the Economic and Monetary Union. It also paved the way for the Euro single currency introduction that formally occurred on January 1, 1999.

The Europeans changed their system once the Euro became adopted. They introduced ERM II as a way to link together those EU countries who were not a part of the eurozone with the euro. They did this to boost extra eurozone currencies' stability. A second goal was to create a means of evaluating the countries who wished to join the eurozone. In 2016 only a single currency uses the ERM II. This is the Danish krone.

The European ERM ceased to exist in 1999. This was the point after the eurozone country European Currency Units exchange rates became frozen and the Euro began trading against them. ERM II then replaced the initial ERM. At first the Greek drachma remained in the ERM II alongside the Danish currency. This changed when Greece adopted the Euro in 2001. Currencies within the newer system may float in a fairly tight range of plus or minus 15% of their central exchange rate versus the euro. Denmark does better than this. Its Danmarks Nationalbank maintains a 2.25% range versus the central rate of DKK 7.46038.

In order for other countries that wish to join the Euro to participate, they are required to be a part of the ERM II system for minimally two years before they can become members of the eurozone. This means that at some point, a number of currencies for member states that joined the EU will have to be in the system. This includes the Swedish krona, Polish zloty, Hungarian forint, Czech Republic koruna, the Romanian leu, Bulgarian lev, and Croatian kuna. Each of these is supposed to join the system according to their individual treaties of accession.

In the case of Sweden, the situation is more complicated. The country held a referendum on becoming a part of the mechanism to which the citizens voted no. The European Central Bank still expects that Sweden will join the system and eventually adopt the euro. This is because they did not negotiate for an opt out of the currency as did the U.K. and Denmark. The Maastricht Treaty requires that EU member states all eventually join the exchange rate mechanism.

Britain participated in the mechanism from 1990 until September of 1992. On September 16, 1992 the British famously crashed out of the system on what became known as Black Wednesday because of manipulation of the pound by currency speculators led by Hedge Fund Billionaire George Soros.

Exchange Traded Funds (ETF)

These ETF's prove to be stock market exchange traded investment funds that work very much like stocks. Exchange Traded Funds contain instruments like commodities, stocks, and bonds. They trade for around the identical net asset value as the assets that they contain throughout the course of a day. The majority of ETF's actually follow the value of an index like the Dow Jones Industrial or the S&P 500. Since their creation in 1993, ETF's have evolved into the most beloved kind of exchange traded instruments.

The first Exchange Traded Fund particular to countries proved to be a joint venture of MSCI, Funds Distributor, and BGI. This first product finally turned into the iShares name that is accepted and recognized all over earth today. In the first fifteen years, such ETF's were index funds that simply followed indexes. The United States Securities and Exchange Commission began allowing firms to establish actively managed ETF's back in 2008.

Exchange Traded Funds provide a number of terrific advantages for smaller investors. Among these are elements like simple and effective diversification, index funds tax practicality, and expense ratios that remain very low. While doing all of this, they also offer the appeal of familiarity for you who trade stocks. This includes such comfortable and helpful options as limit orders, options, and short selling the ETF's. Since it is so inexpensive to purchase, hold, and sell these ETF's, many investors in ETF shares choose to keep them over a longer time frame for purposes of diversification and asset allocation. Still other investors trade in and out of these instruments regularly in order to participate in their strategies for market timing investing.

Exchange Traded Funds boast of many advantages. On the one hand, they provide great flexibility in buying and selling. It is easy for you to sell and buy them at the actual market price any time during a trading day, in contrast to mutual funds that you can only acquire at a trading day's conclusion. Since they are companies that trade like stocks, you can buy them in margin accounts and sell them short, meaning that they can be used for hedging purposes too. ETF's also allow limit orders and stop loss orders, which are helpful for assuring entry prices and protecting profits or safeguarding from losses.

ETF's also provide lower costs for traders. This results from the majority of ETF's not being actively managed. Also, ETF's do not spend large amounts of money on distribution, marketing, and accounting costs. The majority of them do not have the fees associated with most mutual funds either.

ETF's are among the greatest vehicles for diversifying portfolios quickly and easily. As an example, with only one set of shares, you can "own" the entire S&P 500 index. ETF's will give you exposure to country specific indexes, international markets, commodities, and even bond indexes.

ETF's have two other advantages. They are both transparent and tax efficient. Transparent in this regard means that they are clear in their portfolio holdings and are priced all day long. They are tax efficient as they do not create many capital gains, since they are not in the business of buying and selling their underlying indexes. They also are not required to sell their holding in order to meet redemptions of investors.

Extendable Commercial Paper (XCP)

Extendable Commercial Paper, also known by its acronym XCP, represents a promissory note that is unsecured and comes with a set maturity date which can not be longer than 270 days. This paper is also a money market form of security that major corporations issue and sell to raise funds for their short term needs, such as payroll obligations. The paper is backed by a corporate promise to pay back the face value on date of maturity, which the note itself specifies. Alternatively it could be secured by the bank which issues it.

Because these instruments do not carry any collateral backing, it is only those companies that boast of phenomenal credit ratings from at least one of the principal credit ratings agencies which are able to sell such extendable commercial paper for a reasonable rate. Companies commonly sell this debt instrument at a face value discount. It usually comes with a lesser interest rate than would a comparable bond. This is because of the lesser maturity dates inherent with the rules surrounding commercial paper (they must all be under 270 days in maturity to be extendable commercial paper).

In general, the greater amount of time till maturity on any given note, the greater the interest rate will be required of the institution. Though such interest rates do go up and down according to conditions in the market, they are usually less than the rates which banks pay.

Such extendable commercial paper is called extendable simply because it is issued in an open ended fashion within the United States as part of American companies' ongoing rolling programs. In Europe by contrast, these programs are typically a predetermined and set number of years in length.

By the end of the year 2009, over 1,700 different firms within the U.S. were issuing extendable commercial paper. As of month-ending October in 2008, the American Federal Reserve announced that the end of 2007 seasonally adjusted figures demonstrated that a total of $1.78 trillion worth of all forms of commercial paper existed. Of this amount, $979.4 billion of it did not have any assets backing it as extendable commercial paper. Financial companies were issuing $816.7 billion worth of it while $162.7 billion was from non-financial entities.

In the rest of the world outside of the U.S., the next most significant commercial paper market is the Euro-Commercial Paper Market. This market boasts more than $500 billion worth of outstanding paper. These instruments are mostly denominated in Euros, pound sterling, and U.S. dollars.

The history of commercial paper and credit dates back over a century. Promissory notes from companies and corporations have been around since at least the 1800s. In that century, now legendary Goldman Sachs founder Marcus Goldman began his career in trading commercial paper in 1869 in the city of New York.

The whole point of extendable commercial paper is that it does not have to be monitored by the Securities Exchange Commission because the maturities on these obligations are under their targeted 270 days. Companies get around this by using continuous commercial paper arrangements. These renew and replace the maturing commercial paper for as many times as necessary to provide for the corporate obligations. Otherwise, the companies would be forced to file registration statements of the instruments with the SEC. This would cause higher costs for the offerings and lead to lengthy delays.

Two methods exist for extending this commercial paper into markets. Issuers are able to sell the securities right to money market funds and other buy and hold investors. Besides this, they can offload the paper to a commercial paper dealer who will then sell the paper on to the market on their behalf. Dealer fees typically run five basis points, which amounts to $50,000 in fees for every $100 million they issue.

Federal Deposit Insurance Corporation (FDIC)

The U.S. government started The Federal Deposit Insurance Corporation back in 1933. They created it because of the literally thousands of failed banks that went down in the 1920s and 1930s. The FDIC began insuring bank accounts at the beginning of 1934. Since then, no depositors have lost any insured bank account money despite a consistent number of banks failing every year.

The first role of the FDIC is to insure and to increase the public's confidence in the American banking system. They do this in several ways. The FDIC insures minimally $250,000 in bank and thrift accounts. They watch for and take action on any risks to the deposit insurance funds. They also stop the spread of any bank failures when one of the banks does fail.

The Federal Deposit Insurance Corporation only insures deposits. This means that it does not cover mutual funds, stocks, or any other investments that some banks offer to their customers. They offer a standard $250,000 amount for each depositor's account. This single limit amount does not apply to other types of account ownerships and accounts at other banks. To help individuals understand if the insurance provided is enough to cover their various kinds of account, the FDIC provides its Electronic Deposit Insurance Estimator.

Another important role of the FDIC lies in its supervisory position. The outfit oversees over 4,500 different savings and commercial banks to make sure that they are operationally safe and sound. This represents more than half of the banks. Those banks that are set up as state banks may choose to become a member of either the Federal Reserve System or the FDIC. Any banks that are not overseen by the Federal Reserve System are watched over by the FDIC.

Another job of the FDIC is to check on the various banks to make sure they abide by the government's consumer protection laws. These laws include The Fair Credit Reporting Act, the Fair Credit Billing Act, the Fair Debt Collection Practices Act, and the Truth in Lending Act.

Lastly, the FDIC checks banks to make sure the different institutions are abiding by their responsibilities under the Community Reinvestment Act. This law ensures that banks help the communities where they were started to achieve their needs for credit.

Despite all of these roles, the only one that members of the public really encounter on a personal basis is the FDIC protecting insured depositors. When a bank or thrift goes down, the FDIC immediately reacts to the situation. They come in fast with the group that chartered the bank to close it down. The charter group could be the Office of the Comptroller of the Currency or the state regulator.

The next step is for the FDIC to wind up the failed bank. In their preferred method, they sell both the loans and the deposits of the bank to another banking institution. Customers rarely feel the transition in the majority of the cases. This is the FDIC's goal, to make sure that people do not lose access to their accounts and money.

The FDIC carries out its several mandates through six regional branches. It has more than 7,000 staff members that help it to carry out these goals. The organization is based in its headquarters in the capital Washington, D.C. Besides these locations, they also have various field offices throughout the nation.

The leadership of the FDIC is supplied by the Federal Government. The President appoints the board which the Senate confirms. There are five members of their Board of Directors. No more than three of them may belong to one political party to ensure bipartisanship in the decisions.

Federal Trade Commission (FTC)

The FTC Federal Trade Commission proves to be the agency responsible for protecting the American consumers. They strive to stop tricky, fraudulent, and unfair practices in business in the nation's marketplaces. They also disburse valuable information to consumers that helps them to recognize, stop, and sidestep these frauds.

The FTC accepts consumer complaints by phone, email, their website, and through the mail. They take these complaints and enter them into a database that is called the Consumer Sentinel Network. This secure online tool is utilized for investigation purposes by literally hundreds of criminal and civil agencies for law enforcement throughout the United States and overseas.

What the FTC would like to do is to stop these types of deceptive and non-competitive business dealings before they hurt consumers. They are also attempting to improve consumer opportunities so that they are better informed about and comprehend the nature of competition. The agency attempts to perform all of these tasks without putting too many burdens and restrictions on businesses activities that are legitimate.

Congress created the FTC back in 1914. Originally its mandate lay in stopping unfair means of competition in trade and business caused by the trusts. They were a part of the government's stated goal to bust up these trusts. Congress has given them more authority to monitor and fight practices that were against fair competition over the years by passing other laws.

The government enacted another law in 1938 that was broadly addressed to stop any deceptive or unfair practices and acts. They have continued to receive direction and discretion to govern a number of other laws that protect consumers over the subsequent years. Among these are the Pay Per Call Rule, the Telemarketing Sales Rule, and the Equal Credit Opportunity Act. Congress passed another law in 1975 that gave the Federal Trade Commission the ability to come up with rules that regulated trade throughout the industries.

The FTC has a vision for the American economy. They want to see one that has healthy competition between producers. They also desire to see consumers able to obtain correct information. Ultimately the government agency looks for all of this to create low priced and superior quality goods. They encourage innovation, efficiency in business, and choice for consumers.

This agency carries out its vision with three strategic goals. It starts with them protecting consumers by heading off trickery and deception in the business and consumer marketplace. They desire to keep competition going strong. In this role, they stop mergers and business dealings that they believe are against competition. They also work to increase their own performance with consistently improving and excellent managerial, individual, and organizational efforts.

All of these goals and efforts combine to make the FTC one of the government agencies that most impacts each American citizen's economic and personal life. They are the only government entity that possesses a mandate for both competition jurisdiction and consumer protection in large segments of the U.S. economy. They go after aggressive and effectual enforcement of the laws.

The FTC shares its knowledge with international, state, and federal groups and agencies. The group creates research tools at a variety of conferences, workshops, and hearings every year. They also develop and distribute easy to understand educational materials for business and consumer needs in the transforming technological and global market.

The FTC carries out its work through its Bureaus of Economics, Competition, and Consumer Protection. They receive assistance from the Office of General Counsel. Seven regional offices around the country help them to carry out their mandate.

Financial Industry Regulatory Authority (FINRA)

The Financial Industry Regulatory Authority is a congressionally authorized independent and non profit outfit. Congress established them to safeguard the investors of America by ensuring that the stock market industry runs honestly and fairly for all participants.

FINRA is not an agency of the government, even though they have broad disciplinary and enforcement powers. The organization tirelessly works to ensure the integrity of the market and protection for investors by regulating the securities business.

FINRA carries out these duties in a variety of ways. They investigate brokerage firms to make sure they abide by the rules. The not for profit creates and then enforces these rules that govern the actions of more than 3,941 securities companies who have over 641,157 brokers on staff. FINRA also encourages transparency in markets and settles disputes. The group does all of this without taxpayers having to support them via taxes.

The authority works every day to make sure individuals selling securities are tested and licensed. They ensure all advertisements for securities utilized to sell the products are clear and truthful. FINRA holds companies to a high standard for only selling suitable investments to individuals that are appropriate to their needs. They ensure that every investor obtains full disclosure about their investment before they buy it.

The independent agency carried out 1,512 disciplinary actions on registered firms and brokers in 2015. This allowed them to collect fines of over $95 million. They mandated that $96.6 million be given back to investors who where harmed in these and other actions. The group handed over 800 different insider trading or fraud cases to other agencies like the SEC for settling or prosecuting the same year.

Ultimately FINRA's goals are to deter misconduct in the industry. They do this by enforcing rules for everyone. This is not only the rules that they create. The group also enforces the Municipal Securities Rulemaking Board's regulations and federal securities laws as well. They make the qualifying exams and require brokers to come to continuing education classes.

The organization puts hundreds of their own financial examiners in the field to check on the way these brokers carry out their business. Their main concern is for the investors and risks to the markets. They follow up on complaints filed by investors and other suspicious activities.

They also review all advertisements, brochures, websites, and communications to be certain brokers are fairly presenting their products. This amounts to approximately 100,000 different communications and advertisements they examine and approve between broker firms and their investors.

FINRA also disciplines rule breakers. They use their authority, technology, and professional experts to rapidly react to wrongs. The organization has the authority to fine brokers, suspend them, or expel them from the business.

The independent agency also possesses technology that is potent enough for them to be able to review various markets and pick up on possible fraud. They are able to gather data in such a way to keep tabs on insider trading or other practices that give broker firms advantages that are unfair. To this effect they process anywhere from 42 billion to 75 billion transactions daily to have a full picture of U.S. market trading.

The group is also involved in resolving disputes in the securities' business. This pertains to problems between investors and brokers. FINRA handles almost 100% of all mediations and arbitrations that are related to securities. They hear these disputes in 70 different locations. This includes one hearing center in every state, Puerto Rico, and London.

Financial Times Stock Exchange (FTSE)

The Financial Times Stock Exchange represents an enormous group of indices owned by the London Stock Exchange. The acronym originated in the days when it was half owned by the Financial Times newspaper and the LSE. Now this group is an entirely owned subsidiary of only the London Stock Exchange.

When individuals use the word FTSE, they are most commonly referring to the most important benchmark index of the group the FTSE 100. These 100 companies are the hundred largest British companies which the London Stock Exchange lists. As such the Blue Chip companies of the British economy represent the biggest companies by market capitalization in the U.K. Besides this FTSE 100 index, the group produces the FTSE 250, the 350, the Small Cap, and the All-Share.

The FTSE 250 companies are those next 250 largest companies after the FTSE 100. Combining the 250 and the 100 yields the 350 index. Merging the 350 and Small Cap provides the All Share Index.

London Stock Exchange launched the FTSE 100 on January 3, 1984. The companies in the index are calculated for size based on their market capitalization, or number of existing shares times the price per share. The group recalculates the indices every quarter to adjust for any of the companies in the 250 index that have moved up to the 100 index and those in the 100 group that have dropped to the 250 group.

Besides this, they have to remove companies that have been taken over or merged with others. The index must also be updated for name changes, as happened with British Gas becoming BG Group and Centrica, Midland Bank becoming HSBC, and Commercial Union Assurance becoming Aviva. Name changes, mergers, and takeovers are changed as soon as they become effective.

FTSE 100 updates its composite companies based on those which rise to a position in the top 90 largest companies on the London Stock Exchange. Those which fall to the 111th position or lower are dropped. They maintain this overlapping band so that there will not be too much change in the index in any given quarter. The group is concerned about the stability of the index and the rate of change because it forces investment companies and funds to rebalance when the benchmark 100 index changes. This is an expensive process for the large investors that the group tries to mitigate.

The 100 index and other benchmark indices are calculated up every 15 seconds throughout the trading days. The values are published in real time all day. The indices are open from 8am to 4:30pm on all weekdays that are not market holidays.

FTSE 100 is considered to be a good barometer for geopolitical and economic events throughout the world. When the major global markets soar, it does as well. When they plummet, it falls in sympathy. The largest single point drop for the 100 index happened on the day following Black Monday in the U.S. on October 20th of 1987. On this occasion, the 100 index fell 12.22% in a single trading session.

FTSE is not only a series of British stock indices. The group also produces and compiles every day more than 100,000 additional indices around the globe. Among these are the Global Equity, Italy's MIB, the China A50 and 50, the Portugal 20, and the TWSE Taiwan. In 2015 the group merged with Russell to become the FTSE Russell Group. This gave it reach into a number of American stock market indices like the Russell 2000.

Follow-On Public Offer (FPO)

A Follow-On Public Offer is also known by its official acronym FPO. This occurs when a public company which is already listed on a stock market exchange issues additional shares to investors. Such FPOs are useful and practical for those firms which wish to raise extra equity capital from the capital markets via stock issues. These methods are popular with publically traded corporations.

Such firms like to avail themselves of these FPO issues by selling more shares to investors. They have to complete an offer document in order to accomplish this. FPOs are never to be confused with IPOs. IPOs refer to the initial public offering a company uses to issue equity shares to the public for the very first time. FPOs are instead supplementary issues which they make once the firm is already exchange-established and -trading.

There are two main types of Follow-on public offerings available to companies today. The first kind dilutes existing investors. The Board of Directors must agree to boost the level of shares floating. It raises money for paying down debt or internally growing the company business. It ultimately raises the numbers of outstanding shares as well.

The second kind of FPO proves to be non diluting. It is the preferred method when the major shareholders or corporate directors elect to sell their own personal shares of the company stock. Since no new shares become created, it does not dilute the holdings of existing investors in the company. This is generally known as a secondary market offering. Neither the firm nor the present shareholders gain an advantage from this type of method.

Because there are two different means of selling shares with such Follow-On Public Offers, this makes it extremely crucial to know who the stock sellers are on any given offering transaction. This way, investors are able to learn quickly and easily if the new offering will prove to be net dilutive or not.

Such Follow-On Public Offerings prove to be increasingly commonplace within the world of investing. Corporations appreciate that they can quickly and easily collect additional fresh capital to utilize for any common purpose they deem appropriate or expedient. Their share price might drop as a result of such an FPO announcement. This upsets shareholders who are the main losers in such a scenario. Many times these secondary share offerings will be made at prices that are lower than the present market prices. In any case, they will almost certainly dilute the power and voting rights of their presently existing shares of company stock.

It always helps to look at some tangible examples to better grasp a challenging concept such as this one. Back in the year 2013, corporations deployed enough Follow-On Public Offers to raise an impressive $201.7 billion in additional equity. This was the greatest single-year amount that they raised for four years. Facebook outperformed in this respect by selling off an additional $3.9 billion worth of shares. This made them among the biggest single beneficiaries of the FPOs for that year.

Investment banks love secondary offerings. They benefit directly from them since they receive a portion of the fee structure pricing. In that same year of 2013, leading American investment banking operation Goldman Sachs handled $24.7 billion in secondary offerings to be the number one FPO underwriter.

The year 2015 subsequently saw a great number of firms which had only gone public a year earlier decide to issue Follow-On Public Offerings. Shake Shack proved to be one of these. They announced their secondary offering and witnessed their shares decline as a result. The stock plunged an eye-watering 16 percent on the news that a major secondary offering was in the works for a price lower than the then-current share price. Naturally, investors in Shake Shack were unhappy, but they were completely powerless to prevent the deal from going through.

Foreign Account Tax Compliance Act (FACTA)

Foreign Account Tax Compliance Act (FACTA) proves to be an American-issued and -rigorously enforced law. It requires all United States' citizens living either stateside or overseas to make annual report filings of any foreign bank account holdings they possess. This FACTA law came into effect back in 2010 along with the HIRE Act. The goal ostensibly was to encourage and foster greater transparency in the worldwide financial services universe. The ulterior motive lay in knowing any and all U.S. individuals' accounts which they might use to hide income or assets overseas. The ultimate goal is to maximize every last dollar in taxes form overseas-living Americans.

It was former U.S. President Barack Obama who signed the new HIRE Act into law in 2010. With this Hiring Incentives to Restore Employment Act, he was seeking to cut down the stubbornly high rate of unemployment that refused to disappear after the global financial crisis and meltdown of 2008-2009. Among the incentives they dangled in front of employers with the act was the ability to increase their business tax credits on every new staff member which a firm hired and retained for minimally a calendar year. There were still other incentive included in the bill. Companies benefited from a special payroll tax holiday advantage as well as a higher expense deduction limit on any new factory or production equipment which they purchased back in 2010.

Naturally the President and Congress required a revenue stream with which to pay for these business benefits and incentives. What they came up with was the requirement that all American tax payers report all of their assets maintained outside of the United States ever year. The idea was that in taxing such foreign-based accounts and assets, the country would boost its revenue sources enough to pay for the desperately needed corporate job stimulation programs. To provide a sufficient penalty incentive for American citizens to reveal these hidden assets, the IRS created a stiff regimen for any American resident or overseas-living U.S. citizen who chose not to report their international account assets and currency amounts which was greater than $50,000 value during the course of any tax year.

To grow the potential additional revenues by as much as possible, the government applied the new requirements not only to presumably wealthy and foreign-born individual Americans, but also to NFFE Non-Financial Foreign Entities and FFI Non-US Foreign Financial Institutions. These internationally based banks were then mandated to become compliant with the new revenue-catching law by revealing all American citizens' identities and the worth of any and all of their assets kept in their banks. Banks have to report this information to the IRS Internal Revenue Service or alternatively to the IGA FACTA Intergovernmental Agreement.

For those FFI's which elect to not comply with the Internal Revenue Service, they will summarily be banned from the United States' markets and banking system. They will also suffer a 30 percent deduction of any witholdable payments' amounts in the form of a tax penalty.

These payments relate to U.S. financial assets and income generated and kept in the banks. They include dividends, interest payments, remunerations, salaries and wages, profits, and compensations. Those NFFE's and FFI's which comply with the law have to report every year the identities of all their account holding U.S. citizens. This includes their names, addresses, and TIN tax identification numbers for every account. They also have to divulge the Americans' account numbers and balances, and all withdrawals and deposits made using the account during the calendar year.

The real goal behind FACTA is to eliminate tax evasion of American businesses and citizens who invest, earn, and operate in such a capacity as to gain taxable income overseas. It remains legal to own and operate an offshore account. It is in not properly disclosing it to the IRS that it becomes illegal. The reason is because the United States is the only major economy and jurisdiction to tax all of the assets and income from its citizens regardless of where they live, reside, and realize income in the world.

FOREX Markets

FOREX markets are the world wide foreign exchange markets. They are called FX markets as well. FOREX markets are different from all of the other major financial markets in that they are over the counter and decentralized. They exist for the purpose of trading currencies.

Unlike with other markets, the FOREX markets are also open twenty-four hours a day during the week and on Sunday, since the different financial centers around the globe serve as trading bases for a variety of buyers and sellers. This foreign exchange market is the place where supply and demand mostly decides the different currencies' values for nations around the world.

The main point and reason for the FOREX markets are to help out investment and trade internationally through permitting businesses to easily change one currency to the other one that they require. In practice, individuals or businesses actually buy one amount of foreign currency through paying for it with a given amount of a different currency.

As an example, Canadian businesses may import British goods by paying for them in British Pounds, even though their income and base currency are Canadian dollars. The foreign exchange markets allow for investors to speculate on the rising and falling values of various currencies as well. It also makes the infamous carry trade possible, where investors are able to borrow currencies with low yields or interest rates and use them to purchase higher interest rate yielding currencies. Critics have said that the FOREX markets also hurt some countries' competitiveness against other countries.

This market is extremely popular and unique for a variety of reasons. It possesses the greatest trading volume on earth, managing in the three to four trillion dollar range every single trading day. This gives it enormous liquidity. It is also geographically centered all over the world, from Wellington in New Zealand to London in Great Britain to New York in the United States. Traders love that the market runs fully twenty-four hours per day except for on the weekends, when it reopens Sunday afternoon.

Finally, an enormous degree of leverage, that can be as much as two hundred to one, allows for even people with small accounts to make potentially enormous gains. Because of all of these factors and its world wide trading base, the FOREX markets have been called the ones where perfect competition is most evident. This is the case even though central banks sometimes intervene directly in these markets to increase or decrease the value of their currency relative to a trading partners' or trading competitors' currency value.

Generally Accepted Accounting Principles (GAAP)

Generally Accepted Accounting Principles, more commonly referred to by their acronym GAAP, are the mostly American used set of accounting principles, procedures, and standards. These are utilized by companies to put together their corporate financial statements. Such GAAP proves to be a blend of the most accepted means of reporting and recording accounting data in the United States combined with the American policy board set standards.

Companies must use GAAP in order for their investors to have some common standard of consistency with financial statements they compare when considering the various companies in which to invest their money. These standards include such areas as balance sheet items classification, revenue recognition, and measurements of outstanding shares of stock.

Regulators expect that companies will obey these generally accepted accounting principles rules as they release their financial statements to routinely report their financial information. American investors should be leery of company financial statements that are not properly developed utilizing these guiding principles.

Despite this fact, these accounting procedures are merely a cohesive group of guidelines and standards. Crooked accountants are still able to distort and misrepresent the numbers while using these generally accepted procedures. Although a company may utilize the generally accepted procedures, investors should still carefully go through their financial statements with a healthy degree of skepticism.

The competing accounting standards that most of the rest of the world employs is known as the IFRS International Financial Reporting Standards. There has been a recent move to harmonize the two sets of standards in past years. Because of the global financial crisis and economic collapse of 2008 and its terrible aftermath, globalization, the SEC agreeing to accept international standards, and the Sarbanes-Oxley Act, countries like the United States have been severely pressured to close the gap between GAAP and the IFRS.

Doing so would have major ramifications on accounting throughout the U.S. It also would affect investors, corporate management teams, accountants, national accounting standard makers, and American stock markets. Bringing these two sets of standards together is impacting CFO and CPA attitudes regarding international accounting. This influences the International Accounting Standards quality as well as the various endeavors that professionals are making on converging the two sets of standards.

There are some problematic inconsistencies with international financial reporting because the financial reporting standards and rules are somewhat different from one country to another. This dilemma has become more of a challenge for those international investors who are attempting to figure out the various differences in global accounting and reporting. As they are thinking about offering substantial investments to overseas companies which are earnestly seeking capital in good faith, it makes it more challenging since companies report according to the standards of the country where they do business.

The IASB International Accounting Standards Board has been sincerely looking for a practical solution to this international complication, confusion, and conflict that inconsistency in accounting standards for financial reporting has created and continues to encourage. The principle difference with GAAP and the IFRS methods lies in the totally different approaches that either one uses regarding the standards.

Generally Accepted Accounting Practices prove to be based on a set of rules. It employs a complicated group of guidelines that set criteria and rules in any given scenario. The International Financial Reporting Standards alternatively utilizes a method based on principles. The IFRS instead starts with the goal of good financial reporting and gives guidance on the particular needs and challenges of a given scenario.

Government National Mortgage Association (GNMA)

GNMA refers to a United States HUD Department of Housing and Urban Development based government corporation. This agency is different from its cousin Freddie Mac as Ginnie Mae is not a private corporation. Rather it is an actual U.S. government agency.

The roles of GNMA are two-fold. They are to guarantee there is sufficient liquidity for mortgages which are government insured. This comprises all mortgages provided by the FHA Federal Housing Administration, the RHA Rural Housing Administration, and the VA Veterans Administration. The other responsibility of Ginnie Mae is to attract the capital of investors into the marketplace for such loans. This allows for the various issuers to provide still more loans in the future. The majority of those mortgages which Ginnie Mae securitizes and sells are in fact MBS mortgage-backed securities which are guaranteed by the FHA. These are usually mortgages which are offered to lower income borrowers and first time home buyers.

GNMA operates in a fairly straightforward manner. The governmental agency purchases home mortgages off of the financial institutions which make such loans. Then it pools them together into $1 million and higher collections. Ginnie Mae has choices at this point. Some of these pools it holds on to and then directly sells them to investors outright. Others it sells off to financial institutions and mortgage bankers who then sell them on to investors themselves.

After this, either the mortgage banker or GNMA itself will collect mortgage payments off of the pools' mortgage homeowners. For those investors who choose to invest in a GNMA, they typically receive monthly payments which come with at least a portion of the principal (that remains outstanding) as well as an interest payment. The other method has investors just obtaining interest payments. In this case, the principal only comes back to the investors as the mortgage reaches maturity.

Sometimes investors call such bonds from the agency Ginnie Mae pass through securities. This is because the requisite mortgage payments will go through, or pass through, a bank. The bank then collects its fee in advance of passing on what remains of the payment to the appropriate investors. These payments amount to greater returns than comparable U.S. Treasury notes provide investors.

GNMA's also possess other advantages. They are guaranteed not to default and fail by the United States' government and its full faith and credit. They also prove to be extremely liquid. This is partly because they may be easily resold via the active secondary market at any time.

GNMA instruments come with a hefty minimum investment dollar requirement. This amounts to typically $25,000. Once this minimum threshold is met, the size may be increased in only single dollar increments to whatever level is desired. There are opportunities to purchase such Ginnie Mae's which can sell for under the standard $25,000 when they are occasionally offered at face value discounts via the secondary market. This could occur in cases where the applicable interest rates prove to be lower than more current instrument issues' rates or also as the remaining principals have become reduced significantly.

There are also mutual funds which buy into Ginnie Mae's. The cost of shares in such funds are considerably lower than the $25,000 minimum of the instruments themselves. In cases like this, investment trusts or outright Ginnie Mae funds will purchase the bonds directly from the government agency or secondary market. They will then provide their own shares, which represent stakes in such instruments, to the investing public.

It is not only separate investors who purchase the Ginnie Mae's. A great range of different organizations and companies purchase them. Several examples of these other buyers abound. They are credit unions, retirement pension funds, commercial banks, real estate investment trusts, corporations, and insurance companies. There are also a great variety of different institution kinds that actually issue such Ginnie Mae's. Among these are banks, mortgage companies, and credit unions.

Government Sponsored Enterprise (GSE)

A government sponsored enterprise is a financial service operations that the U.S. Congress created by law. Their purpose is to improve the amount of credit that flows into specific areas of the American economy. They were also intended to help those parts of the capital markets become more transparent and efficient as well as to lessen risks for investors and capital suppliers.

The wish of Congress in establishing them was to increase the available finance and lower the cost of obtaining it for certain specific segments of the economy. This was to be accomplished by encouraging investors via lowering the risks of losses to those involved.

The main components of the economy where these were set up were home finance, agriculture, and education. Among these, two of the government sponsored enterprises are best known. These are Fannie Mae, the Federal National Mortgage Association and Freddie Mac, the Federal Home Loan Mortgage Corporation.

The year 1916 saw the first government sponsored enterprise that Congress established. This was the Farm Credit System. Congress moved GSEs into housing finance in 1932 when it established the Federal Home Loan Banks. It focused on education costs and finance when in 1972 Congress chartered Sallie Mae. In 1995, Congress passed a law and permitted this educational GSE to give up its government sponsorship so that it could transform into a fully private company.

The segment of the economy for residential mortgages and borrowing proves to be substantially the largest industry where the government sponsored enterprises function. In mortgages, these GSEs own or pool around $5 trillion in home mortgages.

The way that Congress came up with to boost capital market efficiency and get past the imperfections of the market was to help funds migrate more effortlessly from fund suppliers to fund borrowers in major loan demand areas of the economy. They accomplished this with a type of government guarantee which limited the loss risks for those who offered the funds.

These government sponsored enterprises now mostly serve as intermediaries between agricultural and home borrowers and lenders. Freddie Mac and Fannie Mae remain the two best known and most influential GSEs today. They buy up mortgages and issue them through affiliated companies. Once this is accomplished, they pack them up as MBS mortgage backed securities. These securities come with the important financial backing from Freddie Mac or Fannie Mae. Investors allowed to trade in the TBA to be announced markets find these investments appealing when they carry government sponsored enterprises backing.

These housing GSEs also established a secondary market for loans with their guarantees, securitizing, and bonding. It has helped the main issuers of primary market mortgages to boost their volume of loans at the same time as they reduce the risks of single loans. It also gives investors a wide market of instruments which are securitized and standardized.

The government sponsored enterprise does not actually come with the government's hard guarantee of their credit. Despite this, lenders have always given them better interest rates at the same time that investors in the securities have paid high prices. This stems from the government's implicit guarantee that these critical organizations will not default or fail. It has helped the two main GSEs to save on borrowing costs to the tune of around $2 billion each year.

The subprime mortgage crisis and financial crisis reached a fevered pitch and embroiled Freddie Mac and Fannie Mae in 2007 and 2008. The American government demonstrated the value of the implicit guarantee then by bailing out and putting the two GSEs into conservatorship in September of 2008.

Graduated Payment Mortgage (GPM)

A graduated payment mortgage is a special type of home mortgage where payments are low initially and go up over the term of the loan. These are still considered to be a type of fixed rate mortgages as the interest rates are set and pre-determined even when the payments rise.

The low upfront payment helps financial institutions to qualify the borrowers. Banks only have to take into account the original low rate to approve them. This is why the GPMs assist those who otherwise would not be able to get qualified using the normal FRM fixed rate mortgage. This aids a great number of potential home buyers who might not be able to get qualified to purchase a home. It is best for younger or newer homeowners. Their levels of income should rise with time. This helps them to make the increasing mortgage payments.

The payments rise every year with a graduated payment mortgage until the entire amount has been repaid. The amount that they increase varies from one contract to the next. Typically the payments rises between 7% and 12% each year from the original base amount.

There is a danger with these types of products. If the young home buyers do not see their income rise consistently and significantly enough, the increasing payments on the home will take a greater share of their take home pay every year. Eventually, they may not be able to afford the payments if their salaries do not rise sufficiently.

The original payment for these graduated payment mortgages is not enough to cover the loan's interest. The difference between what is covered and what is not is called negative amortization. This amount adds on to the loan balance with every payment. It takes years for the rising payments to overcome this increase in the loan balance. Lenders do not like the fact that the balance goes up above the initial amount. Because of this they charge greater rates for these types of loans than they do for standard fixed rate mortgages.

The trade-off with a graduated payment mortgage is the larger payment that continues to grow for several years. This generally does not reach its peak level until five years have passed. The higher payment will then stay fixed for the rest of the mortgage term. This is the price to pay for a low upfront payment that a borrower can be approved for and can afford.

There are other kinds of graduated payment mortgages on the market. These alternatives provide varying rates of payment rises for different amounts of time. In one example, homeowners can get a gradually rising rate of 3% per year for ten years rather than pay more than 7% each year for 5 years. These alternative GPMs require a higher upfront payment amount and can also lead to a larger final payment. Because the initial payment is higher, the negative amortization will be less. This will cause the peak loan balance to be smaller.

GPMs are not unique in mortgages that have payments which increase. There are also fixed rate mortgages called temporary buy downs. These come with lower upfront payments during the loan's early years. The advantage to these is that the loan does not incur negative amortization.

Temporary buy downs only work if someone pays for the buy down account. The financial institution takes money from this supplemental account to cover the lower payments in the first two years. This way the lender receives identical payments for the entire life of the loan. Either the home seller or the buyer has to supply the money for the supplemental account.

Gross Development Cost (GDC)

Gross Development Cost (GDC) refers to the aggregate costs of a given company project. It could also be called the sum of all means of finance which a company employs on a particular project. This is similarly the total costs which a firm incurs from the conception of to the final implementation of a certain project. Any costs that occur after the project's completion will be treated as operational expenses. Some analysts refer to the GDC as the expenses associated with developing either improved or new products.

Two main project cost estimate categories exist in the world of business. These are project planning estimates and project design estimates. The former will be deployed in justifying and receiving approval for a given project, analyzing alternative projects, programming the sequence of project events, and receiving the final project go ahead. The latter sum up the projected project costs pertaining to sourced materials and contracted work.

One thing about such cost estimates is that they never become complete until a given project is final. In fact, insightful companies will constantly review their estimates in an effort to ensure they remain current and accurate as possible. Project engineers carry the burden for making sure the projected cost stays updated all during the project development process. At the same time, the responsible project manager carries the responsibility for both reviewing and ultimately signing off on every estimate for the costs of the project.

Current project cost estimates prove to be the ones which are the most current estimates on file in the design and planning phases. Alternatively, project planning cost estimates will be the ones compiled before a project becomes fully approved. Project planning costs estimates can be categorized according to several different breakdowns. These include project feasibility, project initiation, draft estimate project report, and project report.

Projects rarely begin without a company coming up with a project initiation cost estimate. This is an expanded version of the estimates on project feasibility in greater detail. This estimate is the one that ultimately underlies the program project costs. This is why a highly reliable estimate is critical at this juncture. It proves to be the initial benchmark against any other and future estimates.

Next in the natural progression of a potential project comes the draft project report. This estimate utilizes the identical format to the project initiation cost estimates but naturally comes with far greater detail. In such an estimate, every competing project alternative option has to be compiled with current data derived from units actually involved with the project in question. This includes elements like structure design, materials, labor unit costs, hydraulics, right of way, etc.

The next project estimate in the progression of a project will be the Project Report Cost Estimate. Once again, this stays with the identical format as with the previous project planning cost estimates. The estimate for project costs should be more conclusive at this stage. Finally, once a project is fully approved will come the project design cost estimates.

The Project Manager will update such estimates during the project development. The Project Design Cost estimates can be labeled as either final or preliminary. Such design cost estimates concentrate on the project's construction costs. These estimates should be the most detailed, up to date, and accurate of the various planning cost estimates. They should cover everything from upfront project evaluation to construction design data and costs as available. Such data permits the project manager to develop the most detailed cost estimate possible in the ongoing progress of the project in question.

Gross Domestic Product (GDP)

GDP stands for the entire value in dollars of all goods and services that have actually been produced within the nation in a particular period of time, commonly a year. A simpler way of putting GDP is how large the economy proves to be.

The Gross Domestic Product turns out to be among the most closely watched and important measurements for how healthy the economy is. GDP is commonly given out as a comparison against a prior year or quarter. When the financial news reports that the Gross Domestic Product has increased by three percent year on year, it is referring to the economy having expanded by three percent during the last year.

Coming up with the actual measurement of Gross Domestic Product is complex. In simplest terms, it is figured up in one of two methods. The income approach works by totaling up the earnings of all individuals in the country over a year. The expenditure approach simply tallies up the money that everyone in the nation spends over the year. It stands to reason that through both means you should come to approximately a similar total.

With the income approach, economists take all of the employees' compensation in the nation. They add this to all of the profits that both non incorporated, as well as incorporated, companies have made throughout the country. Finally they add on all taxes paid minus subsidies given. This is known as the GDP(I) method of calculation. The expenditure based means proves to be the more typically utilized method. To figure up GDP this way, all government spending, net exports, consumption, and investment in the country have to be tallied up together.

You can not overstate the importance of GDP to an economy's growth and production. Almost every person within the nation is massively impacted by gross domestic product. If an economy is in good shape, then wages will rise and unemployment will prove to be low as businesses require greater quantities of labor in order to produce to keep up with the expanding economy. Major changes to Gross Domestic Product, revised to the downside or upside , have significant repercussions for the stock markets. The reasons for this are simple to grasp.

Economies that are contracting translate to smaller amounts of profits for corporations. This leads to lower prices for stocks. Investors also become nervous about decreasing growth in GDP, since it commonly means that the nation's economy is falling into recession or is already in a recession.

Conversely, economies that are expanding signify that corporations' profits in general will be higher. Investors bid stock prices up on this news as they become increasingly confident in the future economic prospects. Because of these effects of Gross Domestic Product on peoples' lives, it could be said to be the most significant economic measurement for all of the people in the country in general.

High Frequency Trading (HFT)

High frequency trading turns out to be a platform for program-based trades. It works with super computers that are able to run huge quantities of trading orders at incredibly rapid speeds. This HFT works with complicated algorithms. These analyze a wide range of markets and then place a number fast-paced orders depending on the conditions in the markets. The secret of the trading algorithms lies in their speed. Those traders who have the quickest trade executions usually make more money than do traders who have slower trade executions.

This high frequency trading has not always been mainstream or even possible. It grew in popularity as some of the exchanges began to provide incentives for corporations that could increase the stock market's liquidity.

As an example, the NYSE New York Stock Exchange works with a number of liquidity providers. These are known as SLPs Supplemental Liquidity Providers. The strive to provide better liquidity and more competition for the exchange and its already existing quotes.

The companies that participate in this program earn either a rebate or a fee when they increase the liquidity. This amount turned out to be $0.0019 in mid 2016 for securities that are listed on the NYSE or NYSE MKT. It may not sound like an enormous amount of money. It adds up to major profits quickly as some of these companies are engaged in millions of transactions on busy days.

The NYSE and other exchanges introduced this SLP program for a specific reason. After Lehman Brothers collapsed back in 2008, liquidity turned into an enormous concern for market participants. The SLP provided the solution to low liquidity. It also made high frequency trading a major part of the stock market in only a few years.

High frequency trading offers some significant benefits to the stock exchanges and financial markets. The most significant one centers on the significantly better liquidity that the programs provide. It has reduced bid ask spreads substantially. Larger spreads are more or less a thing of the past.

Some exchanges tested the benefits by trying to place fees on the HFT. The spreads then increased as fewer trades occurred. The Canadian government started charging fees for high frequency trading on Canadian markets. A study concluded that the end result was 9% higher bid to ask spreads.

There are many who dislike high frequency trading as well. Opponents are harsh in their criticism. Many broker dealers have been eliminated by the computer programs. The human element has been removed from many decisions on the exchanges.

When errors occur, the critics are quick to point out that human interactions could have prevented them. Part of the problem in the speed is that the programs are making decisions in literally thousandths of a second. This can lead to huge moves in the market with no apparent explanation or reason.

The best example of the mistakes that can lead to enormous and scary stock market moves happened on May 6, 2010 during the Flash Crash. The DJIA Dow Jones Industrial Average experienced its biggest drop of all time on an intraday basis. The Dow plunged over 1,000 points and dropped a full 10% in only twenty minutes. It then recovered back much of the loss in the next few hours. When the government investigated the issue, they found an enormous order which had caused the sell off to begin. The HFT computer algorithms did all the rest.

Another criticism concerns large corporate profiting at the expense of the smaller retail investors. The trade off is superior liquidity. Unfortunately, much of this turns out to be phantom liquidity. It is there for the market at one moment and then gone in another. This keeps the traders from benefiting from the liquidity.

Home Affordable Modification Program (HAMP)

The Home Affordable Modification Program is also known by its acronym HAMP. This stands for a program created by the United States government. They founded it in order to assist those homeowners who were struggling to keep up with their mortgages. For any homeowners who have watched in dismay as their financial conditions deteriorated since they originally purchased their house, they could be able to qualify for loan modifications to make keeping the home possible and affordable.

The program actually helps participants by allowing them to reduce their monthly mortgage payments. This happens as the program approves a lower rate of interest, extends the mortgage's time frame (and term), or alters the type of mortgage to fixed rate from adjustable rate ARM. In some cases, two or even three of these changes may be approved together. The modifications can happen because the United States government backs them.

The Home Affordable Modification Program began as the Departments of Housing and Urban Development HUD combined forces with the Treasury in order to forge a new initiative that they named Making Homes Affordable. Though there were other parts to this ground breaking concept, the HAMP proved to be a key pillar of it. The government recognized in the wake of the Great Recession that many Americans were only one accident, job loss, or illness away from falling hopelessly behind on their mortgages and payments. This is why they decided to come up with their innovative program for modifying mortgages to make them more affordable for those who are in the most need of help.

Becoming eligible for this home modification assistance program requires an applicant be able to successfully meet a particular set of criteria. They must have bought and financed the house before or on January 1st of 2009. They have to be capable of proving a real financial hardship that makes them struggle to meet their monthly mortgage payments. At the same time, they have to show that they are already behind on the monthly payments or even at risk of sliding into foreclosure of their home. In order to successfully qualify, the property can not have been condemned. They may not owe more than $729,750 on the primary residence which is a single family home. Finally, applicants may not show any personal real estate fraud convictions from any time within the past ten years.

If they meet all of these exacting criteria, then interested parties are able to call their specific mortgage servicer to inquire about any additional requirements that could exist with their particular company. It is also important to inquire if the mortgage servicing company even participates with the Home Affordable Modification Program in the first place. If the provider does participate and the applicant actually meets all of the minimum requirements for participation, then the home owner will need to speak with his or her lender in order to obtain all of the necessary paperwork and forms to enroll.

These forms include first the Request for Mortgage Assistance Form, or RMA. There is also the Income Verification Form as well as the IRS' 4605T-EZ form to complete. It is important to note that the final application does not get submitted to the government, but instead to the mortgage servicer. They will require a tangible proof of financial hardship when the individual submits this application.

There are actually a number of key benefits which this Home Affordable Modification Program delivers for successful applicants. They are able to sidestep foreclosure of the home, reduce their costs for keeping the house, obtain a new start on the mortgage, and better their credit history and rating. The home loan will be made to work for the owners so that they can simply modify the mortgage instead of losing the house.

Though the program is one that has helped a number of Americans, it is not the foolproof answer to irresponsible home buying and borrowing. There have been a number of homeowners who availed themselves of the program in HAMP only to re-default a second time. Some of these have actually forfeited their homes in the foreclosure process. The program has been shown in a recently conducted study that it can help a number of the fully 20 percent of homeowners who are not saving money which they might be able to by taking advantage of either a loan modification program such as this one or through refinancing their home.

Home Equity Line of Credit (HELOC)

A home equity line of credit is also known by its acronym HELOC. It represents a viable alternative to the more commonly used home equity loan. Whereas home equity loans provide lump sum amounts, Home Equity Lines of Credit provide cash as and when the borrower needs it. The downside to a HELOC is that a bank can decide to reduce the amount of available credit or cancel the line altogether without warning. This can happen before a borrower has utilized the funds.

In a home equity line of credit, borrowers use the equity within the home to be their collateral with the bank. The lending institution decides on the maximum amount that the borrower can obtain. The home owner then determines how much of this they want to borrow for the amount of time the bank permits. This might be until the monthly payments reduce the line to a zero balance, or it could be for a certain number of months. This makes these HELOCs much like a credit card in the ability to draw on the resources only when and as they need them.

The main difference between a home equity line of credit and a home loan is that the former is a revolving loan instrument. Borrowers are able to use the money then pay it off. They can then draw on it once again. Home equity loans pay a single lump sum up front amount one time. HELOCs also feature variable interest rates that will change over time, while home equity loans come with interest rates that are fixed. The payment amounts on the home equity loans are also fixed every month, while the payment on the HELOC depends on how much of the line is used.

In order to be able to obtain a home equity line of credit, the home owner must have significant equity in the house itself. Banks will insist that owners keep at least 10% to 20% equity within the property all the time. This must be the case after the line is approved as well. The HELOC approval process will also require verifiable proof of income, consistent documented employment, and a high credit score that is generally more than 680.

It is important for prospective borrowers to determine what they will use the home equity line of credit money for before they draw on it. Home renovations lend themselves better to home equity loans. This is because the one time large amount would enable the borrower to finish the renovations and then repay the loan. A HELOC is a better fit for a revolving bill such as the children's college tuition. Borrowers can use them to cover the tuition, then pay them off hopefully before the next tuition payment become due. At this point they can re-utilize the HELOC for the next semester tuition.

The home equity line of credit can also be a good choice for individuals who wish to consolidate the balances on their credit cards which feature high interest rates. The rates for the HELOC are typically much lower. This strategy requires some discipline. Once the credit cards have been cleared, there is the danger that the home owner might be tempted to run them back up again while they are still making payments on the line of credit. This would put borrowers in a worse situation than before they chose to consolidate.

Home equity lines of credit can get a home owner into the bad habit of constantly borrowing and paying them back as with a credit card. This can be a problem if the borrowers take on more debt with the HELOC than they can afford to pay in monthly payments. Missing these payments would put their home at jeopardy of being seized by the bank.

Individual Retirement Account (IRA)

An IRA stands for Individual Retirement Account. IRA's offer two types of savings for retirement. They can either be tax free or tax deferred retirement plans. In the universe of IRA's, numerous different types of accounts exist. These are principally either traditional and standard IRA's or Roth IRA's as the most popular types. The various IRA's are helpful to different individuals based on the particular scenarios and end goals of every person.

Standard IRA's permit contributions of as much as $4,000 every year. These are contributions that are tax deductible, giving the IRA's their primary advantage as retirement accounts. People who are older than fifty are allowed to contribute more than the $4,000 maximum for the purposes of catching up for their approaching retirement. Any money put into the IRA is used to reduce your annual income amount, which lessens your overall tax liability for the year.

The tax is really only deferred though, since monies taken from an IRA will be taxed at the typical income tax rate for the individual when they are withdrawn, even if they are held in such an account until retirement. When the money is taken out earlier than this age of 59 ½, then an extra ten percent penalty is applied as well. There are exceptions to the penalty rule though. When these early withdrawn monies are utilized to buy a home or to pay for the tuition costs associated with higher education, then they are not penalized. The typical tax rate would still apply, although the penalty is waived in these two cases. This makes IRA's a good vehicle for investments that also give you the versatility of making significant purchases with the money.

Roth IRA's are the other principal type of IRA's. The government established these types of IRA account back in 1997 in an effort to assist those Americans in the middle class with their retirement needs. Roth IRA's do not turn out to be tax deductible. The upside is that they offer greater amounts of flexibility than do the typical IRA's. These contributions are allowed to be taken out whenever you want without a penalty or extra tax. Interest that the account earns is taxed if taken out before the first five years have passed. At the end of five years, the earnings and contributions both made are capable of being taken out without having to pay either taxes or penalties. The identical housing and education allowances that permit to standard IRA's pertain to Roth IRA's. The principal attraction of Roth IRA's is that they offer tax free income at retirement time.

It is worth noting that the Roth IRA's have their particular rules that keep them from being for everybody. If your income is higher than $95,000 in a year, then you will be barred from making the full contribution, and if it exceeds $110,000, then you will not be allowed to make a partial contribution. For married, filing jointly, the limits are $150,000 for full contributions and $160,000 for partial contributions.

ING Group

The ING Group is the largest Dutch and Benelux based bank in the world. The acronym ING translates into International Netherlands Group in English. This global bank and financial institution draws on its important European base to provide services on a global scale. Their customers include governments, institutions, major corporations, smaller businesses, families, and individuals. ING is famous for its world class service and well known brand that put their customers at the center of all their endeavors.

Over 52,000 staff work for the ING Group to deliver wholesale and retail banking and financial services and products to their customers located in more than 40 countries. The group calls its advantages the important financial positions it enjoys, its international network, and its all channel distribution strategy. They claim their greatest asset is their brand that is both well recognized and well liked by customers in a number of different countries. They are honored as one of the leading institutions found in the Banks industry sector of the Dow Jones Sustainability Index.

The ING Group acts as a European network bank that extends its range around the globe for its many customers. They boast a range of global franchises as well. ING concentrates on growing into the main bank for new customers. This strategy is to increase the number of customers with recurring income payment accounts that have another product minimally included. ING starts customers with retail banking and offers other anchor products such as lending, wholesale banking transactions, and investments.

The bank's business transformation program is working to help the bank grow into an optimal operating model of Wholesale Banking. To do this, they are increasing their customer base in industry transaction and lending financial services. To better focus on this goal, they divide their principal and target markets into market leaders, challengers, and growth markets.

The market leaders group are those countries of Benelux - the Netherlands, Belgium, and Luxembourg. These are the nations where the ING Group is market leading in wholesale banking and retail banking services. The strategy here is to expand in certain segments and to continue developing into their direct first bank model. They are investing in digital capabilities and providing excellence in their operational programs to this effect.

Challenger markets are those where they are working consistently to increase their current market share. These markets include the important countries of Germany, France, Italy, Spain, Austria, and Australia. The businesses in these nations provide wholesale and retail banking. The focus with retail here is to offer online direct banking services. This gives them a price advantage versus other traditional banks.

In the challenger markets, ING is working to use their already recognized savings vehicles to grow into payment accounts and to create primary banking relationships. They are striving to launch from their expertise in direct banking to build up the consumer lending and small to medium sized business lending. They are also working on diligently increasing their corporate customer base in these countries through new abilities in industry lending and transaction services here.

ING Group's growth markets include their businesses in Turkey, Poland, Romania, and Asia. Here they provide a comprehensive line of wholesale and retail banking. These rapidly expanding economies provide them with solid opportunities for growth. This is why they are investing heavily to build a sustainable market share here. To do this, they are concentrating their efforts on digital technology leadership and also are pushing their direct first bank model.

Initial Coin Offering (ICO)

An Initial Coin Offering refers to a non-regulated process in which the funds for new crypto-currency projects become raised. This is also popularly known by its acronym of ICO. These ICOs allow for entrepreneurs to sidestep the heavily regulated process of raising capital through more traditional means involving banks, venture capital, angel investors, or IPOs initial public offerings on stock exchanges.

With any ICO offer campaign, at least some of the crypto-currency will be sold off to those backers of the venture who become involved early. They receive this in compensation for providing traditional currency or alternative currency investment from the likes of Bitcoin. These ICOs are also known as IPCOs, or Initial Public Coin Offerings sometimes.

The process for engaging in an Initial Coin Offering is straightforward and relatively easy to do. The startup outfit begins by producing and releasing a whitepaper-based plan that reveals all of the key details on the venture. These include the needs this operation will meet when it is up and running, what percentage of the new virtual currency project pioneers will keep, what kinds of funding is allowed, the amount of cash required to make the venture a success, and what time duration the campaign will run.

In this campaign, the investors and supports of the new initiative will purchase part of the alternative coins of the new venture with real or virtual money. Such alt coins will be called tokens. They function in much the same way as do shares of stock which corporations sell their investors during an IPO initial public offering.

In cases where the funds raised are not sufficient to carry out the project requirements as set out by the firm in the white paper plan, invested sums will be given back to the investors as the ICO becomes a failure. Yet in those many cases where the funding objective are attained within the set out duration, then the money will be utilized to fund the new enterprise (or to finish it in other cases).

Naturally the upfront investors have their own motivation in purchasing such crypto-coins in the project. This is because they believe that the operation will be a success following launch. This would lead to a potentially massive gain in the value of their tokens.

One highly successful ICO proved to be the platform for the introduction of smart contracts to the world, known as Ethereum. Its coin tokens are called Ether. The Ethereum project came out in 2014. The ICO garnered $18 million worth of Bitcoins for the project's completion. This meant that the Ether tokens cost forty cents apiece. Following the live launch of Ethereum in 2015 and growing success in 2016, Ether roared higher to more than $14. In 2017, it has even topped $400 each at one point. Early investors who held to $400 realized gains of an eye-watering over 1,000 percent in less than five years.

It is true that many ICO events go off successfully. These Initial Coin Offerings are in fact highly disruptive and innovative means of fundraising. Yet they are not a serious rival to traditional stocks by a long shot. Many ICO campaigns have been deemed to be fraud. Without the imperative regulation provided by the SEC Securities Exchange Commission, their volume is likely to remain a tiny fraction of that done in IPOs on traditional exchanges for at least the foreseeable future.

ICOs have suffered from official national opposition which has hindered them as well. The People's Bank of China fully banned all ICOs in September of 2017. They declared them to be financially unstable and disruptive to an orderly economy. Banks were forbidden to provide any services having anything to do with ICOs. At the same time, these new tokens were no longer allowed to be utilized as a currency on Chinese markets. It caused the Bitcoin and Ether enthusiasts to realize that crypto-currency regulation is in the future cards. This temporarily crushed the prices of both main alternative currencies as investors realized what a serious setback it represents.

Initial Public Offering (IPO)

An IPO is the acronym for an Initial Public Offering. Such IPO's represent the first opportunity for most investors to start buying shares of stock in the firm in question. Initial Public Offerings commonly generate a great deal of excitement, not only for the company involved but also for the members of the investing community.

Private companies decide to issue stock and become publicly traded companies for a few different reasons. The main two motivating factors revolve around the need to raise more capital, as well as the desire to permit the original business owners and investors to take profits on their time and investment that they originally put into starting up the company.

It is true that private companies are limited in the amount of capital that they are able to raise, since their ownership turns out to be restricted to certain organizations and individuals. Public companies have the advantages of allowing any investor to take a stake through buying stock shares on exchanges that are publicly traded. It is far easier for them to raise money as public companies.

Initial Public Offerings that go well translate to large amounts of cash for a company. They use this for future expansion and development. Those who began the company or who were initial investors typically make enormous gains at that time in compensation for their time and effort.

Initial Public Offerings take huge amounts of preliminary work. Great amounts of paper work have to be filled in and filed with the regulatory oversight groups. A prospectus has to be created for investors to study and consider. Advertising campaigns for the first shares that will be sold must be developed. On top of these tasks, the company has to continue its normal operations. Because of this, financial firms such as Morgan Stanley or Goldman Sachs are commonly engaged to perform these tasks on the company's behalf. Such a firm is called the IPO underwriting company. With enormous sized IPO's, these tasks could even be divided up between a few different IPO underwriting companies.

Contrary to what many people think, the majority of IPO's typically do not do well initially. Besides this, a percentage of the companies will not make it, meaning that all of the investment in the IPO stock could be lost. Because of this, there is great risk and often lower rewards for sinking money into Initial Public Offerings than in traditional well established companies and stocks. Many investors buy into the enthusiasm and excitement that surrounds Initial Public Offerings. Another explanation for their euphoria may have to do with believing that there is something special in being among the first investors to acquire the next possible Apple, Coca Cola, or IBM. Whatever their reasoning proves to be, investors continue to love Initial Public Offerings and the somewhat long shot opportunities that they represent.

Initiative for Policy Dialogue (IPD)

The Initiative for Policy Dialogue, also known as IPD, is a Columbia University based American non-profit organization of global economic reach and importance. Joseph E. Stieglitz the famous Nobel winning laureate in economics founded the group back in July of 2000. In this endeavor he had the financial support of such important heavyweight groups as foundations and governments. These included the Rockefeller, Ford, Mott, and McArthur Foundations as well as the governments of both Sweden and Canada.

This Initiative for Policy Dialogue proves to be an international network of over 250 world renowned economists, civil society representatives, political scientists, and active practitioners of various backgrounds from around the whole world. Their backgrounds are diverse and well represented of various inter-disciplines. The IPD uses this wide range of skills and tremendous resources in order to assist nations with effective solutions for urgent challenges, issues, and problems. They are also interested in building up the developing national institutions as well as civil societies.

It is the mission of the Initiative for Policy Dialogue to carry the pressing areas of concern from the developing world to both academics and American and other developed nations' policymakers and governments. Joseph Stieglitz the driving force behind this organization is well-placed and -suited to do this with his connections to governments and academia around the world. He serves as co-President of the organization.

As the Columbia University ranking "University Professor" in Economics at their business school, he is also involved with their School of International and Public Affairs. Stieglitz also serves as their Committee on Global Thought Chairman. He has chaired the United Nations Commission known as the "Experts on Reforms of the International Monetary and Financial System."

The U.N. established this committee after the devastating Great Recession, financial collapse, and economic crisis of 2007-2009 under the auspices of the President of the General Assembly. He has also served as the World Bank's Senior Vice President and Chief Economist, as well as President

Clinton's Chairman of the Council of Economic Advisors. Stieglitz earned the Nobel Memorial Prize in Economics back in 2001. It is hard to find a more impressive resume in the world of economics. He was named among the top four most influential economists in the world.

The other co-President of the Initiative for Policy Dialogue is José Antonio Ocampo. Ocampo also works as Professor for the Columbia University School of International and Public Affairs. He is similarly a Member of the Columbia University Committee on Global Thought. Ocampo is internationally known for his role as the Chairman of the U.N. Committee for Development Policy. He has also served as Under Secretary-General at the United Nation's ECLAC Economic Commission for Latin America and the Caribbean. Previously he held the post of Colombia's Minister of Finance, Planning, and Agriculture.

The Initiative for Policy Dialogue has four main programs that help them to impact public policy and shape the world. Their Task Forces help experts from around the world to collaborate in order to investigate complicated issues of development so that they can offer alternative policies to governments. Their Country Dialogues work to better the quality of decisions which policy makers engage in regarding issues covering economics.

Their Journalism Program is the outlet which they use to improve the economic literacy of journalists so that they are able to more effectively report on the complex economic topics that affect developing nations. The Educational Programs attempt to explain the various issues combating both local and global decision making in the developing nations of the world.

Internal Rate of Return (IRR)

The IRR is the acronym for internal rate of return. This IRR proves to be the capital budget rate of return that is utilized in order to determine and compare and contrast various investments' profitability. It is sometimes known as the discounted cash flow rate of return alternatively, or even the ROR, or rate of return. Where banks are concerned, the IRR is also known as the effective interest rate. The word internal is used to specify that such calculation does not involve facts that are part of the external environment, such as inflation or the interest rate.

More precisely, the internal rate of return for any investment proves to be the interest rate level where the negative cash flow, or net present value of costs, from the investment is equal to the positive cash flow, or net present value of benefits, for the investment. In other words, this IRR will yield a discount rate that causes the net current values of both positive and negative cash flows of a specific investment to cancel out at zero.

These Internal Rates of Return are generally utilized to consider projects and investments and their ultimate desirability. Naturally, a project will be more appealing to engage in or purchase if it comes with a greater internal rate of return. Given a number of projects from which to choose, and assuming that all project benefits prove to be the same generally, the project that contains the greatest Internal Rate of Return will be considered the most attractive. It should be selected with the highest priority of being pursued first.

The assumed theory for companies is that they will be interested in eventually pursuing any investment or project that comes with an IRR that is greater than the expense of the money put into the project as capital. The number of projects or investments that can be run at a time are limited in the real world though. A firm may have a restricted capability of overseeing a large number of projects at once, or they may lack the necessary funds to engage in all of them at a time.

The internal rate of return is actually a number expressed as a percent. It details the yield, efficacy, and efficiency of a given investment or project. This should not be confused with the net present value that instead tells the particular investment's actual value.

In general, a given investment or project is deemed to be worthwhile assuming that its internal rate of return proves to be higher than either the expense of the capital involved, or alternatively, than a pre set minimally accepted rate of return. For companies that possess share holders, the minimum IRR is always a factor of the investment capital's cost. This is easily decided by ascertaining the cost of capital, which is risk adjusted, for alternative types of investments. In this way, share holders will approve of a project or investment, so long as its Internal Rate of Return is greater than the cost of the capital to be used and this project or investment creates economic value that is viable for the company in question.

Internal Revenue Service (IRS)

The Internal Revenue Service is an agency of the United States government. It is an entity that falls under the Department of the Treasury. The IRS' purpose is to collect incomes taxes from businesses and working individuals. Workers generally pay in their incomes taxes to the IRS once a year. There are cases where groups pay taxes quarterly, as with businesses and independent contractors who make more than pre-determined amounts. In practice employers withhold most individuals' taxes are from their paychecks.

For most individuals and small businesses, annual tax payments are due every year on April 15th. They pay these for the preceding year. Submitting these payments and forms is known as filing taxes with the IRS. The agency also permits extensions for filing if the requests are turned in ahead of the due date. Estimated payments have to come with the request for extension.

The Internal Revenue Service figures up taxes for individuals and businesses on a sliding scale. Individuals and entities that earn higher amounts are subsequently placed into higher tax brackets. The more individuals earn, the higher amount they will be required to pay to the IRS.

Any person who earns a yearly salary or who is paid wages by the hour will have taxes estimated and deducted directly from every payroll. This creates a situation where too much or too little money may be deducted throughout the year. Individuals who overpay will receive a refund. Those who underpay will have to make a payment to cover the additional tax if the appropriate amount did not come out of checks during the year.

Income taxes in the U.S. depend on the amount of net income. This is the income that remains once deductions have been calculated and subtracted from the total gross income. Individuals in the poverty bracket are not expected to pay any income taxes. Those people who earn $50,000 will pay around 20% of their net incomes. Over $100,000 earners are more likely to pay near 25% of net income earned. Sometimes those earning millions of dollars per year are able to use tax shelters, business write offs, and accounting strategies to receive substantial tax breaks and actually pay a lower percentage of their net income in taxes. This is why the middle class in America bears the greatest taxation burden.

The IRS was not the original Federal taxing authority in the United States. President Lincoln began its original predecessor the Bureau of Internal Revenue in 1862 with Congressional approval. They set this agency up to collect a new income tax to assist in paying for the Civil War. This tax was intended and enacted to be temporary at the time.

While the first income tax did become repealed in 1872, the government reinstated it again in 1894. Supreme Court legal challenges kept the income tax in a quasi legal state until the 16th Amendment came into force in 1913 and allowed income taxes to be permanent. Eventually the Bureau of Internal Revenue evolved into the Internal Revenue Service.

The IRS website offers consumers and businesses all of their forms in a convenient, downloadable format. It also features instructional pages to properly complete these tax forms. A frequently asked questions page helps individuals with general queries. For people who need assistance in filing, there are a variety of software programs available that will ask questions and prepare the relevant tax forms for individuals. These programs then file the forms online with the IRS. Another option is to hire and pay a CPA certified public accountant to complete and file their tax forms.

International Accounting Standards Board (IASB)

The International Accounting Standards Board is an independent and private entity which arose back in 2001. The group was originally created to replace the former International Accounting Standards Committee. The IFRS Foundation maintains all oversight of the IASB.

Under their auspices, the IASB creates, publishes, and approves the International Financial Reporting Standards for the global accounting community. There are presently 14 members of the IASB. The IASB group is headquartered in London, Great Britain.

The constitution of the IFRS foundation gives the IASB full control over all technical and operating issues. This includes pursuing and developing the technical agenda after consulting with the public and the appropriate trustees of the foundation. They also approve and deliver interpretations that the IFRS Interpretations Committee recommends. Finally, they prepare and publish the International Financial Reporting Standards and all accompanying related drafts as laid out in the constitution of the IFRC Foundation.

The IASB itself was originally organized under the auspices of the IFRS Foundation. The foundation itself proves to be a non profit company incorporated in Delaware in the United States on March 8, 2001. The IFRS Foundation oversees all of the tasks that the IASB pursues as well as its strategy and structure. At the same time, the IFRS maintains the responsibility for fund raising for the IASB.

Another governing agency within the IFRS Foundation is the DPOC Due Process Oversight Committee. This trustee committee bears responsibility for the function of overseeing the IASB, as per the foundation's constitution. The last governing board is the Monitoring Board. It monitors the trustees of the IFRS foundation. It also participates in nominating the Trustees as well as approving all final appointments that the board makes to the Trustees.

There are several technical groups within the framework of the organization of the IFRS Foundation. The International Accounting Standards Board itself is among these. It bears the sole responsibility for setting all International Financial Reporting Standards since 2001.

There is also the IFRS Interpretations Committee. Their job is to create interpretations that the IASB actually approves. It also engages in tasks as requested by the IASB since 2001. Finally there are the various working groups. These different task forces are for particular projects that meet a necessary agenda of the group.

There are also numerous advisory groups within the IFRS Foundation that carry out important functions for the IASB. The ASAF Accounting Standards Advisory Forum gives advice regarding the activities for setting technical standards by the IASB. The IFRS Advisory Council provides advice to both the IFRS foundation and the IASB.

There are also a variety of specific policy committees that serve advisory roles to the IASB and the IFRS foundation. These include the Capital Markets Advisory Committee from 2003, the Effects Analyses Consultative Group of 2012, the Emerging Economies Group from 2011, the Financial Crisis Advisory Group that merged with FASB in 2008, the Global Preparers Forum, the IFRS Taxonomy Consultative Group from 2014, the Joint Transition Resource Group for Revenue Recognition of 2014, and the SME Implementation Group from 2010.

One of the important tasks of the IASB has been to help with the project to converge the differing GAAP and IFRS standards. In order to simplify the understanding of different countries' accounting and financial statements, the group is trying to bring the standards into some sort of harmony. This will especially help out investors who must read and compare the financial statements and reports of various international companies.

International Bank Account Number (IBAN)

IBAN is an acronym which stands for the International Bank Account Number. This standardized numbering system for identifying bank accounts around the world with precision was first conceived of and implemented by the banks of Europe. They wanted to make simpler the means of transacting between bank accounts of financial institutions based in different countries.

This internationally agreed to system for identifying the world's banks and bank accounts was critically needed for banking across international borders. European banks found it necessary to come up with a way to effectively process the cross border transactions. They wanted to dramatically lower the dangers of errors in transcription and subsequent transmission problems which sometimes resulted.

It was the ECBS European Committee for Banking Standards that first adopted the IBAN concept. It later evolved into a global standard under the auspices of ISO 13616:1997. This standard became updated with ISO directive 13616:2007 that now utilizes SWIFT as the official registrar. The system originally arose as a means of facilitating payments made throughout the European Union. It has now been put into place by the majority of European nations along with many countries throughout the globe, especially in the states of the Caribbean and Middle East. Sixty-nine different nations utilized the IBAN account numbering system as of February 2016. More sign up all the time.

The IBAN account number is made up of several components. The two letter national code comes first. This is followed up by the two check digits which enable an integrity check of the IBAN number to be sure it is correct. Finally come as many as thirty alphanumeric characters which are also called the BBAN, or Basic Bank Account Number. Each national banking association decides which BBAN will become the standard for their own national bank accounts. In general, the remaining thirty characters include such information as the domestic bank account number, branch location identifier, and additional routing information.

While the IBAN concept has taken hold effectively throughout the continent of Europe, it is not a universal global standard yet, though it is the closest thing to one. The practice of working with such standardized account numbers as these is growing and gaining in popularity in other countries of the world. This is proven by the fact that nearly forty non- European countries now employ the International Bank Account Number system for themselves on only the twentieth anniversary of the concept being introduced originally.

Before the rise of the IBAN, every country utilized its own national standard to identify bank accounts within their own borders. This proved to be confusing in Europe, particularly as the borders between the 27 different EU countries began to blur thanks to the EU. Free movement of people, capital, and goods meant that money was being drawn from and transferred back and forth between the banks and bank accounts of different European states on an increasingly common basis. Sometimes important and even critical routing information was simply missing from transfers and payments.

SWIFT's routing information does not require transaction specific formats which identify both account numbers and transaction types specifically. This is because they leave the transaction partners to agree on these. SWIFT codes also lack check digits, meaning transcription errors can not be detected nor can banks validate the routing data before they submit the payments without these two digits. Continuous costly routing errors were creating delays on payments and transfers as the receiving and sending banks were also working with intermediary banks for routing.

The ISO International Organization for Standardization overcame these problems in 1997 by creating the IBAN in association with the European Committee for Banking Standards. Because the ECBS simplified and better standardized the original format proposed by the ISO, an update was issued with ISO 13616:2003 and then again in ISO 13616-1:2007.

As of 2017, the United States' banks do not employ IBANs themselves. Instead, they utilize either Fedwire identifiers for the banks or the ABA Routing Number.

International Bank for Reconstruction and Development (IBRD)

The International Bank for Reconstruction and Development proves to be a principal and original organization within the World Bank. It loans money to help out middle income nations as well as poorer countries that are creditworthy. It derives the majority of its funds from selling bonds on the global capital markets.

Over 180 countries participate as members of the IBRD. Every member has a certain amount of voting power. This is based on its subscription of capital. The United States possesses a full sixth of all the IBRD's shares. Besides an enormous amount of voting clout, the U.S. also owns the exclusive rights to veto any changes which are proposed for the bank itself.

The origins of the International Bank for Reconstruction and Development hail back to the end of the Second World War. The United States founded it in 1944. The initial purpose of this organization lay in assisting Europe to rebuild itself from the devastation brought on by World War II. The role of the bank has since shifted to offering loans along with technical assistance, knowledge, and advice to mostly middle income nations.

As the first institution within the World Bank, the IBRD cooperates closely alongside the other institutions within the World Bank Group. Together they serve to encourage economic growth, to assist developing nations in reducing the poverty of their citizens, and to help spread prosperity.

The bank itself is owned by the 189 member nations' governments. A board and directors represent these countries for routine decision making and administration. This board is comprised of 25 members who are Executive Directors. Five of these are appointed and 20 of them are elected by the owning members.

Developing nations are able to benefit greatly from the technical services, knowledge, and strategic advice that the bank provides. This is beyond its financial resources which it distributes as guarantees, loans, and risk management products. The World Bank serves in this capacity its beneficiaries who are also shareholders and global actors as well as being clients of the bank.

Not only national but sub national levels of governments can participate and benefit. The International Bank for Reconstruction and Development finances a wide variety of projects spanning every sector. It simultaneously offers its expert knowledge and technical support for varying phases in an ongoing project.

Some of the financial services and products which the IBRD delivers assist countries with developing resilience to external shocks. They help with product access for alleviating negative affects of interest rates, currency exchange rates, destructive weather and natural disasters, and volatility in commodity prices. The bank is different from a traditional commercial lender in that it does more than serve as a financier. It also has an important role in the international transfer of knowledge and technical assistance.

In times of crisis, the International Bank for Reconstruction and Development serves to help preserve the financial strength of its borrowers to limit the negative effects on the poor. It also works to provide financial market access to these nations at better terms than they would be able to attain by themselves. This helps with attracting private capital as well by encouraging a positive investment environment.

Many of the longer term social and personal development projects that the bank supports, private creditors would not consider. The bank also helps with promoting institutional reforms in areas like anti-corruption and public safety.

International Financial Institutions (IFI)

International financial institutions (IFIs) are international financial organizations which multiple nations founded. They are subject to international law instead of the laws of any one single country. The IFIs are usually owned by national governments of the founding members.

Sometimes other international institutions or organizations are stakeholders as well. Even though there are IFIs that two or three nations created, the best known ones were developed by numerous national participants. The most famous international financial institutions arose following the Second World War in order to help rebuild Europe, as well as to offer the means of multinational cooperation in overseeing the world's financial system.

The largest international financial institution in the world today proves to be the European Investment Bank. In 2013, this organization possessed a balance sheet that amounted to 512 billion euros. This compares to the main component parts of the World Bank, the IBRD with $358 billion in assets as of 2014 and the IDA with its $183 billion in assets as of 2014. By means of comparison, the world's biggest international commercial banks boast assets each totaling between $2 - $3 billion, as with Britain's HSBC and the United States' JP Morgan Chase Bank.

Arguably the most important international financial institutions in the world today remain the ones which the Bretton Woods agreement founded in 1944. These are the World Bank and the International Monetary Fund. Both are participating members of the United Nations system. Their goals are to improve the standards of living in their respective member nations.

Each of these two organizations has its own approach to achieving this mandate, yet they complement each other. The IMF concentrates its efforts on larger macroeconomic issues. The World Bank instead focuses on developing the economies and reducing the poverty of member states over the longer term.

The World Bank and IMF came into being in July of 1944 at the internationally attended Bretton Woods Conference held in New Hampshire. The conference had a goal to build up a new framework of development and economic cooperation which would help to establish a more prosperous and stable global economy. Over 70 years later, this goal is still critical to the operations of both international financial institutions. Only the means they use to reach the goals has changed as different economic challenges and developments arise.

The World Bank mandate is to encourage poverty reduction and economic improvement longer term. They do this by offering financial and technical assistance to aid countries which are trying to reform sections of their economies or to develop particular projects. These projects could be delivering electricity and water, constructing health centers and schools, safeguarding the environment, or fighting disease. Such help as the World Bank provides is typically longer term in nature and funded by contributions from member nations as well as by issuing bonds. The staff of the World Bank is typically specialized in certain sectors, issues, or methods.

The IMF on the other hand operates under a mandate to foster monetary cooperation on an international level while it offers technical assistance and policy advice to help countries to develop and keep more prosperous and stronger economies. As part of this, the IMF offers loans. They also help nations to create policies and programs that will address their imbalance of payments if they are unable to obtain affordable term financing to meet their international financial obligations. These loans are either medium or short term. The funds come from the quota contributions' pool provided by member states. The staff of the IMF is mainly economists who possess vast experience with financial and macroeconomic issues.

International Financial Reporting Standards (IFRS)

The International Financial Reporting Standards prove to be the principally used set of accounting regulations in the world. Their main rival is the United States' based GAAP Generally Accepted Accounting Procedures. These IFRS turn out to be a single collection of accounting standards. They were created and are maintained still by the IASB International Accounting Standards Board based in London.

The IASB developed these IFRS standards with the goal of them being effectively utilized on a consistent basis throughout the globe. They were written with developed, developing, and emerging market economies and nations all in mind. These standards provide both investors and other consumers of business financial statements with the necessary tools to make like comparisons between various companies. Thanks to the IFRS, investors can effectively compare and contrast the financial performances of various publicly traded corporations on a consistent basis against their global peers.

This is a high standard for the IFRS. It of course requires more and more countries sign on to these accounting standards in order for the objective to be effectively and eventually met. This vision of a single set of worldwide accounting standards is well supported by numerous globally active organizations. Among these are the International Monetary Fund, the World Bank, the G20, the Basel Committee, the IFAC, and the IOSCO.

Thanks to the tireless efforts of the IASB and the IFRS foundation along with the support of these other active international organizations, the IFRS account standards have now been made law in over 100 countries. These include all of the 27 core countries in the European Union plus Great Britain as well as over two thirds of the member nations comprising the G20. This makes sense as the G20 and other critical worldwide bodies have always encouraged the important task of the IASB and its goals of achieving a universally recognized set of international accounting standards that everyone can rely on and understand.

Since the year 2001, the International Accounting Standards Board has created and continued to improve and promote the International Financial Reporting Standards. The IASB turns out to be the body that sets the standards for the IFRS Foundation. This foundation is an organization that serves the public good. It has been well recognized for the award winning examples of its organizational transparency as well as the participation of all of its stakeholders and other participants.

The 150 members strong staff based in London hail from around 30 individual countries. The IASB operates under the auspices of a 14 member Board of Directors that is appointed and monitored by 22 different trustees coming from around the globe. These trustees themselves are further accountable to a public authority monitoring board. This way all of the various members of the leadership at the IASB are accountable to someone else.

The work of the IASB via the IFRS allows international accountants to more consistently deliver a standard means of detailing the financial performances of companies and other financial entities. This benefits investors, companies, and regulators. The standards of accounting that the IASB creates and the IFRS represents give the preparers of financial statements a complete set of principles and rules to follow when they are compiling the financial accounts of these organizations. This makes for an international standardization throughout the global markets.

It all works because the various corporations traded on public stock exchanges are required by law to prepare and produce financial statements that follow the appropriate IFRS accounting standards as do their business rivals and peers. The IFRS foundation maintains an online database of profiles on 143 countries and jurisdictions to show whether or not they accept and utilize these standards.

International Monetary Fund (IMF)

The International Monetary Fund represents an international organization with membership of 189 different countries. As such it counts nearly all countries of the world among its almost global membership. This IMF seeks to achieve financial stability, helps to encourage worldwide monetary cooperation, pushes for economic growth that is sustainable and for high unemployment, helps to facilitate international trade, and attempts to lessen poverty throughout the world.

Members of the United Nations created the International Monetary Fund back in 1945 as a result of the idea initially conceived of at the important Bretton Woods UN conference held in New Jersey in the United States in July of 1944. Originally 44 nations attended this conference and looked for ways to rebuild the global economy. They wanted to create a way of fostering economic cooperation. The group collectively hoped to not repeat the mistakes of the 1930s. A currency devaluing race to the bottom had led to the Great Depression in those years.

There were a number of original goals for the IMF. The organization was to encourage stability of exchange rates and monetary cooperation on an international scale. They were to promote and aid in the growth of a balanced international trade. IMF also had to help build up a system for balance of payments that was multilateral in scope. They also were designed to provide emergency resources to member states that suffered from problems with their balance of payments. Safeguards on the resources loaned out would b required.

With the early 1970's dissolution of the fixed exchange rates based on the gold standard set up at the Bretton Woods conference, their role changed some. They were no longer responsible for stable exchange rates and a balance of payments system based on pegged exchange rates. They became more of an organization that helps out member states in emergency economic need.

Today the IMF counts among its largest emergency borrowers Greece, Portugal, Ukraine, and Ireland. It also issues precautionary loans to members who may need to borrow based on particular conditions within their countries. The countries with the largest precautionary loan amounts agreed on include Poland, Mexico, Colombia, and Morocco. Between the two groups, the IMF has committed itself to $163 billion. Of this amount $137 billion has not yet been drawn.

The International Monetary Fund still works to safeguard the global monetary system. They watch over the system of international payments and free floating exchange rates so that nations and their populations can engage in transactions with each other. In 2012, the fund received an expanded mandate in part as a result of the chaos in the Great Recession. This bigger mandate includes all issues pertaining to the financial sectors and all macroeconomic issues that have to do with global stability.

The International Monetary Fund has its headquarters in Washington, D.C. Their governance is by an executive board. The board is made up of 24 directors. Each of these directors represents either a group of nations or a single nation. The IMF maintains a global staff of 2,600 individuals who hail from 147 different countries.

The majority of the IMF's money comes from its quota system. Every member is given a quota that they must contribute. This amount is based on the nation's economic size in the global economy. The member state's maximum contributions are limited to this quota. When countries join, they pay as much as one-quarter of their quota in a widely traded foreign currency like the pound, euro, dollar, or yen or as SDR Special Drawing Rights made up of a basket of these currencies. The other three-quarters they pay from their own currency.

Japanese Bankers Association (JBA)

The Japanese Bankers Association is also known by its internationally recognized acronym the JBA. This is the elite financial institutions' umbrella organization. Its membership is comprised of bank holding companies, banks, and banker associations throughout Japan. Their purpose is to promote planning for the best operating of payment systems, to reinforce compliance and promote CSR, to encourage appropriate transactions for consumers, and to support the individual banking endeavors and operations of its member banks.

Every year the Japanese Bankers Association elects both a chairman and a number of vice chairmen to oversee the organization. It is the JBA's Board of Directors which confers each March to hold this election. The various board members actually vote to decide who will become the two heads of the umbrella banking organization. President and Chief Executive Officer Takeshi Kunibe of Sumitomo Mitsui Banking Corporation is the current chairman of the JBA, as of February 2017.

In Japan, the various financial institutions are actually broken down into a few important categories. These groupings come from characteristics which include either the historical backgrounds or the primary business functions of the institutions in question. Such categories include city banks, regional banks, and member banks from the Second Association of Regional Banks (or regional banks level II). These are not legally binding definitions. Instead they are classifications used to help with publishing statistics and administration efforts.

City banks prove to be extremely large in their geographical representation and size. Their headquarters lie in the major cities of the Japanese islands. They also boast branches in the important and large population centers of Tokyo, Osaka, and other important cities and surrounding suburbs. Today there are only five of the large and impressive city banks remaining in Japan. These are as follows: Bank of Tokyo-Mitsubishi UFJ, Resona Bank, Mizuho Bank, Sumitomo Mitsui Banking Corporation, and Saitama Resona Bank. Mergers and acquisitions in the field have helped to narrow this important category down from the original 13 city banks to the present five.

By contrast, regional banks are typically found and headquartered within the primary city of a given prefecture in Japan. They naturally conduct the overwhelming majority of their business endeavors in their home regional prefecture. It follows that they would have important local ties with area governments and locally based businesses. Today's Japan boasts 64 regional banks such as Hiroshima Bank, Shikoku Bank, and Bank of Okinawa.

The final category of the Japanese based banks is the regional banks level II. Such financial institutions tend to provide services to individuals and smaller companies in their principal geographical regions. The vast majority of the Regional Banks II was once mutual savings banks at some point. There are 41 Regional Banks II in Japan today. Among them are banks including Towa Bank, Aichi Bank, and Ehime Bank.

The banking classification picture has become more clouded in 1999 with the rise of certain specialty financial institutions which were not traditional banks at all. These entered into the banking universe in Japan through founding different kinds of banks like those which are internet based or specialize in settlements. They do not fall under a traditional category of the three mentioned above and so are referred to by the Japanese Bankers Association as "other banks." There are five banks in this non-traditional banking category. These are as follows: Citibank Japan, Aozora Bank, Norinchukin Bank, Shinsei Bank, and Seven Bank.

There is only one single foreign based banking member of the Japanese Bankers Association today. This is the United States' headquartered JP Morgan Chase Bank, National Association. Citibank Japan is of course classified as one of the "other banks" so does not fall under this category as determined by the JBA.

One of the primary ancillary functions of the Japanese Bankers Association is to calculate up and publish the JBA TIBOR. Since 1995, they have released this Japanese Yen TIBOR rate as well as the Euroyen TIBOR rate from 1998. Such rates reveal the unsecured call markets' prevailing rates as well as the interest rates on the offshore market.

Key Performance Indicator (KPI)

Key Performance Indicators are measurements that aid companies and other organizations in assessing the progress they are making towards their key goals. It is important for any organization to start out by deciding on its mission and determining its goals. Once they have done this effectively, they can decide on the best means of measuring their incremental progress to reaching the goals.

A characteristic of Key Performance Indicators is that they are measurements that are quantifiable. They must also be relevant to the organization's particular benchmarks of success. These will be different for various organizations. A business and a community service organization will not have the same KPIs.

Businesses could have KPIs that relate to their total profits or amount of income that they derive from repeat customers. Customer service departments could use KPIs that measure the number of calls they answer in under a minute. Schools' Key Performance Indicators could center on the percentages of students who graduate. Community service organizations might look at a KPI that revolves around the number of individuals they are able to assist in a given year.

There is no one right or wrong Key Performance Indicator. KPIs only need to be measurable, relevant to the goals of the organization, and a core part of the group's success. As an outfit's goals evolve or are met, the KPI goals may shift as well.

Key Performance Indicators have to be definable and measurable to be useful. It is no good setting a KPI that is subjective or a matter of opinion. Their definitions also should be consistent year in and year out. This is the only way that the targets set for each KPI will be meaningful.

If a company sets a goal to be the best employer, then they might use their company Turnover Rate each year as a Key Performance Indicator. This will work so long as they are using the same turnover rate definition and measurement each year. Reducing turnover by a certain percent annually is an understandable goal that different departments can act on and address.

Another important attribute of these Key Performance Indicators is that they have to be relevant to the organization and its goals. A business whose goal is to become the most profitable company in the sector will need to use KPIs that address profits and relevant finances. They might choose profits before taxes. Schools that are not interested in turning profits would not utilize such KPIs.

For Key Performance Indicators to be helpful they also need to be a core part of an organization's success. KPIs are only practical so long as they relate to the elements that the organization needs to work on so that they can attain the goals. Another important facet of these KPIs is that there should not be too many of them.

The idea is for the members of the organization to be able to focus on the identical Key Performance Indicators. It is possible for the organization as a whole to have three to five KPIs while departments have several others that help to support the overall goals. So long as these goals can be neatly categorized under the company's larger ones, this is acceptable.

Key Performance Indicators make a good tool for performance management. When everyone in the organization is aware of the goals, then they can take appropriate steps to help reach them. KPIs can be posted on company websites, in employee break rooms, and in company conference rooms. All of the activities of the members of the organization should be focused towards meeting or even surpassing those KPI goals.

Limited Liability Company (LLC)

A limited liability company is often referred to by its acronym LLC. These business setups combine the best in both worlds of proprietorships and corporations. They offer the sole proprietorship or partnerships' advantages of pass through taxation. At the same time, an LLC provides the same limited liability for the owners which a corporation receives.

With a limited liability company, the owners will file their business losses or profits with their individual tax returns. This is because an LLC is not considered to be its own taxable structure. When lawsuits against the company are involved, it is only business assets that are at risk of seizure.

Creditors and lawsuit parties are not usually able to get to the LLC owners' personal assets, like cars or houses. This is not absolute protection. If the owners of the LLC engage in unethical, illegal, or irresponsible behavior, then they can forfeit this level of security.

Setting up a limited liability company is harder than establishing either a sole proprietorship or partnership. Once this hurdle is cleared, it is much easier to run the LLC than it is a corporation. Officers of corporations are not completely protected from actions they undertake in the business.

LLC owners must be careful not to behave like the entity is a mere extension of their own individual activities. Should the owners not act as if the LLC is its own separate business concern, then courts can determine that the business LLC does not really exist. In these cases, the judge could decide that individuals are masquerading their business affairs and conducing business as a personal venture. They can became liable then for these actions if this determination is made.

Taxes are another major reason that individuals opt to set up a limited liability company. As pass through entities, the income from their business passes on through the entity directly to the members of the LLC. This means that they must report all financial gains or losses from the enterprise directly on their own tax returns. They do not have to file separate business tax returns. The IRS does require that LLC owners make an estimated quarterly tax payment four times per year.

LLCs which are owned by more than one individual do have to file the informational return Form 1065 every year with the IRS. This form clearly states every owner's share of the limited liability company profits or losses. The IRS goes over these to be certain that the owners are all appropriately reporting their share of the earnings.

Limited liability company management is specific in how it has to be conducted. There are two forms of this. Member management involves an equal participation of the owners in the operating of the business. This is the way that the majority of smaller LLC owners run them.

The alternative form of management is called manager management. In this type of business operation, the collective owners of the LLC must choose someone to handle the daily responsibilities of managing the company. This could be an owner or several of the owners. It could also be someone who is not a part of the LLC ownership who professionally manages the business on their behalf. In this arrangement, the owners who are not managing are only tasked with sharing in the profits or losses of the business. This is often the case with family members or friends who invest in a limited liability company.

Loan-to-Value-Ratio (LTV)

The Loan to Value Ratio is commonly known by its acronym LTV. This loan to value ratio states the total value of the first mortgage against the full real estate property's appraised value. The formula for figuring this ratio is simply the amount of the loan divided by the property value. It is expressed as a percent. So if a borrower is seeking $180,000 with which to buy a $200,000 house, then the Loan to Value Ratio is ninety percent.

The loan to value ratio proves to be among the most critical risk factors that lenders consider when they are deciding whether to qualify borrowers for a mortgage loan on a house. The dangers of a default occurring most influence the loan officers in their lending decisions. The chances of an institution having to take a hit in a foreclosure procedure only goes up as the dollar amount of the property equity goes down. Because of this, as the Loan to Value ratio goes up, the qualification tests for many mortgage programs get significantly stricter. Some lenders will insist on a borrower who comes with a high loan to value ratio on the property in question to purchase mortgage insurance. This safe guards the lender from any default realized by the borrower, but it also raises the mortgage's total costs.

Property values used in the loan to value ratio are generally set by appraisers. Still, the most accurate value of a piece of real estate is undoubtedly that determined when a willing seller and willing buyer come together to agree on a sale. Usually, banks decide to go with the lower number when they are offered choices of a purchase price that is fairly recent or an appraisal value. Recent sales are commonly deemed to be those that happened from a year to two years ago, although every bank makes its own rules in this regard.

When a borrower selects a property that he or she will purchase with a lower loan to value ratio that is less than eighty percent, lower interest rates can many times be obtained by borrowers who are low risk. Higher risk borrowers will also be considered in such a scenario, meaning those who have prior histories of late payments on mortgages, who have lower credit scores, who have high loan requirements or higher debt to income ratios, and who have neither sufficient cash reserves nor requested income documentation. Generally, higher loan to value ratios are only permitted for those borrowers who have a reliable mortgage payment history and who possess greater credit scores. Only those buyers with the greatest credit worthiness are considered for one hundred percent financing that translates to a one hundred percent loan to value ratio.

Loans that are made to the standards of lending giants Freddie Mac and Fannie Mae and their guidelines can not have loan to value ratios that exceed or are equal to eighty percent. Any loans higher than this percentage of eighty percent must come with attached private mortgage insurance. The private mortgage insurance premiums simply go on top of the existing mortgage principal and interest payments.

London Interbank Offered Rate (LIBOR)

LIBOR is a main global benchmark interest rate. It stands for London InterBank Offered Rate. This rate represents how much banks actually charge each other for loans based on one year, six months, three months, one month, and overnight timeframes. Banks all over the world use this benchmark rate. Reuters news service publishes this critical rate every day at 11 am. They do this in five different currencies of the U.S. dollar, the Euro, British Pound, Swiss franc, and Japanese yen.

Historically the BBA British Bankers Association oversaw and compiled this rate. The IBA ICE Benchmark Administration assumed this responsibility on August 1st of 2014. They figure up this rate using contributor bank submissions. In every currency for which they calculate it there are between 11 and 18 contributing banks who act as an oversight board.

LIBOR does more than provide a rate for the interbank loans. It is utilized as a bank guide for their setting of credit card rates, interest only mortgages, and adjustable rate loans. Bank lenders add in between one and two points to make money. An incredible $10 trillion in loans are determined at least in part by this interbank rate.

Besides these uses, this rate also serves as a base price for credit default swaps and interest rate swaps. These contracts are a type of insurance in case loans default. The swaps also created the 2008 financial crisis. Hedge funds and banks believed that risk did not exist in the mortgage backed securities because they were protected by this insurance.

The problem arose as the subprime mortgages that underlay the mortgage backed securities started defaulting. AIG and other insurance companies discovered they did not have enough cash available to pay off the swaps. In order to save all swap holders from bankruptcy, the Federal Reserve was forced to rescue AIG with a bailout. Despite the fact that these swaps were supposed to be dispersed after the financial crisis, the LIBOR rate remains the basis on over $350 trillion of such credit default swaps.

Banks created LIBOR in the 1980s in response to a demand for a standard interest rate to establish derivatives. The original rate came out in 1986 in the three currencies the U.S. dollar, British pound, and Japanese yen. The BBA later expanded it to include the additional currencies of Swiss franc and Euro.

A scandal plagued the LIBOR rate starting in 2012. The British Bankers' Association figured out the rate using its panel of banks that acted as representatives from every one of the currencies involved. BBA queried the banks about the rate they would charge in the set currencies for different amounts of time. The BBA's downfall was that they believed the rates the banks provided them with were true.

This unraveled in 2012 as British bank Barclays became charged with deliberately providing lower rates to the BBA then the ones they actually received from 2005 to 2009. They suffered a $450 million fine and the CEO Bob Diamond had to resign. When Diamond went down he told authorities the majority of other banks engaged in the same practice and that the Bank of England was aware.

The reasons that Barclays and others were lying about their rate was for better profits. Lower rates made the banks look stronger and more attractive to borrowers than banks with higher rates. The end result had three bankers found guilty of manipulating rates in 2015 while six others were acquitted of their charges in 2016. The guilty bankers all worked for Rabobank. The rate was taken away from the British Bankers Association and given over to the care of the ICE Benchmark Administration because of the scandal.

Long-Term Capital Management (LTCM)

Long-Term Capital Management refers to an enormous hedge fund that had been created and led by several famed Wall Street investor traders and economists who were Nobel Prize winners. Because of its huge size and connectedness to many other systemically important financial institutions and markets, its demise nearly brought down the worldwide financial system back in 1998. It was the firm's risky arbitrage-styled trading strategies that broke the company and endangered the U.S. financial system. Legendary Salomon Brothers John Meriwether the bond trader founded the company in 1993.

What made Long-Term Capital Management such a systemic risk was that the fund boasted $126 billion worth of assets. Because it traded with significantly leveraged positions, it actually controlled a substantially greater number of positions than the massive $126 billion in assets it held. The near collapse of this hedge fund giant back in the end of 1998 almost started a financial crisis and did cause financial panic throughout the globe.

The success of Long-Term Capital Management lay in its incomparable and unsullied reputations of the founders and owners. Principal stakeholders in the fund included the Nobel Prize winners for Economics--- Robert Merton and Myron Scholes. These three individuals (with John Meriwether) who really were the heart and soul of LTCM all proved to be legendary experts in derivatives investing. They knew how to deploy these highly risky assets in order to beat the market and earn significantly higher than average annual returns.

Admission to this speculative fund cost investors a flat $10 million investment. They had to commit the money for a full three years and not inquire about what kinds of investments the Long-Term Capital Management invested in and traded. These were steep and unheard of restrictions and limitations for a hedge fund at the time, yet investors begged to be let in the fund. Their enthusiasm seemed warranted, as in its first two years, LTCM did provide fantastic returns of 42.8 percent for 1995 and 40.8 percent for 1996. These stellar returns were even after the management received a steep 27 percent cut in fees. These were the golden age years of the fund.

Even in 1997, the Long-Term Capital Management firm managed to successfully hedge the majority of the Asian currency crisis risk to return a still impressive 17.1 percent that year. Yet returns were fast declining from their peak, and the writing was already on the wall. By September of the following year in 1998, the LTCM firm's highly risky trades began to catch up with it. The firm neared bankruptcy. The regulators quickly ascertained that it was simply too big too fail thanks to its enormous size and importance. Because of this realization, the Federal Reserve stepped in to bail out the massive hedge fund.

What led to the downfall of Long-Term Capital Management lay in its core strategies. As with many hedge funds, these relied upon making hedges for a number of volatile events (which were supposed to be predictable) in both bonds and foreign currencies markets. This went awry for the fund giant in 1998 when Russia decided to devalue its currency and to default on the Russian government sovereign bonds.

This catastrophic economic event proved to be outside of the typical range of volatility for which the LTCM had prepared and hedged. European stock markets plunged 35 percent in response. The American stock exchanges declined 20 percent in sympathy. Investors then fled to their usual safe haven suspects, the U.S. Treasury bonds. This enormous increase in buy side volume pushed up the prices which inversely pushed down the longer term interest rates by over a full percentage point.

It all combined to cause the extremely leveraged investment positions of LTCM to begin to crack and fail. By the conclusion of August in 1998, the capital investments of Long-Term Capital Management had drastically declined by fully 50 percent of their original value. Numerous pension funds and banks had invested heavily in the fund. The collapse in their investments also threatened to force many of them to almost bankruptcy condition.

It was bond trading giant Bear Stearns that finished off LTCM. As manager of their derivatives and bond settlements, Stearns demanded a $500 million payment all at once. LTCM had been outside of its agreements with the investment bank for three months at this point, and they could not meet the margin cash call.

The banking system now stood on the verge of collapse in the U.S. This is when the FRBNY (Federal Reserve Bank of New York) President William McDonough leaned on 15 banks to jointly bail out the fund with a $3.5 billion investment that gave them 90 percent ownership of LTCM. The Fed also aggressively began cutting their benchmark Fed funds interest rate. They pledged to U.S. investors that they would take any action necessary to support the markets and economy.

Money Market Account (MMA)

Money Market Account refers to a type of savings account which commonly includes advantages such as a debit card and check writing privileges. Besides this, it usually has interest rates which are higher than those which normal savings accounts provide. Such money markets generally have a higher minimum account balance than the average savings accounts do. These accounts are sometimes referred to by their acronym of MMA.

For those individuals who are contemplating a safe depository vehicle for bigger sums of cash and who wish to earn some interest while keeping the funds entirely liquid, these money market accounts can be an optimal solution. Among their pros are that the balance funds are available without advance notice, that they earn a relatively higher interest rate, that they provide the capability of writing as many as six checks each month, and that the debit card attached to them can be utilized as many as six times every month.

For any person who is going to place at least a few thousand dollars into a bank account and desires the clear cut safety provided by the FDIC Federal Deposit Insurance Corporation guarantee of funds, these can be a solid choice. Both credit unions and banks offer them as a reliable place to keep customers' emergency day purpose funds. The money is kept segregated from an account holder's daily utilization checking account funds this way. It can grow quicker than money kept in a comparable savings account thanks to the higher interest rate commonly attached to these MMAs. They provide the added convenience of check writing, which allows for easily covering any unexpected or emergency expenses.

Yet these accounts should not be confused with either checking or savings accounts. In fact they have stark differences from either of the two competing types. For starters, MMAs are not at all checking accounts. They may include the debit card maximum use feature or limited check writing privileges. Yet as with a savings account, they are Federal Reserve-regulation limited to maximum of six monthly withdrawals or transfers in a given month. This includes transactions made by check, debit card, or online/in person transfer. For those individuals who will need more than these half a dozen uses, interest bearing checking accounts make more practical sense than do money market accounts.

Besides this MMAs are similarly not strictly savings accounts either because of their debit cards and check writing capabilities. For those people who do not feel the need of having checks or even the debit card convenience with the account, there are sometimes better interest rates on balances available through what are known as high yield online savings accounts.

One of these types is the CD or certificate of deposit. Cd's may require that the owners agree to tie up their funds for as little as from months to as long as for years. MMAs will certainly permit more convenient and immediate time framed withdrawals than this. Yet CDs will pay better rates for those who can afford to lock it down for some time.

Finally, such money market accounts should not be confused with money market funds. The latter are instead investments whose principal value will decline if the market plunges. All MMAs carry the full FDIC backing when they are operated by banks, and by the NCUA National Credit Union Administration when they are held at credit unions. This amount of protection is equal to $250,000 per depositor or account.

For those individuals who decide that money market accounts are well suited for them, the best policy is to pursue those that come without any associated monthly fees and that pay the highest possible interest rates. It is also critical to ensure that they do not require too high a minimum account balance. This is critical to pay attention to since some financial institutions mandate that depositors open the account with and maintain a $10,000 account balance for these MMAs.

Money of Zero Maturity (MZM)

Money of zero maturity represents a way of measuring the money supply. This measurement for money which is circulating in an economy only covers money that is available to be spent and utilized. As such, this MZM is really a counting of all of the money supply that is liquid in a given economy.

Individuals can figure up the money of zero maturity with some basic math. This starts with obtaining the M2 measure of the money supply. From this M2 figure, all time deposits must be subtracted, such as with certificates of deposit. Next this result must be taken and added to the amount of money market funds which are available. This sum finally provides the MZM.

In practical terms, this measure of money includes several different components. All physical currency, including bank notes and coins, are a part of it. Checking account balances are also included. Savings account totals similarly comprise the MZM. Finally, money market accounts round out the figure. These are all configurations of money which are immediately available for par value to both companies and individuals.

Other forms of money are not included in the measure. Money of zero maturity never considers money held in accounts such as certificates of deposit or any other types of time deposits. This is because these funds contained in such financial instruments can not be instantly accessed for full par value. Similarly investments held in stocks and bonds must be first sold and settled before they can be obtained.

A number of analysts like to utilize the money of zero maturity because it proves to be an extremely liquid measurement. In fact this has grown to become among the most preferred means of measuring the country's money supply exactly because it does more completely depict the readily available money in the economy that can be employed for consumption and other spending. The name for this money measure comes from its combination of all available liquid and money with zero maturity that the three M's contain in M1, M2, and M3.

There are practical applications for the money of zero maturity measurement. The figure presents a reliable indicator of a nation's actual money base for the entire economy. As such it depicts the quantity of money which is literally moving throughout the economy as a whole. Since the Federal Reserve quit tracking and following the M3 number for money supply back in 2006 on March 23rd, this has become a preferred measurement of money supply, if not the most popular one.

When economists and analysts are aware of the amount of money which is moving throughout the economy, they can develop a feeling for two important trends. They are able to learn at a fairly quick glance whether or not the economy is growing or is instead contracting. By studying this figure, they can also determine how high the danger for inflation is over the near term.

When economists look at a chart of the MZM, they are interested in the rate of growth on a year to year, quarter to quarter, or month to month basis. As this growth rate improves, the economy is likely to expand along with it, and the threat of inflation increases apace. If instead the growth rate in the MZM decreases, the economy stands a solid chance of shrinking. This would mean inflationary threats are lower.

Mortgage Backed Obligations (MBO)

Mortgage Backed Obligations are also called mortgage backed securities, or MBS. These are real estate-based financial instruments. They represent an ownership stake in a pool of mortgages. They can also be called a financial security or obligation for which mortgages underlie the instrument.

Such a security offers one of three different means for the investor getting paid. It might be that the loan becomes paid back utilizing principal and interest payments that come in on the pool of mortgages which back the instrument. This would make them pass through securities. A second option is that the security issuer could provide payments to the investing party independently of the incoming cash flow off of the borrowers. This would then be a non-pass through security. The third type of security is sometimes referred to as a modified-pass through security. These securities provide the security owners with a guaranteed interest payment each month. This happens whether or not the underlying incoming principal and interest payments prove to be sufficient to cover them or not.

Pass-through securities are not like non-pass through securities in key ways. The pass through ones do not stay on the issuer of the securities' or originators' balance sheets. Non-pass through securities do stay on the relevant balance sheet. With these non pass through variants, the securities are most frequently bonds. These became mortgage backed bonds. Investors in the non-pass through types often receive extra collateral as a letter of credit, guarantees, or more equity capital. This type of credit enhancement is delivered by the insurer of the mortgage backed obligation. The holder of the MBO will be able to count on the security which underlies the instruments in the event that the repayments the pools of mortgages make are not enough to cover the payments (or fail altogether) for the bond holder investors.

These offerings of Mortgage Backed Obligations, Mortgage Backed Bonds, or Mortgage Backed Securities are all ultimately backed up by mortgage pools. Analysts and investors usually call these securitized mortgage offerings. When such types of investments are instead backed up by different kinds of assets and collateral then they have another name. An example of this is the Asset Backed Securities or Asset Backed Bonds.

They are backed up with such collateral as car loans, credit card receivables, or even mobile home loans. Sometimes they are referred to as Asset Backed Commercial Paper when the loans that underlie them are short term loan pools.

With these Mortgage Backed Obligations, they are often grouped together by both risk level and maturity dates. Issuers, investors, and analysts refer to this grouping as tranches, which are the risk profile-organized groups of mortgages. These complicated financial instrument tranches come with various interest rates, mortgage principle balances, dates of maturity, and possibilities of defaulting on their repayments. They are also highly sensitive to any changes in the market interest rates. Other economic scenarios can dramatically impact them as well. This is particularly true of refinance rates, rates of foreclosure, and the home selling rates.

It helps to look at a real world example to understand the complexity of Mortgage Backed Obligations and Collateralized Mortgage Obligations like these. If John buys an MBO or CMO that is comprised of literally thousands of different mortgages, then he has real potential for profit. This comes down to whether or not the various mortgage holders pay back their mortgages. If just a couple of the mortgage-paying homeowners do not pay their mortgages while the rest cover their payments as expected, then John will recover not only his principal but also interest. On the other hand, if hundreds or even thousands of mortgage holders default on their payments and then fall into foreclosure, the MBO will sustain heavy losses and will be unable to pay out the promised returns of interest and even the original principal to John.

Mortgage Backed Securities (MBS)

Mortgage backed securities turn out to be a special kind of asset which have underlying collections of mortgages or individual mortgages that back them. To be qualified as an MBS, the security also has to be qualified as rated in one of two top tier ratings. Credit ratings agencies determine these ratings levels.

These securities generally pay out set payments from time to time which are much like coupon payments. Another requirement of MBS is that the mortgages underlying them have to come from an authorized and regulated bank or financial institution.

Sometimes mortgage backed securities are called by other names. These include mortgage pass through or mortgage related securities. Interested investors buy or sell them via brokers. The investments have fairly steep minimums. These are generally $10,000. There is some variation in minimum amounts depending on which entity issues them.

Issuers are either a GSE Government Sponsored Enterprise, an agency company of the federal government, or an independent financial company. Some people believe that government sponsored enterprise MBS come with less risk. The truth is that default and credit risks are always prevalent. The government has no obligation to bail out the GSEs when they are in danger of default.

Investors who put their money into these mortgage backed securities lend their money to a business or home buyer. Using an MBS, regional banks which are smaller may confidently lend money to their clients without being concerned whether the customers can cover the loan itself. Thanks to the mortgage backed securities, banks are only serving as middlemen between investment markets and actual home buyers.

These MBS securities are a way for shareholders to obtain principal and interest payments out of mortgage pools. The payments themselves can be distinguished as different securities classes. This all depends on how risky the various underlying mortgages are rated within the MBS.

The two most frequent kinds of mortgage backed securities turn out to be collateralized mortgage obligations (CMOs) and pass throughs. Collateralized mortgage obligations are comprised of many different pools of securities. These are referred to as tranches, or pieces. Tranches receive credit ratings. It is these credit ratings which decide what rates the investors will receive. The securities within a senior secured tranche will generally feature lesser interest rates than others which comprise the non secured tranche. This is because there is little actual risk involved with senior secured tranches.

Pass throughs on the other hand are set up like a trust. These trust structures collect and then pass on the mortgage payments to the investors. The maturities with these kinds of pass throughs commonly are 30, 15, or five years. Both fixed rate mortgages and adjustable rate ones can be pooled together to make a pass through MBS.

The pass throughs average life spans may end up being less than the maturity which they state. This all depends on the amount of principal payments which the underlying mortgage holders in the pool make. If they pay larger payments than required on their monthly mortgages, then these pass through mortgages could mature faster.

National Association of Securities Dealers (NASDAQ)

The NASDAQ is the acronym for the National Association of Securities Dealers Automated Quotation Systems, though the organization has dropped the Automated Quotation Systems part of the name as obsolete. This NASDAQ is the country's second largest stock exchange. It represents the principal rival to the NYSE, or New York Stock Exchange, which is the largest stock exchange in the country and only one larger than it.

The NASDAQ is also the largest equity securities trading market in the U.S. that is based on an electronic screen. When market capitalization, or the value of its stock per share multiplied by the number of outstanding shares, is considered, it is the fourth largest trading exchange in the world. The NASDAQ actually records a higher trading volume than does any competing electronic stock exchange on earth with its actively traded 2919 ticker symbols.

NASDAQ became established in 1971 by the NASD, or National Association of Securities Dealers. The system originally represented the successor to the OTC, or Over the Counter traded market. It later developed into an actual stock exchange of sorts. By 2000 and 2001, the NASD sold off the NASDAQ into the NASDAQ OMX Group, who presently own and operate it. Its stock is listed under the symbol of NDAQ since July 2 of 2002. The FINRA, or Financial Industry Regulatory Authority, oversees and regulates the NASDAQ stock market exchange.

The NASDAQ made major contributions to the world of electronic stock exchange trading as the first one of its kind on earth. When it began, it started out as a computer bulletin board system that did not literally put buyers and sellers in touch. Among its great achievements, the NASDAQ proved to be responsible for decreasing the spread, or the bid and the asking prices' difference for stocks. Many dealers disliked the NASDAQ in the early days, as they made enormous profits on these higher spreads.

In subsequent years, the NASDAQ evolved into a typical stock exchange through adding volume reporting and trade reporting to its new automated trading systems. This exchange became the first such stock market in America to advertise to the public. They would highlight companies that traded on the NASDAQ, many of which were technology companies. Their commercials closed out with the motto the stock exchange for the nineties and beyond, that they eventually changed to NASDAQ, the stock market for the next one hundred years.

The NASDAQ is set to become a trans Atlantic stock exchange titan with its purchase of the Norway based OMX stock exchange. This will only enhance its European holdings that presently include eight other stock exchanges throughout Europe. Besides its NASDAQ stock exchange in New York City, the group possesses a one third stake in the Dubai Stock Exchange in the United Arab Emirates. With its double listing arrangement in place with the OMX exchange, the NASDAQ OMX is set to become the major competitor for NYSE Euronext in bringing in new listings.

National Bureau of Economic Research (NBER)

The NBER National Bureau of Economic Research is an organization whose purpose centers on creating and disbursing economic research. They are committed to encouraging better understanding of the way the economy functions for individuals, businesses, and policymakers. As part of this they write and distribute unbiased economic reports.

The NBER got its start in 1920 as a not for profit, private, non-political group. Their objectives from the start were undertaking research on economics and sharing it with business people, politicians, and academics. The researchers who are connected with NBER study a great range of different economic and business subjects.

Along with this they utilize numerous research methods in their studies. The group focuses on numerous different topics. Chief among them are creating quantitative economic behavior models, coming up with new ways to measure statistics, and studying the impacts that public policies cause.

The history of the NBER shows they covered many important ground breaking economic issues within American society. Their early efforts centered on longer term growth for the economy, the full business cycle, and the aggregate economy. In the formative years Wesley Mitchell wrote an important paper about the business cycle. Simon Kuznets pioneered the topic of national income accounting.

Milton Friedman researched and argued for money demand and what determined consumer spending. All of these proved to be in the earlier studies performed by the National Bureau of Economic Research. In 1984, Solomon Fabricant wrote a summary of their initial work and development entitled Toward a Firmer Basis of Economic Policy: The Founding of the National Bureau of Economic Research.

The NBER has greatly expanded and grown in influence over the years. Today it is considered to be the foremost group for not for profit research on economics in the United States. Among the economists who were affiliated with NBER are 25 Nobel Prize winners. There have also been 13 heads of the Presidential Council of Economic Advisers among their affiliated members.

NBER researchers today include over 1,400 business and economics professors who teach throughout universities and colleges around the U.S. and Canada. These researching scholars are considered to be the leaders within their own fields. The vast majority of those researchers who hold NBER affiliation have a title of RA Research Associates or FRF Faculty Research Fellows. These Research Associates are tenured by their home university or college. Their appointments to this senior status must be NBER Board of Directors approved. Faculty Research Fellows usually prove to be junior scholars in their fields.

The NBER does not receive direct tax dollar support. It operates based on a variety of research grants. These supporting grants come from private foundations, government agencies, corporate and individual contributions, and investment income.

The NBER is well organized and run by a board of directors that governs it. Its headquarters are based in Cambridge, Massachusetts. The group also maintains a branch office in New York City. The members of this board come from and represent both important national economics entities and foremost American researching universities. The board also hosts members who are important economists at academia, trade unions, and corporations. Being a board member of this national economics group is a prestigious honor.

In 2016 the Chief Executive Officer and President of the NBER is James Poterba. He is served by 45 personnel who staff the organization. These employees are besides the Faculty Research Fellows and Research Associates located around North America. The research group is governed by various important documents. These include their NBER by-laws, incorporation certificate, and the conflict of interest policy for directors and officers.

Net Operating Profit After Tax (NOPAT)

Net operating profit after tax is also called by its acronym of NOPAT. This refers to the potential earnings (in cash) of a corporation working under the pretense that it has no debt. This NOPAT metric is often utilized in so-called EVA economic valued added calculations. The formula for determining NOPAT is as follows: the operating income times the result of one minus the tax rate. For companies which are debt leveraged, this NOPAT proves to be a more precise and exact way of examining their operating efficiencies. As such it does not factor in the tax advantages which a number of corporations enjoy from their debt load.

Analysts and accountants consider a number of varying performance metrics when they are evaluating a corporation in which to invest. The two most frequent performance measures turn out to be sales (or revenue) and net income growth. With the revenue/sales figures, this delivers a top line performance metric. It does not say anything about the company's operating efficiency value though. Similarly the net income does include the operating expenses of a firm, yet it also factors in the net tax benefits and savings from the company's particular debt leverage.

This is where the Net operating profit after tax comes in as a useful hybrid form of alternative calculation. It permits the analysts to compare and contrast a company's performance against past metrics and other companies by removing the effects of debt leverage from the equation. This allows analysts to truly fairly measure one company against another, regardless of the two firms' net debt positions.

It always helps to consider a real world, concrete example with these complex terms. If a company's EBIT Earnings Before Interest and Taxes was $12,000 and their tax rate was 25 percent, then the calculation for NOPAT would translate to $12,000 times the result of one minus .25,(or .75). This equals $9,000 as a NOPAT. It is an after tax cash flow estimate that does not include the tax benefits of debt. For those companies without debt, Net operating profit after tax equals the same amount as does the net income after tax.

It is worth noting that analysts prefer to compare and contrast firms within the same industry when utilizing the NOPAT metric. This is because every industry has its own normal range of operating costs. Some industries' typical expenses turn out to be dramatically lower or higher than others' do.

For example, cable utilities would have extremely high operating costs associated with initially putting in, continuously upgrading, and maintaining their technology and physical hard-wired distribution networks. Soft drink businesses like Dr. Pepper/Snapple Group (DPS) have relatively low costs since they generally license out their products to other companies which produce and distribute them on their behalf.

Net operating profit after tax has other uses besides the helpful view of a company without its debt leverage being considered. Those analysts who follow and predict mergers and acquisitions utilize this NOPAT value all the time. It helps them to figure up the FCFF free cash flow to firm. This is equal to the NOPAT less any changes to working capital. It also equates to the net operating profit of the firm after taxes less the firm's capital.

These two metrics NOPAT and FCFF are commonly utilized by those types of analysts who hunt down targets for acquisition. The reason for this is that the financing of the acquiring firm will then substitute in for the present financing arrangement (their corporate debt).

Net Present Value (NPV)

Net Present Value refers to a principal profitability measure that companies utilize in their corporate budget planning process. It helps them to analyze the possible ROI return on investment for a particular proposed or working project. Thanks to the involvement of time value and its depreciating effect on dollars, the NPV is forced to consider a discount rate and its compounding effect throughout the term of the entire project.

The actual Net Present Value in an investment or business project considers the point where revenue (or cash inflow) is equal to or greater than the total investment capital that funds the project or asset in the first place. This is particularly useful for businesses when they are comparing and contrasting a number of different projects or potential projects. It allows them to draw a valuable comparison of their comparative profitability levels to make sure that they only spend their limited resources, time, and management skills on the most valuable ventures. The higher the NPV proves to be, the more profitable it is as an investment, property, or project in the end.

Another way of thinking about the Net Present Value is as a measurement of how well an investment is meeting a targeted yield considering the upfront investment that the firm made. Using this NPV, companies can also determine precisely what adjustment they need in the initial investment in order to reach the hoped for yield. This assumes that all else remains constant.

Net Present Value can also be utilized to effectively visualize and quantify investments in real estate and other asset purchases in a simple formulaic expression. This is that the NPV is equal to the Current value minus the cost. In this iteration of the NPV, the current value of all anticipated future cash flow is discounted to today utilizing the relevant discount rate minus the cost of acquiring said cash flow. This makes NPV essentially the value of the project less the cost. When analysts or corporate accountants examine the NPV in this light, it becomes easy to understand how the value explains if the item being purchased (or project being funded) is more or less valuable than the cost of it in the first place.

Only three total categories of NPV ultimate values are possible for any property purchase or project funding. NPV could be a positive Net Present Value. This means that the buyers will pay less than the true value of the asset. The NPV might also be a Zero NPV. This simply means that the buyer or project funder is paying precisely the value of the asset or project worth. With a negative NPV in the final categorization, the buyer will be paying too much for the asset technically. This will be more than the asset is actually worth. There are cases where companies or buyers might be willing to pursue a project or acquire an asset with a negative NPV when other factors come into play.

For example, they might be interested in purchasing a property for a new corporate headquarters whose NPV is negative. The reasoning behind such a decision could be the unquantifiable and intangible value of the location of the property either for visibility purposes or because it is next to the present company headquarter premises.

It is always helpful to look at a concrete example to de-mystify difficult concepts like Net Present Value. Consider a corporation that wishes to fully analyze the anticipated profits in a project. This given project might need an upfront $10,000 investment to get it off the ground. In three years time, the project is forecast to create revenues amounting to $2,000, $8,000, and $12,000. This means that the project is expected to provide $22,000 on the initial $10,000 outlay.

It would appear that the return will amount to 120 percent for a gain greater than the initial investment. There is a reason why this is not the case though. The discount rate for the time value of money has to be factored in, and this means a percentage of several points per year at least. The figure of 4.5 percent is often utilized on a three year project like this. This takes into consideration the fact that dollars earned three years from now will not be so valuable as today's earned dollars. This is why the corporate accountants will use business calculators in order to plug in the discount time value rates to figure the true NPV. Discounting by the 4.5 percent means that the project actually will return somewhere near $21,000 in terms of today's dollar value.

New York Mercantile Exchange (NYMEX)

The New York Mercantile Exchange proves to be the biggest physical commodity exchange for futures buying, selling, and trading in the world. Since they merged, it is comprised of both the NYMEX Division and the COMEX Division. At NYMEX, traders are able to trade platinum, palladium, and energy markets.

COMEX is where they trade FTSE 100 index options as well as silver, gold, and copper futures. NYMEX still keeps a place for the open outcry system where traders shout and make hand gestures to indicate their purchases. This operates only during the day time. After normal business hours, the electronic trading system takes over for the night.

The NYMEX origins go back to an association of Manhattan dairy merchants. In 1872, a group of them came together and formed the Butter and Cheese Exchange of New York. Once eggs joined the various dairy businesses handled on the exchange, they changed the name to Butter, Cheese, and Egg Exchange. By 1882 they had added canned goods, dried fruits, and poultry to the offerings. The name received its final change to reflect the broader product offerings as the New York Mercantile Exchange at this time.

Though COMEX Commodities Exchange and NYMEX used to be separately owned and run exchanges, they merged together to become two divisions of the NYMEX Holdings, Inc. back in 1994. They listed on the New York Stock Exchange on November 17, 2006 trading under the NMX ticker symbol.

In March of 2008, the CME Group of Chicago committed to a conclusive agreement to buy NYMEX holdings for $11.2 billion combination in cash and stock offerings. In August of 2008 the deal finished and NYMEX and COMEX began to function as DCM Designated Contract Markets for the CME Group. They joined sister exchanges the Chicago Board of Trade and Chicago Mercantile Exchange as part of the four DCMs.

In 2006, the New York Mercantile Exchange became almost entirely electronically traded. NYMEX keeps a smaller venue operating for those traders who prefer to engage in the open outcry historic and sentimental form of trading. There they utilize complicated hand signals and shouting while standing on a physical trading floor to buy and sell. The hand signal system is being preserved by a project published on the subject.

NYMEX's headquarters is found in the Battery Park City area of Manhattan in Brookfield Place. They also maintain offices around the world in such cities as Washington D.C., Boston, San Francisco, Atlanta, London, Dubai, and Tokyo. The options and futures traded here on precious metals and energy commodities have developed into important tools for companies that are seeking to mitigate their risk through hedging their own positions. Because these various instruments are traded so easily and liquidly, companies are able to discern future prices and to hedge their future needs. This is why NYMEX has grown to become such a critical part of global activities in hedging and trading environments.

Today the NYMEX manages literally billions of dollars in metals, energy carrier, and other commodities that companies and traders sell and buy every day for delivery in the future. This is handled on either the physical trading floor or the electronic trading system by computers.

These prices on the exchange and its numerous transactions become the basis of pricing for individuals and companies who purchase commodities around the globe. The Commodity Futures Trading Commissions agency of the U.S. government actually regulates the NYMEX floor. Trading on the exchange is performed by independent brokers sent by specific companies.

New York Stock Exchange (NYSE)

The NYSE is the acronym for the world's largest stock exchange, the New York Stock Exchange. With a market capitalization of companies listed on it totaling at $11.92 trillion dollars in August 2010, it also possessed an average day trading value of around $153 billion in 2008. By market capitalization, the NYSE has no rivals for size.

The New York Stock Exchange is owned and operated by the NYSE Euronext company. This outfit came into being in 2007 when the NYSE merged with the completely electronic Euronext stock exchange. Four rooms make up the trading floor of the NYSE that is found at 11 Wall Street. Its main building is found at 18 Broad Street on the corners of Wall Street and Exchange Place. This building became a National Historic Landmark back in 1978, along with its sister 11 Wall Street Building.

Occasionally known as "the Big Board," the New York Stock Exchange allows for sellers and buyers of stocks to exchange shares in all of the companies that are listed for public trading. Its trading hours prove to be 9:30 AM to 4:00 PM on Monday to Friday. Holidays are spelled out in advance by the exchange itself.

The NYSE has always operated as an in person trading floor since its inception in 1792. Today, this works in an auction format that is ongoing. Floor traders here are able to make stock transactions for investors. They simply gather together surrounding the particular company post where there is a specialist broker working as auctioneer in open outcry format to get buyers and sellers together and to oversee the auction itself. This specialist works directly for the company that is an NYSE member and not the exchange itself. These specialists will commit their own money to assist the trades about ten percent of the time. Naturally, they also give out information that serves to bring together sellers and buyers.

In 1995, NYSE began making the automation transition for the auctions. This started with hand held computers that were wireless. Like this, traders were capable of executing and getting orders electronically. This ended a 203 year tradition of paper based trades.

From January 24 of 2007, most every stock on the NYSE is able to be traded on the electronic Hybrid Market. With this ability to send in customer orders for electronic confirmation immediately, orders can also be sent to the floor for auction market trade. More than eighty-two percent of the NYSE order volume came to the floor electronically in only the first three months of that first year.

Only those who own one of 1,366 actual seats on the exchange are permitted to trade shares directly on the exchange. Such seats are sold for enormous sums. The highest price paid for one amounted to $4 million in the tail end of the 1990's. The highest price ever paid adjusted for inflation proved to be $625,000 in 1929, which would amount to more than six million dollars in terms of 2010 dollars. Since the exchange became a public company, the seats have been instead sold in one year licenses.

Non Performing Asset (NPA)

A Non Performing Asset is also known by its acronym NPA. This pertains to a certain way of categorizing loans on a banks' balance sheet. Such NPA loans are those which are in arrears on their regular payments or are otherwise in outright default. In the majority of instances, loans become categorized as nonperforming as the payments on the loans are not received consecutively over 90 days. It is possible for the time lapse to be less or more than the typical 90 days in order for NPA classification to occur. It all comes down to the individual conditions and terms which each loan spells out in the documents and the policies of the bank in question.

Following 90 days of non-payment, most banks will commonly reclassify the loans as Non Performing Assets or loans. This might happen during the term for the loan or as a failure ultimately to pay off the balance principal of the loan which becomes due upon maturity. It always helps to consider a real world example in order to better understand a somewhat complicated topic.

Consider a firm that takes out a $20 million loan with associated payments that are interest-only in nature for a $100,000 payment amount each month. If the borrower misses payments for three months in a row, the bank which originally made the loan could be forced to classify the loan as a Non Performing Asset in order to comply with its government-mandated regulatory requirements. It is also possible for loans to finally become nonperforming if the borrower pays out all of its interest payments but is unable or alternatively fails to pay back the final principal that becomes due at maturity date.

Banks which carry such Non Performing Assets on their books and balance sheets create three separate drags for themselves. The cash flow of the bank lender in question becomes reduced as principal and/or interest payments do not become made. This can reduce earnings or even upset budgets. Provisions for loan losses must be set aside in order to compensate for possible defaults. These provisions actually lower the amount of total capital with which the bank can issue additional loans. After the realized losses are booked, the bank or financial institution will have to write them off versus their earnings.

There are as many as four different means for lenders to recover all or part of their losses that arise because of Non Performing Assets. Smart lending institutions will be willing to restructure loans in order to keep cash flow incoming. It also permits them to keep the loan from becoming categorized as a nonperforming asset. Banks might also seize the underlying collateral of the loans. They can then sell this off in order to reduce their losses as much as the market value of the assets will allow.

Thirdly, financial institutions might also choose to convert their NPA loans into equity. This could grow back all the way to full value over time. As bonds become converted to new equity shares, the original stakes' value typically disappears. Finally, banks might sell off their bad debts for substantial discounts to such firms as specialize in collections on loans. Lenders will tend to sell off their NPA loans which do not come collateral-secured. This is particularly the case when the other methods of recouping their losses do not prove to be especially cost effective for the bank or other lending institution.

Office of Financial Research (OFR)

OFR is an abbreviation and stands for the Office of Financial Research. This government organization that has its headquarter in the Treasury Building works to supply information in support of the Financial Stability Oversight Council.

The OFR strives to encourage financial stability throughout the United States. They do this by scanning throughout the American financial system in order to find, measure, and consider risks. They also engage in gathering critical research and then compile and homogenize the financial data so that it can be easily referenced, understood, and compared.

The Office of Financial Research says about itself that its job revolves around illuminating the darkest parts of the financial system. As they do this, they are looking to see where the risks to the system are heading. They then determine the level of threat such risks pose to the system and the economy. Finally, they deliver financial analysis, data, and insight on these threats along with an available policy tools' evaluation in order to effectively address and diffuse the threats.

Congress created this Office of Financial Research back in 2010 under the Dodd-Frank Wall Street Reform and Consumer Protection Act. They established this new organization in order to provide material support to the all important new super regulatory entity the Financial Stability Oversight Council.

The OFR was also to deliver useful information on the risks to the system to the member organizations of the Council as well as to any interested and concerned members of the public. The Director of the OFR is both appointed at the discretion of the President and must be confirmed by a majority vote of the Senate. In 2016, this Director was Richard Berner. The group was created to work around two offices of a Data Center and a Research and Analysis Center.

The mission of the Office of Financial Research is to encourage American financial system stability via providing high quality financial standards, data, and analysis of the information on behalf of the Financial Stability Oversight

Council, its various member organizations, and the general public. To this effect, they maintain the vision of a financial system that is efficient, effective, stable, and transparent.

Every year, the Office of Financial Research produces several publications. Two of these that have become annual productions are the Annual Report to Congress on Human Capital Planning and the Annual Report to Congress. The Dodd-Frank Act itself requires that the OFR produces, compiles, and presents this general annual report once a year before Congress.

Every general annual report must include a complete analysis of the various threats to the American financial system and overall stability, the progress in their endeavors to meet the mission of the OFR, and the critical discoveries regarding threats from their research and analyzing of the whole United States' financial system.

The 2015 Office of Financial Research Annual Report to Congress is the fourth such yearly report since the office became established under the requirements of the Dodd-Frank Act. This particular report reviewed and analyzed the possible threats to American financial stability, reported on their important discoveries of risk, detailed their progress in meeting the OFR overall mission, and laid out the agenda of The Office for 2016.

The 2015 report stated that the various threats to United States' financial stability increased slightly from the prior year's report. They still consider the risks to be in the moderate to medium range. They did not change their threat assessment after the Federal Reserve FOMC raised the short term interest rates. A major portion of the 2016 agenda for the OFR is to affect a new programmatic approach in their work. They are striving to concentrate their initial efforts on the core areas of eight programs.

OPEC Fund for International Development (OFID)

The OPEC Fund for International Development, or OFID, proves to be the developing world assisting, intergovernmental development financing organization. The member states of OPEC organized this group in 1976. They actually conceived of the idea while they were at a meeting in Algiers, Algeria in March of 1975. The Solemn Declaration of the Conference stated that it "reaffirmed the natural solidarity which unites OPEC countries with other developing countries in their struggle to overcome underdevelopment." They sought ways to build up cooperation between the two groups of fellow developing nations.

The goal of the OPEC Fund for International Development seeks to establish stronger financial ties and coordinate projects between the various OPEC Member Nations and other non-OPEC developing states. They work to deliver financial assistance to these poorer fellow developing nations in order to aid their socioeconomic progress. This makes the primary mission of the group to encourage South on South Partnerships with those other developing nations throughout the globe in order to finally eradicate poverty.

They pursue this noble goal from their global headquarters in Vienna, Austria. Today's Director-General is Saudi Arabia's own Suleiman Jasir Al-Herbish. This is his third term heading the OPEC Fund for International Development. The man was unanimously re-elected in June of 2013 by the Ministerial Council, the highest authority within the institution.

Because of the decision at the First OPEC Summit held in Algiers, the capital of Algeria, back in 1975, the Member Nations had their various Finance Ministers from the Member Nations meet to create the OPEC Special Fund. This pool permitted the Member Nations to funnel aid to those developing countries most in need of financial and developmental assistance. In 1976, this OPEC Special Fund began life with a then-impressive $800 million reserve.

By the conclusion of 1977, the OPEC Fund for International Development had provided 71 loans to a substantial 58 nations. They had also funneled donations from the Member Nations to various other developmental intergovernmental organizations including the IMF International Monetary Fund and the IFA International Fund for Agricultural Development.

The fund performed so spectacularly that the Member Nations chose in 1980 to change the temporary capital facility into a permanent legal organization renamed the OPEC Fund for International Development. They achieved the status of international development agency by May of 1980.

The member nations of OFID are 13 separate countries. These include the following: Venezuela, United Arab Emirates, Saudi Arabia, Qatar, Nigeria, Libya, Kuwait, Iraq, Iran, Indonesia, Gabon, Ecuador, and Algeria. Ecuador had suspended its membership in the developmental organization in the early 1990s. They returned to full membership status in June of 2014, 22 years later.

The OPEC Fund for International Development has at least five different ways they have disbursed their largess to help fellow developing nations most desperately in need of financial - developmental assistance. They offer developmental loans for programs and projects, trade financing, and support for balance of payments needs. They also offer grants to support food aid, technical assistance, research, and humanitarian relief in disasters and emergencies.

A third operation has them finance activities of the private sector in developing nations. The group similarly makes generous contributions to developmental institutions and their resource bases when their work helps out developing nations. Finally, they represent the various OPEC Member Nations internationally when they find themselves in the global financial arena in need of a collective action.

The resources of the OFID come from a build up of the reserves of the operations of the organization itself as well as voluntary member state contributions. In June of 2011 in response to the many and growing developing world needs brought on by the global financial crisis, the OPEC Fund for International Development replenished their funds with an additional $1 billion U.S. dollars.

Open Market Operations (OMO)

Open Market Operations are also called by their acronym OMO. These describe both the purchasing and selling of open market-based government securities. The Federal Reserve central bank of the United States has a committee which engages in these transactions with the goal of expanding or contracting the total quantity of money flowing through the banking system.

When the Fed buys up instruments, it forces money into the banking system to stimulate growth. When it sells its various securities, this has the opposite effect and contracts the economy. The idea behind the Federal Reserve's thinking with this technique is to tweak through manipulating the federal funds rate. This rate represents the price for which the banks will loan money to each other.

This Open Market Operation proves to be the most frequently deployed and highly flexible tool from the toolkit of the Federal Reserve. It permits them to both control and implement their monetary policy for America. They also work with the reserve requirements for the banks and the discount rate. While they have all three tools at their disposal, the buying and selling of government securities proves to be their favorite and also most often deployed tool. This permits them to precisely control the amount of bank reserve balances. It assists the Federal Reserve in decreasing or increasing the short-term interest rates as they deem to be appropriate for any given time.

The Federal Reserve committee which determines the monetary policy is called the FOMC Federal Open Market Committee. They carry out this monetary policy through actually setting the target for the federal funds interest rate and also by implementing their Open Market Operations, along with manipulating the reserve requirement and discount rate strategies to get the federal funds rate to their desired levels. This fed funds rate turns out to be incredibly important for them to finely control since it impacts practically every other interest rate found in the United States today. Among these are the prime rate, car loan rates, and home loan mortgage rates. Only the London-based LIBOR is more important today.

When the FOMC is attempting to attain a desired federal funds rate, they first fall back on the Open Market Operations. They carry out either the contractionary or expansionary monetary policy to achieve their desired movement and ultimate ends.

When the Fed sets its sites on expanding the economy this way, they want an expansionary policy. They need to reduce the fed funds rate in order to facilitate this goal. They will buy government securities off of private bond dealers to deposit funds into the accounts for the financial institutions, entities, and investors who sold them the government bonds. These deposits then became a component of the commercial bank held-cash on account with the Federal Reserve. It grows the money supply available to commercial banks for their various lending operations. It is these commercial banks which seek to loan out their cash reserves. To do this, they will lower their interest rates to bring in more customers.

The Fed also occasionally has moments when it seeks to cool off an overheating economy in the U.S.A. To do this they will begin their contractionary monetary policy and seek to boost the federal funds rate. In practice, this involves them selling off their seemingly limitless supply of government securities to the financial institutions and banks. It reduces the amount of money the commercial banks have left to loan out. This makes the cost of money more expensive and so boosts the associated interest rates, including the federal funds rate too.

Operating Cash Flow (OCF)

Operating Cash Flow is also known by its abbreviated acronym OCF. It refers to a metric for the quantity of cash which a corporation or company's typical daily business operations produce. As such, it provides a good insight into a firm's ability to generate enough cash flow in order to either grow or at the very least maintain its existing operations. It might also prove that a going concern requires outside financing in order to fund its expansion plans.

Publically traded firms must calculate their Operating Cash Flows through employing an indirect method of calculation. This GAAP Generally Accepted Accounting Principles mandate means that they have to adjust their net income into a cash basis. They do this by making alterations to their accounts that are not cash. This includes accounts receivable, depreciation categories, and inventory changes.

In fact the Operating Cash Flow is a true representation of the cash portion of the firm's net income. This will also take into account other non-cash items thanks to the requirements which the GAAP sets out for net incomes to be done as accrual-based reporting. This means that amortization, compensation which is based upon stock shares, and incurred but as of yet not paid for expenses would be included in the calculations.

Besides this the actual net income has to be adjusted to reflect changes to working capital kinds of accounts in the balance sheet of the corporation. Especially important is the fact that any accounts receivable increases actually equate to booked revenues for which no collections have been completed. Because of this, these increases have to be taken off of the net income figure. This is partially offset at least by any reported accounts payable increases that are due but as of yet not paid, since this remains in the net income number.

Analysts have opined that such Operating Cash Flow represents the most accurate and basic form of outflows and inflows of cash as a company engages in its normal operations of the daily business. Where the health of a firm is concerned, this represents among the most crucial of metrics. Yet it most appropriately and usefully works for those corporations that are not overly complex.

The Operating Cash Flows focus on the both outflows and inflows which a corporation's principal business activities involve. This includes buying and selling inventory, paying employee salaries, and delivering services. It is important to remember that all financing and investing activities will not be included in the Operating Cash Flow. These become reportable separately. A part of these excluded activities would be purchasing equipment and factories, borrowing money, and engaging in share holder dividend payouts. Finding this cash flow number is easy by looking at the corporation's cash flows statement. This statement will break out the numbers into several categories including cash flows from operations, from financing, and from investing.

Operating Cash Flow is a very important number on a company balance sheet. Many financial analysts and investors would rather consider such cash flow measures since they reduce the impacts of confusing and opaque accounting tricks. It also delivers a better, sharper big picture for the business operations' health and reality.

Consider the following examples. When a firm concludes a big sale, this delivers a major increase to its revenues. This is irrelevant though if the firm can not collect on the money owed. It does not represent a real gain for the corporation. At the same time, firms could be producing elevated operating cash flow numbers. Despite this, they might have an abysmally low net income number if they employ an accelerated depreciation calculation or possess many fixed assets.

OTC Bulletin Board (OTCBB)

The OTC Bulletin Board (OTCBB) proves to be a service for electronic trading that the NASD National Association of Securities Dealers maintains and provides to investors and dealers. It delivers live quotes on volume and pricing data to both investors and traders on stocks which trade OTC over the counter.

Every company which is listed on this backwater exchange has to be current in its filings of financial statements with regulatory oversight group the SEC Securities and Exchange Commission or some other applicable regulatory body. Other than this, there are no minimum listing requirements on the OTC Bulletin Board exchange; unlike with sister monster exchanges the NYSE New York Stock Exchange or the NASDAQ.

The OTCBB turns out to be a fairly young stock quoting system. It began in 1990 following the passage of the Penny Stock Reform Act of 1990. This legislation mandated that the SEC had to come up with some form of system for electronic quotes for those firms which were not able to qualify for listing on one of the rival major stock exchanges such as NYSE or NASDAQ. Those securities which trade on the over the counter basis does so between individuals who are utilizing either phones or computers to place trades. Every stock which trades on the OTCBB contains an ".OB" in its suffix.

It is important for potential investors in OTC Bulletin Board stocks to remember that this is not an extension of any major stock exchange. Instead, it is because these stocks are not well known, heavily traded, or largely capitalized that they are trading on the over the counter electronic quoting system basis in the first place.

These stocks are well known for their substantial risk and rampant instability and volatility. This is why the very few of the OTCBB stocks which enjoy great success eventually migrate over to the NASDAQ or even NYSE once they are able to meet the strict listing requirements of the relevant larger exchanges. The bid-ask spreads on OTCBB are commonly much higher since the volume is so much less.

OTC Bulletin Board serves a critically important role and fills a much-needed vacuum with its existence and services. In truth there are many individual tiny companies which will never qualify for the stronger listing requirements so that their issues are allowed to trade on the major national stock exchanges.

The OTCBB gives them another avenue to float stock shares to a national investor audience so that they can obtain significant capital for their expansion needs. As long as investors recall that this is not a true exchange in any practical sense of the word, but merely an electronic quotation system, then investors will go into a potentially severely loss-making investment scenario with their eyes wide open. These securities which trade through the OTC Bulletin Board are actually a bunch of shares that exist in a tangled web of market makers who are trading them using the various quotes the system provides on a secure network computer which is only accessible by pay to play subscribers.

Another form of exchange network trading is via the so-called Pink Sheets. There are some parallels between the two systems. They are not at all related in fact though. Pink Sheets is an individually and privately held company which offers its own proprietary system of quotations. Companies whose securities trade as part of the Pink Sheets are not required to file any financials with the SEC. They also do not have to make any certain minimum docs available to members of the public or investing community at large. This is why some smaller firms prefer the simplicity and anonymity provided by the Pink Sheets operations and service.

Over The Counter (OTC)

OTC is the acronym for Over the Counter. In the business and financial world, Over the Counter trading is also known as trading off of the exchange. Such OTC trading goes on when financial instruments of various kinds, including stocks, commodities, bonds, or derivatives, are traded literally between the buying and selling party themselves, without having an exchange in the middle of the transaction.

Over the Counter trading can be said to be the opposite of exchange trading. Exchange trading happens in facilities or over electronic market places that are specially created for the trading of these instruments. Stock exchanges and futures exchanges are the places that exchange trading takes place and Over the Counter trading does not.

Within the United States, Over the Counter stock trading is done via market makers who ensure that there are markets in both Pink Sheet and OTCBB, or bulletin boards, securities. They do this through the utilization of quotation services that are between dealers, like Pink Quote, run by the Pink OTC Markets, and OTC Bulletin Board for the OTCBB. While Over the Counter stocks typically do not either list or trade on any form of stock exchange, stocks that are listed on exchanges may be traded on the third market over the counter.

OTCBB quoted stocks have to follow the reporting rules as set out by the United States SEC, or Securities and Exchange Commission, regulatory body. Pink Sheet stocks are not governed by such reporting requirements. Still other stocks that are traded as OTCQX meet different disclosure guidelines that they are permitted to work under in the OTC Pink sheet markets.

OTC can also relate to contracts created between two entities. In these contracts, the two parties concur on the way that a specific trade will be settled at a certain future point. These typically come from investment banks and go out to their own clients. Good examples of these types of OTC arrangements are swaps and forwards. Such contracts are typically arranged over the phone or via computer. Derivative OTC contracts fall under the governance of an agreement provided by the International Swaps and Derivatives Association. This type of OTC market is sometimes called the Fourth Market.

In the Financial Crisis of 2007-2010, many of these OTC derivative contracts created and wreaked havoc in international financial markets specifically because they were traded over the counter, and no one exactly knew what risk and credit were entailed in the contracts that totaled in the tens of trillions of dollars and were made between mysterious partners. To address this critical problem, the NYMEX, or New York Mercantile Exchange, set up a mechanism for clearing many of the most frequently traded energy derivatives that were previously traded only OTC. Now, many of these customers can simply hand over the trade to the exchange's clearing house ClearPort. This removes the dangers associated with both performance and credit risk that were previously seen in these OTC transactions. Other exchanges are endeavoring to do the same thing to try to take derivatives and credit default swap contracts away from the shadowy world of Over the Counter trading. The G20, or Group of Twenty Industrialized and Industrializing nations, is considering ways of rewarding parties for bringing such OTC derivative transactions onto regulated exchanges as well.

Peer to Peer Lending (P2P)

Peer to Peer Lending helps consumers who have some extra money to invest to help out those who need to borrow it. It is often abbreviated as P2P Lending. The idea behind peer to peer lending is not a new one. It has grown exponentially online in the past ten years thanks to the Internet. The benefits of this form of lending are that it reduces usurious interest rates dramatically. This means that both consumers and the overall economy benefit as it decreases the amounts of payday loans.

Prosper is one of the largest P2P lending companies in America. It loans out amounts as high as $35,000. For this they charge a closing fee of 5%. Their interest rates range from 5.9% for extremely good credit to 30% for credit that is only fair. These rates are often lower than what credit card companies charge and substantially lower than payday loan companies which can command over 600% in a single year.

Loans with Peer to Peer Lending companies like Prosper are unsecured. The applicants' credit history earns the approval, though it does not require perfect credit to obtain them. The money itself comes from surplus money which normal people across America wish to invest.

These Peer to Peer Lending companies generally allow their loans to be utilized for most any type of need. They encourage ones that are financially responsible. Debt consolidation is one of the big reasons why individuals take out these loans. The interest rate is often more affordable than the ones the credit card companies charge. Such a loan helps individuals to pay off loans quicker and with a larger amount of the money attacking the principal rather than interest.

Home improvement is another commonplace reason that consumers employ these peer to peer loans. The traditional means of financing such loans comes from bank issued home equity loans or lines of credit as well as from credit cards. The home equity loans often require a great amount of time for approval and commonly include expensive fees. This has encouraged smart home renovators to seek out Peer to Peer Lending companies.

Small businesses like these loans which help them to increase their capital for expansion. Traditional banks will often require a lot of paper work and documentation in order to issue an approval. P2P lending operations such as Prosper only need credit scores that are decent.

Many consumers have turned to these companies for financing for car loans as well. Having this money pre-approved and in hand can save more than just dealer approved financing costs. It can strengthen the buyer's hand in negotiating the final price on the vehicle as the money for the purchase is effectively offered to the dealer in cash instead of financing.

One of the many advantages to these Peer to Peer Lending companies is that they do not charge early repayment penalties. This makes them effective financing vehicles for many different types of needs. Individuals have employed them in place of short term loans and to pay for surgeries not covered by insurance, among other uses.

Besides this, P2P lenders do not require the prime credit scores that most banks do. Consumers can access substantial loans of as much as $35,000 with credit scores that start at a fair 640.

Pension Benefit Guaranty Corporation (PBGC)

Pension Benefit Guaranty Corporation is also referred to many times by its government given acronym the PBGC. This federal agency arose as a result of the ERISA Employee Retirement Income Security Act of 1974. Its mission is to safeguard the benefits of pensions provided by private sector benefit plans that are defined. These plans commonly promise to pay out a fixed amount per month when retirement begins.

Should a plan end in the event of plan termination, and there not be enough money to pay out all of the promised benefits, then the insurance program of the Pension Benefit Guaranty Corporation will pay out the pension plan-provided benefit to the limits which the law establishes. This means that the majority of plan participants will actually still get the full benefit which they had already earned and been promised before termination of the plan occurred.

Some people have wondered where the money for the PBGC comes from so that they can cover failed plan benefits this way. The answer is that those firms whose plans the Pension Benefit Guaranty Corporation protects are required to pay insurance premiums for the insurance. PBGC similarly has investments as well as seized assets that they assume when they become trustee of a terminated pension plan. They also have assets from recoveries of firms which used to manage the plans. They do not derive any of this benefit-covering money from the general tax base. Even if a given employer does not pay its insurance premiums properly into the fund, the defined benefits pension plan will still be insured.

Employers may close out these defined benefit plans in what the PBGC calls a standard termination. They are only allowed to do this once they have demonstrated that the plan is sufficiently capitalized to pay out all owed benefits to the plan participants. To do this, the plan will be required to do one of two things. They might buy an annuity off of an insurance company. This annuity will pay out the promised lifelong benefits upon retirement of the participants.

Alternatively, they may provide one time single large payments that amount to the full benefit value amount. The PBGC provided guarantee of the plan will then cease to exist once the employer either buys this annuity or provides the beneficiaries of the plan with the one time, single payment.

Should the plan lack the money needed to cover all promised pension benefits to the participants of the plan while the employing firm finds itself in financial trouble, then the employers are able to request a distress termination from the PBGC fund. The plan will only be terminated under these scenarios when the employing firm proves to either a bankruptcy court or the PBGC itself that they will not be able to continue operating the firm if the plan does not become terminated. Once such an application request is approved, the PBGC typically becomes trustee and administrator of the plan. They would then pay out the promised plan benefits to the extent allowed by law.

The law similarly allows the Pension Benefit Guaranty Corporation to act alone in order to close out a pension plan where necessary to safeguard the participants' interests or that of the insurance program of the PBGC itself. As a standard procedural example, they will terminate any plan that is sure to be incapable of paying out the promised benefits when they become due.

The PBGC covers the overwhelming majority of defined benefit plans which private sector businesses provide. The lion's share pledge to pay out a set benefit (typically in a once per month distribution) upon commencement of the beneficiaries' retirement. Some pledge to deliver a single-value lump sum payment for their benefit. It is important to know that the PBGC will never insure any defined contribution plans that do not pledge to deliver a guaranteed benefit amount.

PBGC insures defined benefit plans offered by private-sector employers. Most promise to pay a specified benefit, usually a monthly amount, at retirement. Others, including cash-balance plans, may state the promised benefit as a single value. PBGC does not insure defined contribution plans, which are retirement plans that do not promise specific benefit amounts, such as profit-sharing or 401(k) plans.

PBGC does not commonly insure any plans that lawyers and doctors offer if they have under 25 active participants. They also do not cover the plans provided by local, state, or Federal governments. Finally, church group pension plans will not be covered.

Plunge Protection Team (PPT)

The Plunge Protection Team is a nickname given to the President's Working Group on Financial Markets. It came into existence to make economic and financial recommendations on the economy when there are periods of economic chaos. On the team are the heads of the most critical U.S. financial regulatory organizations. This includes the Secretary of the U.S. Treasury, the SEC Securities Exchange Commission Chairman, the Chairman of the Federal Reserve, and the Chairman of the CFTC Commodity Futures Trading Commission.

The Washington Post newspaper created the nick name Plunge Protection Team only a decade later in 1997. President Ronald Reagan originally convened the team as a response to the terrible Black Monday stock market crash. The government was desperate to restore investor confidence in U.S. financial markets. President Reagan called together the group to improve on the efficiency, integrity, and order of them.

The Working Group on Financial Markets was instructed to find out what happened with the financial markets in the U.S. on and around trading day October 19, 1987. They were told to come up with government actions for coordinating efforts and making contingencies to prevent them from happening again when possible.

To carry this out they were told to talk with various representatives from the business world. This included individuals from clearing houses, exchanges, significant market players, and regulating bodies to learn what the market might suggest for non-government solutions.

Finger pointing at first characterized the investigation. The NYSE held the various futures exchanges responsible for the crash. The CME group engaged in a number of studies to refute this by having market experts rationally analyze the events. They refuted the accusations for the problems with these studies.

One positive mechanism came from these initial meetings with the Plunge Protection Team. NYSE and CME group worked to establish circuit breakers between the securities and futures markets. This slowed down or stopped wildly erratic moves in the market. These circuit breakers remain in effect to this day.

The PPT had 60 days from the Executive Order to give this initial report to the President. They were to report from time to time after this as they reached more findings and solutions for recommended changes to the legislation. When the report and finished recommendations were completed, the President did not disband the group as many had expected.

Instead it stayed together to be reconvened on any subsequent crisis and threat to the financial system. This caused some observers to believe that the group had a secret purpose to manipulate markets and ensure they stayed higher. The group covered such issues as the almost collapse of Long Term Capital Management, Terrorism Risk Insurance from September of 2006 and Over the Counter Derivatives Markets and the Commodity Exchange Act in November of 1999.

Most famously the group reconvened during the financial crash of the Great Recession in 2008. In March, 2008 they issued their Policy Statement on Financial Market Developments. It had the PPTs analysis and report on what continued to plague the markets and cause the ongoing market turmoil.

Their final conclusions had to do with the subprime market mortgages. The determined that the main cause of the destructive chain of events started with the rise in delinquencies of these mortgages. They issued another statement on the continuing crisis on October 6 of 2008. In this they announced that the situation in worldwide financial markets continued to be very strained. They assured investors that they were working with global regulators and market participants to take on the problems and restore stability and confidence to markets.

Private Mortgage Insurance (PMI)

PMI is the acronym for Private Mortgage Insurance, also known sometimes as Lenders Mortgage Insurance. PMI proves to be insurance that is paid to a lending institution that is required much of the time when an individual gets a mortgage loan. Such insurance is used to cover any losses that arise if a person is not capable of paying back their mortgage loan.

Should the lender not be able to recoup all of its costs in foreclosing on and selling the mortgaged property, then PMI insurance covers the remaining losses that exist on the balance sheet of the bank or other lender. The general rates for this Private Mortgage Insurance turn out to be around $55 each month for every $100,000 that is actually financed. On a $250,000 loan, this amounts to $1,875 each year in premiums.

Private Mortgage insurance yearly costs range though. They are usually given out in comparison against the entire loan's value. This depends on a number of factors, such as loan type, loan term, actual coverage amount, amount of home value that the person finances, the premium payment frequency that might be monthly or yearly, and the individual's credit score. While PMI can be paid in advance with closing costs, it can also be worked into the loan payments with single premium PMI.

Private Mortgage Insurance is generally only necessary when the down payment proves to be smaller than twenty percent of either the appraised value of the property or alternatively of the sales price. When then loan to value ratio is greater than eighty percent, you can expect to be required to carry it. As the principal is reduced with monthly payments, or the home value rises through real estate appreciation, or a combination of the two occurs, then this Private Mortgage Insurance might not be required any longer. At this point, the home owner is allowed to discontinue paying for the PMI insurance.

There are some banks and lenders who will insist that PMI be paid for minimally for a pre fixed period of time, such as two to three years. This is regardless of whether the principal value of the property exceeds eighty percent in a shorter amount of time. Banks do not have to permit a person to cancel this insurance legally until the loan has amortized down to a Loan to Value ratio of seventy-eight percent of the original price for which the house is purchased.

A cancellation request must originate from the mortgage servicer. They must send it to the issuing company that made the PMI policy in the first place. Many times, such a mortgage servicer will insist on a current home value appraisal being done in order to ascertain the actual loan to value ratio.

Premiums paid for mortgage insurance were not tax deductible according to the Internal Revenue Service in the past. In 2007 this changed. Now all PMI premiums are considered to be fully reducing of your income for the year in question.

Public Company Accounting Oversight Board (PCAOB)

The Public Company Accounting Oversight Board turns out to be another regulatory group that Congress established to provide oversight on the auditing of public companies. This not for profit corporation is not a government agency. It does provide protection to the public and investors who are interested in the independent, accurate, and revealing audit reports that this group encourages. Besides this, the PCAOB oversees dealers and brokers' audits in order to foster protection for investors. This includes oversight of compliance reports that federal security laws require from public corporations.

This accounting oversight board arose as a result of the Sabanes-Oxley Act of 2002. It mandated that the firms which audit public companies in the United States endure independent and external oversight for the first time ever. Before Congress passed this 2002 regulatory law, auditors were completely self regulating.

The PCAOB Board and chairman of this board are made up of five members who receive appointments to five year terms each from the SEC Securities and Exchange Commission. They select these individuals after consulting first with both the Secretary of the U.S. Treasury and the Federal Reserve System Chairman of the Board of Governors. Given this SEC appointing role, it is not surprising that the SEC also maintains oversight responsibilities for the PCAOB. As part of this oversight, they must approve the Board's various standards, budget, and rules before they become final.

The SOX Act became amended by the Dodd-Frank Act. It created the necessary funding for all PCAOB pursued activities. This money mostly comes from the accounting support fees assessed annually on all publicly traded companies. These fees are actually figured from their average monthly market capitalization. Brokers and dealers are instead levied fees which are dependent on their quarterly average tentative net capital.

The mission of the PCAOB lies in providing oversight of public companies' audits. This ensures that they prepare and deliver reliable, honest, and unbiased audit reports for the benefit of both the interested investors and members of the public. Along with this oversight role, the PCAOB monitors the broker dealers and their audits to encourage protecting investors from fraud. This includes monitoring their federal securities law required compliance reports filing.

PCAOB has a particular vision they seek to fulfill. Their overriding goal is to prove themselves a model for regulatory organizations everywhere. They seek to reduce the numbers of audit failures throughout the public securities markets in the United States, to improve the overall quality of audits, and to foster the public's trust of auditing as a profession and the process of financial reporting itself. They aim to do this while utilizing cost efficient and cutting edged tools.

The PCAOB maintains two special advisory groups as part of its mandate. The first of these is the PCAOB Investor Advisor Group, also known by its acronym IAG. It presents advice and viewpoints to the general board pertaining to investor concerns and regarding work related matters and important policy issues. The board is able to count on the IAG to deliver it expert and quality insight and advice for carrying out its important mandate to safeguard investors as outlined in the Sarbanes-Oxley Act.

The board also relies on its Standing Advisory Group, refereed to by its acronym SAG. The SAG advises the board regarding standards of professional practice and continuing developments within the world of auditing. Among the members of the Standing Advisory Group are investors, auditors, executives of publicly traded companies, and other individuals. This SAG group holds meetings between two and three times each year. They are chaired by the Chief Auditor and Director of Professional Standards of the PCAOB.

Purchasing Power Parity (PPP)

Purchasing power parity is a method for comparing the various standards of living of different countries and through different times. It also allows economists to compare one nation's economic productivity to another nation's. This economic theory believes that it is possible to compare the various currencies of different countries by analyzing the cost of a basket of goods. The idea states that two currencies are at a fair market value to each other when the basket of goods becomes priced identically in the two countries.

There is a formula for calculating purchasing power parity. It is $S = P1/P2$. S stands for the exchange rate of a first currency against a second one. P1 is the symbol for the price of goods in the first currency. P2 symbolizes the price of goods in the second currency.

Coming up with a meaningful comparison of goods requires that a considerable range of services and goods should be analyzed. This requires gathering a great amount of information. To help make the process easier, the United Nations worked with the University of Pennsylvania in 1968 to establish the International Comparisons Program.

The purchasing power parity numbers which come from the ICP uses price surveys from around the world which compare and contrast costs for literally hundreds of different goods. These results give international economists the tools they need to create global growth and productivity estimates.

The World Bank compiles a special report on PPP once each three years to compare the nations of the world by both U.S. dollars and their PPP values. Both the OECD Organization for Economic Cooperation and Development and the IMF International Monetary Fund base their recommended policies and economic predictions on the purchasing power parity measurements.

Forex traders have also been known to employ PPP to scout for undervalued and overvalued currencies. Finally investors with foreign corporation stocks or bonds can consider these figures to forecast how exchange rate fluctuations will impact the economy of the country where their investments are based.

When individuals or companies employ PPP, they are utilizing it in place of the market determined exchange rates. This figure provides them with the quantity of currency required to purchase the basket of goods and services used in the equation. This means that inflation rates and cost of living ultimately determine a nation's PPP.

Economists are also able to utilize purchasing power parity to determine which countries have the largest amount of purchasing power. To do this, they take the GDP gross domestic product of countries as a starting point. This is the aggregate dollar amount of every good and service a nation produces in a particular year. The number is among the preferred means of analyzing the economy of a country. Economists can determine this in either market exchange rates or PPP terms.

The PPP measurement will consider the costs of localized services and goods of a given nation as measured in U.S. prices. It contemplates both the inflation rates and the exchange rates in this calculation. The GDP using PPP demonstrates a citizen's purchasing power compared to that of the citizen in another. Since a shirt will usually cost more in one nation than in the other one, purchasing power parity helps to make the calculation fairer. While the 2016 rankings for GDP by market exchange terms show the top five countries as the U.S., China, India, Japan, and Germany, when PPP is used, China ranks ahead of the U.S.

Quantitative Risk Management (QRM)

Quantitative Risk Management represents the discipline which deals with the ability of an organization to quantify and manage its risk. This scientific approach to business is becoming increasingly critical in today's world as organizations need to satisfy stakeholders who demand it.

Government regulators similarly insist on clarity within organizations now, especially regarding the amount of capital financial institutions are holding. The firm executives are hunting for the best allocation of capital. Corporations and their boards are seeking justification to control expenditures. Project managers need to be assured they will make their timelines and meet budgets. All of these individuals and entities are looking for effective QRM nowadays.

These QRM capabilities give decision makers the facilities to both analyze their applicable risk data as well as to forecast the likely positive and negative effects in the future. It provides the organization with enormous advantages. Analyses that are more dependable and finely detailed will deliver information which management requires to make superior decisions that are ultimately better informed. As the Quantitative Risk Management process yields higher quality information and becomes more easily accessible to the relevant organizational members, the decision makers are able to more effectively utilize the techniques of QRM to decrease the amount of guesswork involved in the daily decisions of their business operations.

This allows them to obtain valuable insights into possible risks, so they can estimate their overall exposure to them and discern any weaknesses in their oversight controls. It also permits them to determine how practical new services and products will be and to consider the opportunities for up selling and also cross selling of company goods, information, and services. Finally, organization leaders will be able to evaluate any degrees of variance in their company cash flow so that they can streamline and better their ultimate operations.

Quantitative Risk Management is important as every one of those activities just mentioned contains at least some degree of risk. By quantifying and considering them all using a combination of techniques such as trending, modeling, stress tests, and metric evaluations, company decision makers can create faster and more effective responses. This allows them to benefit from any uncovered opportunities and simultaneously to deal with any possible negative effects before they actually materialize and cause significant damage.

There are numerous examples of the uses of and needs for Quantitative Risk Management in business organizations. Cash flow at risk, or CFaR, represents one of the most significant drivers of business. Company leaders require effective prognoses of their future cash flow in order to firm up important decisions for the business. These include confirming or pushing off investments, reducing expenses, reinvesting capital in the business model, or choosing to reengineer their critical operations. Correctly extrapolating cash flow involves proper understanding of such underlying factors as currency changes, sales, pricing of products and services, vendor viability, and operational costs.

Value at Risk, or VaR, is another critical measurement in an organization that benefits from Quantitative Risk Management. Bigger, international, and more complicated financial institutions such as JP Morgan Chase, Citigroup, HSBC, Standard Chartered Bank, BNP Paribas, and Banco Santander have to constantly evaluate where their risk exposures are in order to appropriately allocate the correct capital amounts to be capable of absorbing losses which they do not anticipate.

Project risk management is another area where this Quantitative Risk Management can save the day. So many projects exceed their allocated budgets, deadlines, and milestone markers simply because there is not a sufficient evaluation of the variables, uncertainty, and risk involved with the project itself. This is where the process of QRM can save enormous amounts of time, frustration, and ultimately resources by delivering on deadlines and budgets.

Real Estate Investment Trusts (REIT)

Real Estate Investment Trusts are also known as REITs. These turn out to be investment companies which finance or outright own real estate that produces income. REITs were created along the model of mutual funds. They give all levels of investors the access to the benefits that real estate typically provides.

This includes diversification, income streams, and capital appreciation longer term. Usually these REITs pay their investors 100% of their taxable income in the form of dividends. The shareholders are responsible for paying taxes on the dividends as income tax.

The beauty of Real Estate Investment Trusts lies in the ability for any investor to participate in major properties. They are able to do this by buying shares of stock to become involved as they would with any other industry Just as a shareholder obtains benefits through stock ownership in companies, the stock holders in a REIT gain a percentage of the income that the underlying real estate produces. They do not have to locate, purchase, or finance any of the properties in the process.

The majority of Real Estate Investment Trusts trade on the bigger stock exchanges. Despite this, some of them are privately held or public companies that are not exchange listed. With these REITs there are two principle types, Mortgage and Equity REITs.

The mortgage REITs buy mortgage instruments or outright mortgages that are connected to residential or commercial properties. The Equity REITs produce their income by collecting rent from and selling properties they hold over longer time frames.

Real Estate Investment Trusts have expanded into practically every part of the economy today. There are REITs connected to timberlands, student housing, storage centers, shopping malls, company offices, nursing homes, infrastructure projects, industrial facilities, hotels and resorts, hospitals, and apartments. Every state in the United States has properties which are owned by REITs. Ernest and Young has funded a study that shows REITs provide for around 1.8 million jobs in the United States every year.

These American REITs have become so successful that they are now a model for other countries. Over 30 nations throughout the globe have approved legislation that allows the Real Estate Investment Trust.

Real Estate Investment Trusts offer diversification that does not correspond to the overall stock market and its performance measured longer term. Their dividends give investors a reliable stream of income. They are so liquid because these stock exchange based ones may be simply and quickly purchased and sold.

Their performance is standout. REITs which are publically listed and traded have outperformed the Dow Jones Industrial Average, the S&P 500, and the NASDAQ Composite when measured over the longer term. Like publically traded companies, they offer the transparency and oversight of quarterly financial reporting and commonplace regulatory standards.

There are many qualifications a company must meet to be considered a Real Estate Investment Trust. They have to place minimally 75% of all assets they possess into real estate. They also must obtain 75% or more of their gross income from sales of real estate, rents on property, or interest on mortgage holdings that finance property. These companies have to pay out a minimum of 90 % of their taxable income as dividends to shareholders every year.

The prospective REIT must have the status of corporation that is taxable. It must also have either trustees or a board of directors that manage it. They can not have over 50% of their entity shares owned by less than six individuals. The REITs also must possess at least 100 different shareholders.

Required Minimum Distribution (RMD)

The Required Minimum Distribution is a concept that pertains to retirement accounts and IRS rules which govern their distributions. Many individuals are not aware that they can not simply choose to hold retirement money in their retirement vehicle forever. They must begin accepting withdrawals from their traditional IRA, SEP IRA, Simple IRA, or other type of retirement plan and account after they turn age 70 ½. The notable exception to this rule is for Roth IRAs, which do not mandate disbursements while the owner is still alive.

The required minimum distribution is literally the minimum legal dollar amount that account holders have to take out of the retirement account every year. Naturally most people choose to withdraw a larger amount than this required minimum. Withdrawals that are received must be detailed in the individuals' taxable income. The exception to this is for any income that had been previously taxed as with Roth IRA contributions or any earnings which accrued on a tax free basis. This relates to distributions from Roth IRA accounts.

Figuring out the actual amount of the RMD is not so easy. The simplest way to do it is to work with the IRS published Uniform Lifetime Table. In this method, people figure their RMD in any given year by taking the balance from the end of the prior calendar year and dividing this amount by a distribution period taken from the Uniform Lifetime Table. There is also a different table to be utilized if the owner of the account's spouse is the only beneficiary and he or she is at least ten years younger than the owner.

The IRS provides worksheets on their website to help account holders figure up the mandated minimum amount. They also provide several tables to help with this. As mentioned, the Uniform Lifetime Table is for every IRA account owner who is figuring up his or her own withdrawal. The Joint Life and Last Survivor Expectancy Table is for those whose spouse is at least ten years younger and who is the only beneficiary.

The initial date for the first RMD on an IRA is figured out by taking the April 1st of the year that comes after the calendar year in which the account holder turns 70 ½. With a 401(k), 403(b), profit sharing plan, or similar defined contribution plan, either this same April 1st deadline applies or the April 1st that follows the calendar year in which the owner actually retires.

The individual turns 70 ½ on the calendar date which falls 6 months following his or her 70th birthday. The plan terms themselves govern whether the individuals can wait until the year in which they actually retire to take the initial RMD. Other plans will require distributions begin on the April 1st following the year of turning 70 ½ whether or not the person has retired.

Once account holders have received the first RMD, they must take their subsequent ones on or before December 31st. It is possible to avoid having the first and second RMD's included in a single tax year. In the year individuals turn 70 ½ they can simply go ahead and take that first RMD by the end of the year to avoid the double distribution taxation in one calendar year.

People who do not take their full minimum required distribution will suffer an IRS penalty. Any amount which they do not take as the law requires will suffer a 50% excise tax that will be levied on it. This failure to take the RMD must be reported on a Form 5329, Additional Taxes on Qualified Plans.

Return on Assets (ROA)

Return on Assets is also known by its acronym ROA. It is also sometimes called return on investment. This proves to be an indicator of a company's profitability compared to its aggregate asset base. With ROA, investors and analysts can learn about the big picture of the efficiency of an organization's management compared to the deployment of their company assets which produces earnings.

This is figured up relatively easily. To calculate the ROA, simply take the corporation's annual earnings (or income) and divide these by the firm's total assets. The final answer is the percentage amount of ROA. Other investors will do a slight variation on the formula by adding back in the corporate interest costs to the net income. This allows them to employ operating returns before the net cost of debt.

Thanks to Return on Assets, analysts and investors can learn the amount of earnings that the invested capital or assets produced. Such a figure ranges dramatically from one publically traded company to the next. Every industry's ROA varies substantially. For this reason, analysts prefer to compare and contrast the ROA primarily against the company's own prior figures or alternatively versus another company which is both similar and in the same industry.

Company assets are made up of equity and debt together. The two kinds of financing will jointly fund most corporations' various operations and projects. Because of this Return on Assets number, investors are able to discern the efficiency with which the firm converts its investable money into actual net income. Higher ROA numbers are always considered to be superior. They mean that the corporations can bring in larger revenues and earnings on a smaller amount of investment.

Consider a real world example for clarification. If Imperial Legends Strategy Games produces a net income of $2 million on aggregate underlying assets of $6 million, then it has a Return on Assets of 33.3 percent. Another company Joy Beverages may enjoy the same earnings but against a full asset base of $12 million. Joy Beverages would have an ROA of only 16.7 percent in this scenario. This means that ILSG does twice the job of converting its all around investments into profits as does Joy Beverages. This matters because it speaks volumes of the quality of management. There are not too many managers who are able to turn over significant profits utilizing small investments.

The Return on Assets provides observers with a snapshot and analysis of a business that is distinctive from the usual return on equity formula. Consider that certain industries need to pay more careful attention to the ROA figure than other ones do. In banking, some firms managed to avoid the various banking crises of the last few decades. The ones that sidestepped the problems better than others had something in common. It was that they were more conservative based on the ROA they deployed. The more successful banks did not allow their return on assets numbers to become too unnaturally high. They did this by contemplating the underlying fine details in the loan book. Too many loans that yielded too high a return indicated that management was taking excessive risks. Yet in the business of software development firms, these enterprises are not leveraged, so this ROA comparison is less important.

An important difference separates asset turnover from Return on Assets. Asset turnover specifies that companies have sales which amount to a certain amount per asset dollar on the corporate balance sheet. Conversely, the ROA explains to investors the amount of post tax profit that a firm creates for every $1 of assets it has. This is to say that the ROA compares all of the company earnings relating to the entire resource base the company claims, including both long-term debt and the capital from shareholders. This makes the relevant ROA a strict test of shareholder returns. When companies possess no debt, then their two figures of ROA and ROE Return On Equity will be identical.

Return on Equity (ROE)

Return on equity proves to be a useful measurement for investors considering a given company. This is because it takes into account three important elements of a company's management. This includes profitability, financial leverage, and asset management. Looking at the effectiveness of the management team in handling the three factors gives you as an investor a good picture of the kind of return on equity that you can expect from an investment in such a company.

Return on equity is very easy to calculate. You can figure it up by collecting two pieces of information. You will need the company earnings for a year and the value of the average share holder equity for the same year. Getting the earnings' figure is as simple as looking up the firm's Consolidated Statement of Earnings that they filed with the Securities and Exchange Commission. Alternatively, you might look up the earnings of each of the last four quarters and add them up.

Determining share holder equity is easiest by looking at the company's balance sheet. Share holder equity, which proves to be the difference of total liabilities and total assets, will be listed for you there. Share holder equity is a useful accounting construct that reveals the business assets that they have created. This share holder equity is most commonly listed under book value, or the quantity of the share holders' equities for each share. This is also an accounting book value of a corporation that is more than simply its market value.

To come up with the return on equity, you simply divide the full year's earnings by the average equity for that year. This gives you the return on equity. Companies that produce significant amounts of share holder equity turn out to be solid investments, since initial investors are paid off using the money that the business operations generate. Companies that create substantial returns as compared to the share holder equity reward their stake holders generously by building up significant amounts of assets for each dollar that is invested into the firm. Such enterprises commonly prove to be able to fund their own operations internally, which means that they do not have to issue more diluting shares of stock or take on extra debt to continue operating.

The return on equity can also be utilized to determine if a corporation is a cash generating machine or a cash consuming entity. The return on equity will simply show you this when you compare their actual earnings to the share holder equity. You can learn at almost a glance how much money the company's present assets are producing. As an example, with a twenty percent return on equity, every original dollar put into the company is creating twenty cents of real assets. This is also useful in comparing subsequent cash investments in the company, since the return on equity percentage will demonstrate to you if these extra invested dollars match up to the earlier investments for effectiveness and efficiency.

Return on Investment (ROI)

ROI is the acronym for return on investment. This return on investment is among the most often utilized methods of determining the financial results that will arise from business decisions, investments, and actions. ROI analysis is used to compare and contrast both the timing and amount of investment gains directly with the timing and amount of investment costs. Higher returns on investment signify that the results from investments are positive when you compare them against the costs of such investments.

Over the past couple of decades, this return on investment number has evolved into one of the main measurements in the decision making process of what types of assets and equipment to buy. This includes everything from factory equipment, to service vehicles, to computers. ROI is similarly utilized to determine which budget items, programs, and projects should be both approved and allocated funds. These cover every type of activity from recruiting, to training, to marketing. Finally, return on investment is often employed in choosing which financial investments are performing up to expectations, as with venture capital investments and stock investment portfolios.

Return on investment analysis is actually used for ranking investment returns against their costs. This is done by setting up a percentage or ratio number. With the vast majority of return on investment calculation methods, ROI's that are higher than zero signify that the returns on the investment are higher than the associated expenses with it. As a greater number of investments and business decisions compete for funding anymore, hard choices are increasingly made using the comparison of higher returns on investment. Many companies believe that this yields the better business decision in the end.

There is a downside to relying too heavily on the return on investment as the only consideration for making such business and investment decisions. Return on investment does not tell you anything regarding the anticipated costs and returns and if they will actually work out as forecast. Used alone, return on investment also does not explain the potential elements of risk for a given investment. All that it does is demonstrate how the investment or project returns will compare against the costs, assuming that the investment or project delivers the results that are anticipated or expected. This limitation is not unique to return on investment, but similarly plagues other financial measurements. Because this is the case, intelligent investment and business analysis also relies on the likely results of other return on investment eventualities. Other measurements should also be used along side the return on investment to help measure the risks that accompany the project or investment.

Wise decision makers will demand more from return on investment figures than simply a number. They will require effective suggestions from the person making the return on investment analysis. Among these inputs that they will desire are the means of increasing an ROI's gains, or alternatively the means for improving the ROI through decreasing costs.

Securities and Exchange Commission (SEC)

The SEC is the acronym for the Securities and Exchange Commission. This Federal government agency actually governs the buying and selling of stock securities and other types of related investments. The SEC also works to safe guard investors against impropriety and fraud. They encourage the development of the market with the end goal of keeping America in the first place as the world's leading economic giant.

The Securities and Exchange Commission came into existence in 1934. The stock market crash in 1929 prompted a tremendous regulatory response where the national government observed that it had to oversee and monitor investments within the U.S. The SEC is headquartered today in Washington D.C. Its staff is comprised of five commissioners who are appointed, as well as the personnel working in eleven different regional offices throughout the country. They work together to create, amend, and enforce the laws that regulate investments in the country.

The SEC has various critical missions. Among the most significant one is their role in ensuring that the markets are transparent. To do this, they significantly regulate securities trading within the U.S. Companies are required to turn in a variety of legal financial documents during the year so that investors may obtain a true picture of the total financial health of the firm in question.

The documents are kept on file in a database that is available to the public. Anyone who is interested is allowed to inspect them by logging on to the SEC's website and working through their system of electronic documentation. The SEC has great powers that it exercises in enforcing the rules. It is able to mandate company audits if it has suspicions of illegal behavior. Those it finds in violation of its rules may be brought by the SEC to court.

In keeping with the SEC's mandate to help safe guard investors, they monitor the trading of stocks and the individuals responsible for selling them. This means that exchanges, their dealers, and all stock brokers are required to work through the Securities and Exchange Commission. They can be subjected to inspection from time to time to be certain that they are properly taking care of their customers. Consumers have the right to report practices that are unfair to the SEC directly. If you are an investor, you ought to avail yourself of the SEC's wide range of documents on the various publicly traded corporations that they keep in their database on their website.

The SEC additionally governs companies that are interested in undergoing Initial Public Offerings in order to become public companies. Such interested firms have to file a significant quantity of documents with them first. To help them accomplish this, the SEC engages a big staff. Their document database includes regulations and directions for filing such documents. Consultation help is available if companies run into difficulties.

The SEC also promotes education. If you are an investor who wants to learn more about safe investing, then simply go to their website. They have workshops and publications on the site to help all investors. This is in addition to all of the companies' documents kept on file there.

Special Drawing Rights (SDR)

Special Drawing Rights are currency units of the International Monetary Fund. These units were originally worth .888671 grams of gold and $1 when they were initially created under the gold standard in 1969. In 1973 the pegged currency system set up at the Bretton Woods conference collapsed.

The IMF then re-defined these SDRs as a basket of the major world reserve currencies. Until October 1, 2016, SDR baskets are comprised of U.S. dollars, euros, British pounds, and Japanese yen. On October 1 this definition will be broadened to add in the Chinese renminibi. The IMF created these unique currency units in order to supplement the existing currency reserves of countries who are members.

Every day the IMF figures up the SDR value and puts it up on their website. The value is a composition of its various parts. They figure the value as measured in U.S. dollars by adding up the value of each currency in the basket in dollars. To do this, they utilize the noon time exchange rates from the London market fixing.

Every five years, the IMF has an Executive Board meeting to review the components of the Special Drawing Rights. They have the ability to hold this meeting earlier should financial circumstances call for it. The idea is to make certain that the basket continuously mirrors how important various currencies included are in the financial and trading systems of the world. The review that ended in November of 2015 decided that the Chinese renminbi currency had become freely usable enough to include as the basket's fifth currency alongside the dollar, euro, British pound, and Japanese yen.

They also adopted a new method for determining how much of each reserve currency will make up an SDR. Equal weighting is now being given to the exports of the currency issuing nation and a composite financial indicator. With the financial indicator, each of the components is being given an equal weighting. It is based on the reserves in the currency held by other countries, the amount of foreign exchange turnover for that currency, and the total of international debt securities and bank liabilities which are held in that currency.

Until October of 2016, the Special Drawing Rights components are U.S. dollars at 41.9%, euros at 37.4%, British pounds at 11.3%, and Japanese yen at 9.4%. As of October 1, 2016 the new SDRs are instead comprised of U.S. dollars at 41.73%, euros at 30.93%, Chinese renminbi at 10.92%, Japanese yen at 8.33%, and British pounds at 8.09%. This represents the new SDR value in a change more significant than any made in decades. The next scheduled review for the SDR is set to occur on September 30 of 2021.

Special Drawing Rights can be given out to member states of the IMF as a proportion of their IMF quotas. This gives every member an international reserve asset that will not cost them anything. Charges are made on allocations and then utilized to cover any interest owed on SDR holdings. Member countries that do not utilize their holdings which are allocated do not pay since any charges equate to the interest they receive. Members whose holdings become greater than what they are allocated receive interest on the extra ones.

SDRs today are only used in limited capacity as reserve assets. Their main purpose is to function as the account unit of the IMF and a few international organizations. The SDR is not actually a claim against the IMF or a true currency. Instead it represents a possible claim against the IMF members and their currencies.

Standard and Poor's (S&P)

Standard and Poor's is a global ratings agency that is also responsible for the S&P and Dow Jones indices in the stock market. Besides providing ratings on companies and products, they also rate governments' sovereign credit ratings. This company is based in the United States but has 26 offices throughout the globe. The corporation has shortened its name from Standard and Poor's Ratings Services to S&P Global Rating as of April 28, 2016.

The history of Standard and Poor's goes back over 150 years. Today they provide market intelligence that is high quality and well respected. They offer this in the form of their well known credit ratings, global research, and thought leadership. The company operates primarily as S&P Global Market Intelligence and S&P Dow Jones Indices.

Their division S&P Global Market Intelligence proves to be among the world leaders in delivering research and information on a variety of asset classes. They provide this with thought provoking analysis via a number of advanced platforms. Every year the company gathers more than 135 billions individual points of data in the pursuit of this goal. They cover 99% of all the market capitalization in the world. Standard and Poor's wants to be more than just the provider of financial data and intelligence. They are looking to be a creative force for transparency, growth, and the provision of value in the world's capital markets.

Each day this division of the company gathers, scrubs, analyzes, and interprets enormous amounts of data and content. They take this raw information and transform it to intelligence investors can act on covering industries and companies in the worldwide financial markets. Standard and Poor's Global Market Intelligence offers not only data but also valuable insight that helps readers to make more educated and intelligent investment and business decisions that impact the future.

This division boasts several core beliefs. These are relevance, accuracy, timeliness, and completeness. The group proves to be a foremost purveyor of analytics, news, research, and information to a variety of groups around the globe. Beneficiaries of this information include corporations, government agencies, universities, and professionals.

The solutions and data which lead the industry come from their subsidiaries SNL Financial and S&P Capital IQ. These combine to put together data from individual sectors and the comprehensive market with news and analytics. The tools that result allow the group's clients to perform a wide variety of functions. They can track their performance, identify ideas for investments, generate alpha, grasp dynamics of the competition in an industry, determine credit risks, and produce valuations.

This division boasts over 10,000 employees operating in 20 countries around the globe.

The other principal division of Standard and Poor's is the S&P Dow Jones Indices. This group turns out to be the biggest international source for concepts, research, and data on indices. It counts among its legendary financial indicators the Dow Jones Industrial Average and the S&P 500 indices. It has been working with these indicators for more than 120 years to create forward thinking market solutions which help to meet needs of both retail and institutional investors.

They began with launching the Dow Jones Industrial Average in 1896 and later produced the S&P 500 in 1957. This has made them an engine in many of the most critical financial creations of the 20th century. They now offer in excess of 1 million different indices that run the spectrum of many different asset classes throughout the world. The company claims that more assets have been invested in different products that are based on their indices than with any other company on earth.

Swiss Interbank Clearing (SIC)

Swiss Interbank Clearing is the interbank clearing system that Switzerland uses for payments within the country and between its banks. SIX Interbank Clearing Limited launched the system on June 10, 1987. They have been operating it since then for the Swiss National Bank.

The primary eligible users of the SIC are all of the Swiss banks along with German Post Finance. Cash handling companies, insurance companies, and securities dealers which are based in either Switzerland or Liechtenstein are also able to participate. The system allows for foreign based banks to utilize it once they fulfill the added requirements and conditions which the Swiss National Bank sets.

Swiss Interbank Clearing handles large transactions as well as retail transfers that connect service providers to the banks. This includes automatic debits, card payments, and bank transfers. The system has grown continuously in the amount volume it settles and quantities of transactions it processes since SIX first launched it.

Ten years after SIX created and launched the Swiss Interbank Clearing, they developed a similar system to enable the Swiss financial center and Liechtenstein to have access to the European Union's TARGET2 clearing system. This is called the euro Swiss Interbank Clearing, or simply euroSIC. It permits Swiss banks settle any payments in Euros between themselves quickly, simply, and cheaply. Thanks to this expansion of the system, they do not have to keep mutual euro accounts. It saves them the additional trouble, paperwork, and expense.

EuroSIC also makes it possible for Swiss and Liechtenstein banks to send payments in real time to other Euro zone banks. The participating members can process Euro payments across borders with almost any Euro zone institution. The system works effectively both ways. Euro zone banks and institutions gain convenient access to more than 3,200 banks and branches throughout both Switzerland and Liechtenstein.

Banks and financial institutions which the Swiss National Bank supervises may participate in euroSIC. This also applies to any of their branches, joint institutions, or clearing organizations that are located outside the country of Switzerland. These groups must be able to demonstrate that they have a comparable amount of operational and legal standards in the countries where they are based as do their partners or parent organizations in Switzerland.

The Swiss Euro Clearing Bank manages the system. This joint venture between SIX, UBS, Credit Suisse, and Post Finance bears the responsibility for both monitoring and supervising the euroSIC system. SECB has the advantage of being a German licensed bank as well. This means it provides a link to the real time clearing system of the Deutsche Bundesbank.

The system manager the SECB Swiss Euro Clearing Bank provides access to make rapid payments to Germany. The payments which euroSIC processes must be non urgent payments. Banks can send as much as much as 50,000 euros on behalf of their clients with reasonable transaction costs thanks to the system that the Deutsche Bundesbank provides. This is handled through the German EMZ bulk payment system. The SECB also provides its euroSIC members with a means for making inexpensive transfers and payments using the STEP2 system. This is the European Union wide bulk payments system.

Euro Swiss Interbank Clearing operates using the settlement accounts of the member institutions. SIX actually runs the system in Zurich, the Swiss financial center. Every transaction processes through the settlement accounts. There must be enough funds in the bank's account in the system at the Swiss Euro Clearing Bank for the transaction to go through in real time. Otherwise, the transaction is put aside until enough funds are present to cover the transaction.

Swiss National Bank (SNB)

The Swiss National Bank is one of the important central banks of the world. It carries out its monetary policies and other roles independently of the government of Switzerland. In 2007, the SNB celebrated its one hundred year anniversary from its founding in 1907.

Switzerland's central bank has a wider mandate than some other national central banks do. The mandate of the Swiss National Bank is to conduct itself per the best interests for the whole country. It does have a main goal to guarantee price stability for Switzerland by considering the impacts of economic developments. Beyond this it also performs numerous other functions.

Switzerland has adopted a goal of price stability that is comparable with other internationally important central banks. The goal of the SNB is to see under 2% per year increases in the cost of consumer prices. They are concerned with inflation not getting out of hand as it misallocates capital and labor and also unfairly distributes wealth and income. The bank also has a special concern to avoid deflation, the continuous decline in the levels of prices. It is the middle ground of just below two percent which they work towards with their monetary policy decisions.

The SNB actually implements monetary policy to control inflation by guiding the interest rates for on sight deposits and by directing the money market liquidity. This influences the country's overall interest rate. The bank uses the three month Libor measured in Swiss francs for the interest rate it references. One thing the SNB is not shy about is participating in the foreign exchange markets. They do this whenever necessary to impact monetary levels as they deem appropriate.

The Swiss National Bank also issues the Swiss franc notes and coins. The banknotes are created according to high standards for security as well as quality. They determine how many banknotes to issue based on payment purpose demands. As far as cashless payments go in Switzerland, the bank participates in the SIC Swiss Interbank Clearing System. They hold the accounts for the various institutions to clear the checks and other cashless payments.

Asset management is an area in which the Swiss National Bank is proactive. They manage both the country's currency reserves and their gold reserves. Switzerland is unusual in keeping a 25% gold to franc note gold reserve and standard. They keep enough of currencies on hand to have ample room to adjust their monetary policy.

For several years, the bank instituted a 1.20 floor on Euro to Swiss franc exchange rates. Defending this level required massive purchases of Euros and sales of Swiss francs as conditions in the Euro zone deteriorated. Finally, Switzerland abandoned this three year old policy without warning in 2015. This caused massive chaos in world foreign exchange markets as speculators had built up enormous positions in Forex based on the SNB's policy.

Like many central banks, the SNB is tasked with maintaining stability for the national financial system. They analyze risks to the system and find areas where they need to respond. They are also responsible for assisting with both designing and implementing the regulatory framework that governs the financial sector. The bank regulates financial market institutions that are considered to be systemically important.

Another interesting role that the Swiss National Bank carries out is as the banker to the Swiss Confederation. This means that it handles payments for the Confederation. The bank also issues any bonds and money market debt and is custodian for their securities. They carry out all transactions in foreign exchange on behalf of the Confederation as well.

The SNB is renowned for cooperating on the international monetary stage. They offer technical assistance and advice as needed, participate actively in the IMF, and coordinate international monetary actions in crises.

Finally, the Swiss National Bank compiles and releases statistics. These cover financial markets and banks in the country, direct investment, Swiss financial accounts, the balance of payments, and the country's international investment position.

Term Auction Facility (TAF)

In response to the bank lending freeze that followed the outbreak of the banking and financial crisis in 2007, Ben Bernanke created and launched his Term Auction Facility TAF in December of 2007. The Fed was able to utilize its long mostly dormant discount window from December 2007 through to March 2010 as a creative new means of helping out struggling banks to access extra funds. They were then able to loan out these additional funds to consumers and businesses at their discretion. A primary new way of lending out such money to the banks lay in this Term Auction Facility.

Using the Term Auction Facility TAF, the Fed set up a system to auction out term funds to interested banking institutions. Any bank or credit union that already was able to borrow money via the primary credit program had eligibility to be a participant in these TAF Fed auctions.

The Fed was willing to accept bad loans as collateral for these funds. At every TAF auction, the Fed loaned out a set amount of money. They utilized the auction process starting with minimum bid rates in order to set the interest rates on these loan facilities. Banks could participate in the bidding process via phone through their local area Reserve Banks. The last of these TAF auctions occurred back on March 8 of 2010.

For the nearly three years that it ran, the Term Auction Facility worked according to a set out regular process. On a two weekly basis, the Federal Reserve would decide on the amount of money which it would then loan out on any given day. They would determine the minimum interest rate at which they would consent to loan out the funds. Banks which were interested in extra funds could then make bids for the dollar amount of money they wished to obtain at the interest rate they would agree to pay. Next the Federal Reserve sorted out the various competing bids by the level of interest rate that each participating bank offered them.

The Fed started with the greatest interest rate and then went on down from there, adding up the totals of money requested until they reached the maximum dollar amount which they were willing to lend out. Interest rates on each loan equaled the lowest interest rate which had been offered by the banks that had bids accepted.

The Fed was willing to do this so that there would not be funding shortfalls at a single institution which might cause the circular flow of credit and money in the whole American banking system to seize up and stop. In reality, most of the banks who borrowed from the Fed through the Term Auction Facility ended up leaving this money in their accounts with the Federal Reserve.

The Term Auction Facility served a useful purpose as the Federal Reserve Bank was willing to offer loans to member banks at rates that were lower than the associated market rates in exchange for putting up collateral in the form of bad loans that no one else would accept. On March 11, 2009, the banks had drawn total credit in the amount of $493.145 billion. The balance sheet of the Fed swelled to nearly a trillion dollars worth of collateral at its maximum extent.

In the end, the program proved to be successful for increasing confidence the banks had in each other, even though they did not loan out these borrowed funds generally. The TAF was originally intended to be more temporary than it turned out to be. Bernanke never envisioned it reaching the trillion dollar mark by June of 2008. All TAF funds have been repaid without taxpayers having to subsidize any of these loans which the Fed issued to the various banks.

Trans Pacific Partnership (TPP)

The Trans Pacific Partnership TPP represents a trade agreement that has been put together by twelve countries with borders on the Pacific Rim. Participants signed the final version of the deal in Auckland, New Zealand on February 4, 2016. This signing culminated the end of seven long years of negotiating the treaty. In order to enter into effect, the treaty must be ratified by the member states' legislatures. This includes the U.S. Congress, where opposition to the treaty has been intense and bipartisan from many members of both parties.

There are 30 different chapters to the Trans Pacific Partnership. Their goal is to encourage job creation and retention, economic growth, innovation, higher living standards, competitiveness and productivity, poverty reduction, better government and transparency, and better protection of the environment and labor. This TPP is made up of agreements that reduce tariff and non tariff barriers to trade. It also creates a means of resolving disputes through investor state settlement.

Originally the Trans Pacific Partnership was born from the Trans Pacific Strategic Economic Partnership Agreement that Singapore, New Zealand, Chile, and Brunei signed back in 2005. Starting in 2008, other nations on the Pacific Rim began to discuss a wider arrangement. This included The United States, Vietnam, Peru, Mexico, Malaysia, Japan, Canada, and Australia. This increased the nations who were a part of the trade negotiations to 12 countries.

Previously in force trade agreements of the countries participating will be amended to not conflict with the TPP. Deals that offer better free trade will still be in effect. The Obama administration looks at the TPP as a pair of treaties. Its twin is the still under discussion TTIP Transatlantic Trade and Investment Partnership between the European Union and the United States. The two deals are generally similar.

The original goal of the talks was to conclude negotiations in the year 2012. The final deal stretched on for another three years because of conflicts over difficult issues like intellectual property, agriculture, investments, and services. The 12 nations at last came to an agreement on October 5, 2015.

The U.S. Obama administration has made implementing this TPP one of its principle goals for trade. On November 5, 2015, President Obama announced to Congress he would sign the deal and released a public version of the treaty for any interested American individuals and organizations to review. The U.S. President along with the other 11 leaders all signed the TPP February 4, 2016.

In order for the Trans Pacific Partnership to take effect, all of the signors have to ratify it within two years. In case it is not completely ratified by all parties in advance of the February 4, 2018 deadline, there is an alternative arrangement. It will become effective after minimally 6 signing countries with a combined GDP of greater than 85% of all the signing countries ratify it. This means that the U.S. must ratify if for it to ever take effect.

Other countries may be able to join the trade block in the future. Countries that have shown an interest in joining include South Korea, India, Bangladesh, Cambodia, Indonesia, Laos, Thailand, Colombia, the Philippines, and Taiwan. South Korea did not get involved with the original 2006 agreement. The U.S. invited it to join after South Korea and America concluded their own free trade agreements. South Korea is likely to be the first country to join in a next wave expansion of the group. First it will have to work through TPP treaty issues in agriculture and vehicle manufacturing.

Transatlantic Trade Investment Partnership (TTIP)

The Transatlantic Trade and Investment partnership represents a U.S. and European agreement for mutual trade and investment. In essence it is a free trade deal that the two economic superpowers are working to ratify. The two parties began the initiative in the June of 2013 G8 meeting. U.S. President Obama, European Commission President Barroso, and European Union Council President Van Rompuy introduced the idea and began working on the project.

The goal of the TTIP is to encourage both trade and investment. Governments on both sides believe that this will result in more economic growth and jobs for citizens of both sides of the Atlantic Ocean. Negotiations have been complex and mostly held in secret. The U.S. side is headed by the USTR, or Office of the United States Trade Representative. The Europeans are led by the European Commission. This EC handles negotiations for all 28 EU member countries.

TTIP turns out to be the largest and grandest vision for a trade agreement that has ever been attempted. This is because the United States and European Union economic blocks make up nearly fifty percent of the GDP of the entire world. The impacts on trade are expected to be substantial. Small to medium sized enterprises will gain several benefits in access to the new markets. They will have other countries to which they can export. They will also gain the ability to import input materials from other countries. It is anticipated they will have the ability to gain investments in their businesses at a cheaper, better price as well.

Consumers are supposed to benefit also. Lower prices are expected in both economic blocks because of the reduced tariffs and increased competition. This will improve the purchasing power of residents on both sides of the Atlantic and also help to create more jobs.

Twenty-four different chapters comprise the actual Transatlantic Trade and Investment Partnership. These have been divided into three principal topics. The topics are Market Access, Rules, and Regulatory Cooperation.

Market Access pertains to opening up markets. The goal is to allow for improved competition. Besides this, the architects of the agreement are trying to make it easier for products to flow back and forth across the Atlantic.

The rules section has to do with trade and investment. This area's goal is to increase the fairness and ease of importing, exporting, and investing for American businesses in Europe and European businesses in America. Rules cover a number of different important concepts. These include Energy and Raw Materials, Sustainable Development, Small and Medium Sized Enterprises, Customs and Trade Facilitation, Competition, Investment Protection, Geographical Indications, Intellectual Property, and the Government to Government Dispute Settlements.

The area of Regulatory Cooperation pertains to important regulation differences between the United States and the European Union. Both groups often have the same quality and safety levels that they insist on from specific goods. The problem is that each side employs its own procedures in considering the identical product. This imposes high costs on companies who produce the items. It can be prohibitively expensive for smaller to medium sized businesses.

There have been a number of objections raised by protestors to this free trade agreement, particularly in Europe. Many individuals on both sides of the Atlantic oppose the secrecy that surrounds the negotiations. The protesters have concerns that interest groups are creating special rules for larger companies.

The European labor markets are worried that their working conditions and benefits will suffer. Environmental groups are all concerned that environmental standards and safeties that are higher in Europe will be watered down as a result of the free trade initiative.

Treasury Inflation Protected Securities (TIPS)

Treasury Inflation Protected Securities (TIPS) are a unique and useful form of Treasury issued securities. What makes them special is their expressed and close linkage to inflation levels in their coupon payments. They are set up this way to safeguard investors from the interest destroying impacts of inflation.

TIPS prove to be lower risk investments because they enjoy the expressed and unlimited backing of the U.S. government. Besides this, their par value increases at the same pace as the official rate of inflation as depicted by the CPI Consumer Price Index. The interest rate itself stays fixed with these investments.

The interest earned by these Treasury Inflation Protected Securities pays out twice a year on the same fixed dates. TIPS may be bought directly off of the U.S. government by utilizing the Treasury Direct system. This allows for simple $100 increment purchases of the TIPS in a minimum of only $100 order size. They can be obtained from the site with 30 year, 10 year, and 5 year maturity date options.

Unfortunately for the Treasury Inflation Protected Securities holders, the inflation adjustments of the TIPS bonds fall under the IRS definition of taxable income. This is the case despite the fact that investors do not realize any of those inflation adjusted gains until the point where the bonds mature or they sell out their holdings. Because of this, some investors opt to obtain their TIPS exposure by utilizing a TIPS mutual fund or ETF. Otherwise, they could simply buy and hold them within tax deferred retirement accounts like IRAs. This would save them the tax headaches of having to pay the IRS now on money they will not obtain for possibly years or even decades.

On the other hand, buying TIPS directly means that investors sidestep the costs and fees applied by mutual funds and even ETFs. TIPS bought directly also feature complete exemption from the double or even triple taxation of local income and state income taxes which some investors must pay, depending on where they reside. Residents of Puerto Rico do not have to pay any federal income taxes on these inflation adjusted gains or interest payments because of the Commonwealth's completely unique status which it enjoys within the U.S.

If investors purchased $1,000 worth of TIPS and held them through year end and received one percent coupon rates while there was no CPI measured inflation within the United States, the investors could count on obtaining $10 payments for the entire year in interest payments. Assuming inflation increases by two percent, the principal of the bond would increase by two percent or in this specific instance by $20, to reach a total value of $1,020. The coupon rate would remain locked at one percent, yet it would apply to the entire new principal amount of $1,020 to help the holder receive interest payments of $10.20.

In the extremely unlikely event that deflation reared itself, the bonds would similarly decline in total face value. Should the CPI decline by three percent, the principle would drop by three percent, or $30, resulting in a new par face value of $970 on the formerly $1,000 Treasury bond. This would reduce that next year's interest coupon payments total to $9.70.

When the bonds mature, investors would then get the principal equity which equated either to the $1,000 original par face value, or an applicably higher adjusted principal based on the CPI adjustments higher. Interest payments throughout the life of the bond will be calculated from the principal amount as it rises or falls. This does not apply to the downside if the investors hold their TIPS until they reach maturity. Investors who do not wish to hold their TIPS until this interval can choose to receive a lower amount of principal than the par face value by selling their investment via the secondary bonds market if they so desire.

Troubled Asset Relief Program (TARP)

The Troubled Asset Relief Program is also known by its clever acronym the TARP. This represented a series of national relief programs which the United States Treasury Department developed and administered. They did this to attempt to restore stability to the American financial system, to rebuild economic stability and growth, and to forestall housing foreclosures after the 2008 Global Financial Crisis and Great Recession wrecked the national and Western portion of the global economy. The idea was to buy up threatened firms' equity and toxic assets so that they could continue to operate and make loans.

In the first round, the Troubled Asset Relief Program provided Treasury with an mind boggling $700 billion of purchasing ability with which to purchase the dubious and at that point entirely illiquid MBS mortgage-backed securities as well as additional assets. They were to buy these from systemically important banks and financial institutions with an eye on rebuilding the shattered liquidity of the stricken money markets. It was the congressionally approved Emergency Economic Stabilization Act they passed on October 3rd in 2008 which allowed them to develop the program. With the Dodd-Frank Act for banking reforms, the Congress reduced their $700 billion amount of authorization down to a still-impressive $475 billion.

The series of events that led to this de facto bank bailout originated from the freeze up of the worldwide credit markets that ground to a screeching halt in September of 2008. This became worse as a few of the systemically important financial institutions like American International Group, and the GSE government sponsored enterprises Freddie Mac and Fannie Mae became victims of intense financial trouble. Lehman Brothers' went bankrupt which nearly overthrew the global financial system. At the same time Goldman Sachs and Morgan Stanley altered their charters to evolve into commercial banks which provided them with the backing of the FDIC Federal Deposit Insurance Corporation. This did stabilize the attacks on their two market capitalizations and shore up their capital positions, though it required some time to have effect.

It was with the Troubled Asset Relief Program that the government through the U.S. Treasury was finally able to buy up the root of the crisis, the Mortgage-backed securities. In decreasing the possible unknown toxic asset losses from the financial institutions which held them, they saved the banking system in not only the United States but likely the entire Western world.

Critics of the Troubled Asset Relief Program called it the largest bank bailout scheme in the history of the world. Without these cash infusions into the important national banks throughout the U.S. though, they would have been unable to continue operating at all. When the program had successfully stabilized the banking system and the too big too fail, systemically all-important banks, and the market had sufficiently calmed down, TARP was allowed to expire on October 3rd of 2010.

Treasury utilized the TARP funds wisely and well. They deployed some of them to make loans, others to invest in companies in need of cash infusions, and still more to guarantee toxic assets like the MBS. They received bonds or shares off of the collapsing financial companies and banks in consideration for this accommodation. The first program was known as the Capital Repurchase Program. In this initiative, Treasury purchased preferred shares of stock in eight major banks. These included Citigroup, Bank of America/Merrill Lynch, Goldman Sachs, Morgan Stanley, Bank of New York Mellon, Wells Fargo, J.P. Morgan Chase, and State Street Bank.

The banks had to provide the government with a full five percent dividend return which had to increase to nine percent in 2013. This gave the banks huge incentive to purchase back their own stock from Treasury before the conclusion of the five year windows. Then-Treasury Secretary Hank Paulson understood the government would make money off of the program in the end as he believed the stock prices of the banks would rebound at least somewhat by or before 2013.

Four other groups and entities would have collapsed without additional help from the Troubled Asset Relief Program and Treasury. Each of these received either direct cash infusions via preferred stock purchases or loans. AIG (the largest insurance company in the world) received $40 billion. Various community banks obtained a collective $92 billion. A number of these did fail in spite of this help. The American Big Three car makers got

$80.7 billion collectively. Bank of America and Citigroup also received an additional $45 billion between them. TARP also loaned out $20 billion to the sister TALF program which the Federal Reserve managed.

Though critics heavily maligned the government for saving the banking system and national banks, the bailout did not cost the government anything by the time it had been concluded. In fact, by May of 2016, the banks had paid the government back all of their principal (collectively, despite some failing anyway) plus $25 billion in profits for a total repayment of $275.04 billion.

Trustee Savings Bank (TSB)

Trustee Savings Bank refers to a now defunct type of British financial institution. It is also known by its acronym TSB. These banks began as savings deposit institutions for those who had only meager financial means. The shares of these banks were not stock market exchange traded. Rather they were something like the mutually owned building societies of Great Britain. A key difference between the two types of financial institutions was that the depositors of the TSB's did not have any voting rights or ability to direct the organization's managerial or financial goals and direction.

In consequence for a lack of owner-voting rights, the boards of directors for the Trustee Savings Banks were appointed as volunteer basis trustees. This explains where the name for the TSB's came from in the first place. Reverend Henry Duncan from Ruthwell in Dumfriesshire established Britain's very first TSB in Scotland. He set this up to help out his poorest members of the congregation in 1810. The only reason for the organization lay in serving the local community members.

During the inter-war years a hundred years later, the Trustee Savings Bank model demonstrated that it could effectively compete throughout the retail banking model market with the major commercial banks and building societies throughout the nation. At one point by 1919, these types of financial institutions counted an impressive 100 million British pounds in combined deposits and assets. This amount reached 162 million pounds by 1929 and an incredible 292 million pounds at the outbreak of the Second World War in 1939.

Despite enjoying two centuries of success and growth as independent institutions, the Trustee Savings Banks became combined into one financial institution called the TSB Group plc from the years 1970 to 1985. Their stock traded on the famed London Stock Exchange until 1995 when the group merged with the Lloyds Bank to become the enormous conglomeration Lloyds TSB. At that moment, the new Lloyds TSB combined unit represented the largest bank in the United Kingdom by market share. It was second only to HSBC by market capitalization, as HSBC has absorbed Midland Bank in 1992.

The group which now represented the legacy of the Trustee Savings Banks expanded again in 2009 with the acquisition of the HBOS Halifax Bank of Scotland group. Its name changed again to the Lloyds Banking Group at this point. The TSB name was not lost, as the primary retail banking subsidiaries were Lloyds TSB Bank and Lloyds TSB Scotland. Lloyds again resurrected the TSB name and brand when it divested the 632 branches from Scotland, Gloucester, Cheltenham, and some of the Welsh and English Lloyds TSB bank branches into the TSB Bank plc.

The new operation came into being on September of 2013 and underwent an IPO initial public offering during 2014. The rest of the Lloyds Banking Group changed its name back to Lloyds Bank. This spin off happened because the Lloyd's Banking Group had to be bank rescued by Her Majesty's Government. Thanks to the 43.4% government stake in the group as a result of the Global Financial Crisis, European Union state aid rules required that it spin off a portion of the business.

Trustee Savings Bank plc did not continue for long as an independent entity. It began life in 2013 with a national network of 631 bank branches throughout especially Scotland, and also England and Wales. They counted over 4.6 million customers as well as more than 20 billion British pounds worth of customer deposits and loans. The group had its headquarters in Edinburgh, Scotland.

As the reestablished TSB, the group had a listing on the London Stock Exchange and remained a member of the FTSE 250 index of British based companies until it received and accepted a takeover bid from Spanish-based bank Sabadell. Sabadell made its offer for TSB Bank in March of 2015 and completed the acquisition of the last remaining Trustee Savings Bank on July 8, 2015. TSB Bank still operates as a wholly owned subsidiary of Sabadell, so the TSB brand name remains.

Uniform Commercial Code (UCC)

The UCC is the acronym for Uniform Commercial Code. This set of standardized rules arose as a means of covering the majority of United States' based commercial transactions. This code does not represent official national law. Yet the potency of it lies in the fact that the majority of American states have chosen to adopt the UCC in some variation. This makes the code legally binding in all but one of the state jurisdictions throughout the U.S. It is safe to say this means most locations in the country.

It also means the Uniform Commercial Code is confusing, as in any given state, interested parties must research it to uncover how that particular jurisdiction has chosen to interpret the code and implement its policy guidelines. In most locales, it lays out the best practices and rules which govern consumer protection regulations, goods' sales, and those commercial transactions which occur between financial institutions (primarily banks and credit card processors) and merchants. The code has a variety of goals, yet one of the most important is to create transparency so that individuals who engage in business at any place in the United States will understand what they can anticipate from other businesses. It also provides them with guidelines on how they should conduct themselves in business in general.

In general though, the intentions of this code center on reducing conflicts and opaqueness between the various laws of states regarding sales and trade. As such, the UCC covers nine separate articles. Among the significant variety of topics it addresses are bank instruments, selling of goods, letters of credit, negotiable instruments, bills of receipts, investment securities, bulk transfers, and secure transactions. Such regulations and guidelines also attempt to reduce the complexity of any and all relevant commercial paper transactions. This would include the ways that checks become processed. The code makes a valid point of distinguishing the differences between consumers who do not understand business well and merchants who must grasp it thoroughly.

Louisiana is now the lone state in the country that has not adopted the overwhelming majority of the Uniform Commercial Code. The reason is because the state of Louisiana still clings to its civil law system which dates back to the early French Napoleonic Code and their lonely tradition as a French colony. This means that they refuse to update their regulations on selling goods. There are some state laws in Louisiana that work hand in glove with the ideas set out in the UCC, yet it is important to realize that this does not mean all of them do.

The Uniform Commercial Code proves to be critically necessary precisely because commerce is hard to consistently regulate in a realm as enormous as the U.S. is. Clearly goods will typically have a point of origin in one side of the nation, be sold in another state and region, then finally become used in a third state or region. When all of the states possess their own rules, regulations, and laws, it becomes confusing and costly for firms to engage in business around the country.

This UCC originally became drafted back in the 1940s decade. The NCCUSL National Conference of Commissioners of Uniform State Laws dating back to 1892 jointly sponsored it with their fellow organization the 1923-originating ALI American Law Institute. While neither groups can claim to make laws, they each possess a vast respect and influence in national and statewide legislations. Professionals and lawyers from all American territories and states receive appointment to the NCCUSL to determine which laws throughout the nation ought to be the same. The ALI is made up of judges and lawyers from the whole of the United States who seek to clarify and explain the common laws in America based upon the changing needs of society.

Unique Selling Proposition (USP)

A Unique Selling Proposition, or USP, refers to the slogan or idea that sets apart the particular company's products, goods, and services from their main business competition. It is typically expressed by a single, often short, sentence which succinctly sums up the point and purpose of the company's primary line of business. Another way of putting this is that the USP acts as the overriding theme of a firm's marketing plan and endeavors. Ultimately, this proposition strives to answer the customers' query of why they should purchase a given company's products instead of their competitors' goods.

It is critical that the Unique Selling Proposition offers customers and possible customers alike a precise and well-defined benefit which appeals to them directly. This means that the USP can not simply describe better service or that which offers more value. Instead, the proposition should answer two questions directly. The first is what will set apart a service or product from those the competition offers? The second is what can the product offer that consumers determine to be worthwhile or worthy of spending their money on it?

Small businesses in particular find the Unique Selling Proposition critical for their ongoing operations. This is because they must compete against both larger retail corporations as well as other smaller businesses like themselves. It does not matter how superior a given product or service may be if consumers are not aware of its value and do not see a viable reason to purchase it over those which the competition offers them.

The history of the Unique Selling Proposition dates back to the middle years of the twentieth century. It was then that Rosser Reeves developed the concept. He was an American advertising executive who operated in the depression, Second World War, and post world war eras of the United States. Reeves held a personal conviction about the point of advertising. He felt that its only reason for being lay in conveying the specific slogan of a firm which got across their service or product message effectively.

He fiercely believed that such a slogan should never be changed. Among his best known USPs Reeves developed was one for candy maker

Mars/M&M's. This M&M's candy slogan so memorably claimed, "The milk chocolate melts in your mouth, not in your hands."

There have been countless effective other Unique Selling Propositions throughout modern marketing history. Some of the most effective are the ones consumers never forget. Hallmark Corporation's USP is "When you care enough to send the very best." Subway sandwiches are memorably referred to as "Subs with under six grams of fat." The Men's Warehouse has its, "You're going to like the way you look – I guarantee it." FedEx Corporation claims effectively, "When it absolutely, positively has to get there overnight."

Some Unique Selling Propositions became so well remembered that they are even remembered years after a company chooses to abandon them for some reason. Wendy's Hamburger chain, Taco Bell, and Dr. Pepper represent three classic examples of companies which had a USP that embodied this multi-generational slogan appeal. Wendy's famously asked Americans, "Where's the beef?" for years before finally moving on with other far less memorable selling propositions. Taco Bell's little Chihuahua Dinky emphatically claimed, "Yo quiero taco bell!" and "Bless you, Taco Bell" for literally years. Dr. Pepper /7 Up Corporation famously reminded Americans for many decades that their flagship American iconic soft drink Dr. Pepper really is "Just what the Dr. ordered."

According to the strict insistence of USP creator Rosser Reeves, all of these companies broke his cardinal rule of changing slogans which were wildly successful. Many of them paid the price in their subsequent decline in business brand appeal and resulting falling sales and profits.

Universal Basic Income (UBI)

Universal basic income (UBI) is known by a variety of names in different countries and continents. Among the more popular are basic income, citizen's income, unconditional basic income, basic income guarantee, universal demo grant, and UBI. This represents a type of social security welfare program and safety net. In it, all residents or citizens of a nation periodically receive an amount of money which the government or another public institution gives them unconditionally. They receive this on top of and regardless of any other income they earn from work or investment returns. When the money is given out to any persons who live with less than the government-mandated poverty line, it is also known as partial basic income.

This universal basic income and its distribution systems could be financed by the revenues and turnover of publically owned enterprises. These are many times referred to as a citizen's dividend or a social dividend. Such a strategy is a component of a market socialism model, as opposed to market capitalism in which participants' incomes are based on their abilities, hard work, and opportunities. Taxation is another means of paying for such basic income schemes.

It was Thomas Paine's _Agrarian Justice_ published in 1795 where he wrote about capital grants to be provided at the age of majority that began the debates concerning universal basic income within the United States. Up through the year 1986, the phrase which referred to this basic income concept most commonly was "social dividend." After that year, the universal basic income wording gained universal appeal. There are many well-known proponents of the social and economic philosophy. Among them are Ailsa McKay, Philippe Van Parijs, Hillel Steiner, Andre Gorz, Guy Standing, and Peter Vallentyne.

In the United States, this Universal Basic Income has been discussed on a number of different occasions as a serious idea for public policy. The numbers which have been bandied about for Americans amount to approximately $1,000 per month, which would be sent via check to every American. Among the conservatives who espoused the concept and argued for it to be implemented were legendary Nobel prize-winning economist Milton Friedman and former Republican President Richard Nixon.

The base case for this Universal Basic Income has been most effectively argued and written extensively about by Andy Stern, who was once the Service Employees International Union president and who serves as a Columbia University professor since then. He published a book called _Raising the Floor_ in which he argued dramatically and effectively for the UBI.

Stern argues that the concept of a basic guaranteed income has become more necessary for two reasons. On the one hand, the wars on poverty programs have not been so effective nationally. On the other, the rapid advance of technology has led to unparalleled job dislocation and disruption for millions of American workers. This program would deliver an effective floor, or social safety net, to every American.

Critics of the plan in the U.S. have asked how the Federal Government would possibly afford to pay for this proposed program. Stern referenced the 126 existing separate government programs which each already distribute money to American citizens. Some of these might be rolled into the Universal Basic Income program. Besides this, additional taxes would have to be introduced in order to make the proposal a reality. Economists have predicted that implementing such a UBI would require around $3 trillion each year in funding.

Despite the fact that this concept has many critics, it is also possibly the only significant ideology in the early twenty-first century which has supporters on both the right and the left sides of the political, economic, and social spectrum.

The Swiss were given a vote on the UBI issue for their own country in the late spring of 2016, and they soundly rejected it. Interestingly though, the same voters answered an exit poll claiming they expected to see this policy implemented in Switzerland within the next 25 years.

Value-Added Tax (VAT)

Value-Added Tax (VAT) turns out to be a kind of tax on consumption which governments place on all products. What makes this different from a sales tax is that whenever any value becomes added along the stages of production as well as at the final register, the VAT tax is applied.

These Value-Added Tax fees are commonly utilized within the European Union which is also the heaviest user of them in the world. The total VAT which end-users pay proves to be the difference between the product's cost minus the materials' cost which were utilized in making the product (which have already been taxed).

A good example to look at is a television set constructed by a manufacturer in Germany. The maker pays VAT on each of the various components it buys in order to produce the TV. After the set arrives in stores, the individuals who buy it must also pay the appropriate amount of Value-Added Tax.

Value-Added Tax is not based on income as with other forms of taxes. Rather it relies on the amount of goods which consumers purchase and consume. Over 160 different nations rely on VAT for at least partial funding of government budgets. The United States is strangely absent from this list of well over 75 percent of the countries on earth.

Advocates for implementing a VAT in the U.S. argue that by replacing the present inefficient income tax system in America with such a national VAT, this would offer numerous advantages. Among these are that it would lower the national deficit and debt, pay for critical social services, and boost government revenues.

Critics of the Value-Added Tax for the U.S. claim that such a tax is inherently regressive. This means that it would require the poor and low income workers to shoulder a greater economic burden and responsibility for funding the government outlays.

Both sides of the debate are in fact correct. In the advantages column, such a Value-Added Tax would bring in massive revenues on every product which traditional American stores, businesses, and Internet-based businesses sell. This would be a boon for government coffers that typically miss out on sales taxes which can not be levied on businesses that avoid sales taxes with customers (in those states where the businesses do not have any physical offices). It would collect presently unpaid billions in taxes from online sales that could be deployed then to pay for law enforcement, schools, and many other social services. Besides this, a VAT would ensure it is far harder to avoid paying taxes. It would further simplify the complicated and bureaucratic federal tax regulations so that the Internal Revenue Service could be massively downsized and made more efficient at the same time.

There are also a number of possible downsides to the VAT, per opponents of the concept. Business owners would suffer from higher costs all along the chain of goods production. A national VAT would also cause potential disputes between the Federal government and those many local and state governments which already charge sales tax rates set on local and statewide levels.

Critics also correctly point out that the consumers bear the ultimate brunt of the tax in the form of higher consumer goods prices, thanks to a VAT. The theory is that the burden of the tax spreads out through each phase of making goods from inputs to the ultimate product. The reality is that higher costs are nearly always passed off on the poor consumers.

As VAT applies equally to all purchases and for all types of salary and wage earners throughout the jurisdiction in which it applies, this would harm lower wage workers than higher ones. Higher wage earners are able to save massive percentages of their income, which would then not be taxed. Lower wage earners live from paycheck to paycheck. As they spend all of their earnings each month, their share of the VAT tax would be proportionally far higher than the wealthy Americans' share.

War Production Board (WPB)

The War Production Board, or WPB, proved to be a one time agency of the United States Federal Government which was established to order and oversee World War II production and materials procurement from January of 1942 by an executive order of the then-President Franklin D. Roosevelt.

The chairman of the board obtained broad and wide ranging powers over the economic output and production of the entire United States economy, factories, and facilities. Two different men served as chair of this important war effort board. Donald M. Nelson served from 1942 to 1944. He was succeeded by final Chair Julius A. Krug from 1944 to 1945.

The War Production Board expanded the national peace time economy and converted it to serve in the ultimate production of weapons of war to assist the young men who fought in Europe and the Pacific theaters. Controls were established that gave priority of production to such scarce materials delivery and which prohibited industrial activities that were then deemed to be less significant or unimportant to the war efforts.

The board may only have existed and operated effectively for three years, but in this span of time, it directed or oversaw the production of an astonishing $185 billion in supplies and weapons. This represented fully 40 percent of all munitions and ammunition production in the world during the years of the Second World War. By way of comparison, Great Britain, Russia, and all the other allies combined produced 30 percent of all war materials while all of the Axis powers including the Nazis and Japanese only managed to produce 30 percent of war time materials.

It was on January 16, 1942 that President Franklin D. Roosevelt created the War Production Board by implementing an Executive Order numbered 9024. This new WPB then replaced the Supply Priorities and Allocation Board as well as the Office of Production Management. It started by rationing important and limited commodities such as heating oil, gasoline, rubber, metals like copper and aluminum, steel, plastics, and paper.

As such the WPB was converting industries from peacetime production to wartime output, creating important national priorities in distributing services and goods, and stopping all non important production nationwide. The board became dissolved at the conclusion of the war with the final defeat of the Japanese in 1945. The Civilian Production Administration then replaced it in an effort to reconvert production back to a normal market forces controlled peace time economy in late 1945.

Thanks to the efficiency of this board, the war effort in both Europe and the Pacific proved to be ultimately successful. The chairman and his council decided to channel production into a set military hardware production and distribution. This led to a quarter of all national output going into the production of warplanes, while another quarter became allocated to naval warships. Other munitions and civilian needs comprised the balance 50 percent of national production and output.

The War Production Board proved to be so effective on a national and local scale because it operated through 12 regional offices as well as over 120 field offices scattered throughout the country. There were also statewide war production boards that worked hand in glove with the federal board. The state boards kept critical records on state levels of war production facilities and factories. They assisted state based businesses in obtaining loans and war production contracts.

This board also engaged in patriotic propaganda efforts to rally American citizens around the war effort. They had slogans such as "Give us your scrap metal to help the Oklahoma boys save our way of life." It created important national efforts like nationwide scrap metal drives that happened on local levels all throughout the United States with impressive results. As an example, the national scrap metal drive from October of 1942 produced so much metal that it amounted to almost 82 pounds of scrap metal on average per American.

Weighted Average Cost of Capital (WACC)

Weighted average cost of capital (WACC) refers to a calculation of the cost of a capital for a company. It involves every category of the company's capital being weighed proportionately. Each source of capital for the relevant corporation will be considered by this designation. This means that preferred and common stock, bonds and all types of longer-term debt will all be included in the WACC calculation. It will go up with the rate of return on equity and beta increases. When the WACC increases, this means that the risk has increased while the valuation for a firm has decreased.

Calculating weighted average cost of capital requires taking each part of the capital components and multiplying them by their appropriate proportional weight. These individual calculations are then added together to come up with the WACC.

Companies can finance their needs through one of two main types of funding. This is either via equity issuing in the form of primarily stock shares or through debt issuance as with bonds. This measurement actually weights appropriately the two main forms of corporate financing, with each weighted according to its relevant utilization in a particular situation. It allows companies and analysts to decide how much every dollar they are financing will cost them in interest, making it imminently practical.

The reasons this is important are evident. The holders of equity and lenders of a corporation will demand specific minimal returns on their capital or lent money they have delivered. This is why WACC proves to be so useful. It shows the cost of capital for both the stake holders (as equity owners) and the lenders (as the debt holders). This means that both groups will be able to understand the levels and amounts in returns they can anticipate receiving. Another way of looking at the weighted average cost of capital is that this is the opportunity cost of any investor for assuming the risk which investing in the corporation entails.

A firm's WACC represents the all around return on capital for the company. This means that the directors of the corporation will commonly utilize the numbers internally to make appropriate decisions for the organization. Such decisions might include evaluating opportunities for expanding the business or the financial practicality of engaging in an acquisition or a merger.

It is helpful to consider examples to best understand this complex concept of weighted average cost of capital. Assume that a corporation is a money pond. Money comes into this pond out of two separate streams which are the sources. These streams represent the equity and the debt of the company. Money which the daily business operations bring in does not count as another source. The reason for this logic is that once a firm pays down its debt, any remaining money that they do not pay out as dividends or for share buybacks becomes what analysts call retained earnings held in trust for the shareholders.

Consider lenders that want eight percent return for their funds they loaned to a given company. At the same time, the stakeholders possessing the stock share may want a minimum 16 percent return on their investments or they will not hold onto the shares of the company. This means that the projects which the corporation funds using its money pond will need to provide an annual recurring return of 12 percent so that both their lenders and equity holders will remain happy. This 12 percent represents the weighted average cost of capital.

Going back to our original example of the money pond, if it contained $100 in debt holder money and $100 in investments from shareholders, the company might invest $200 in one of its projects. They would then require an annual return of 12 percent total, or $24 from the project funded by the pond. This would mean that $16 of this return was for the share holders while $8 of the total return was for the debt holders.

World Trade Organization (WTO)

The World Trade Organization, or WTO, proves to be an organization that is intergovernmental in scope and signatories. Its ultimate purpose is to regulate international trade. This WTO began in 1995 on January 1 under the auspices of the Marrakesh Agreement that 123 different nations signed on April 15th of 1994. It then replaced the preexisting General Agreement on Tariffs and Trade, or GATT that had begun functioning from 1948.

The World Trade Organization handles the legal regulating of trade between those nations that participate. It does this via a framework that helps to negotiate trade agreements and resolve disputes, all the while enforcing the obedience of participating members to the agreements of the WTO (which member nation governmental representatives have previously signed). Their parliaments or congresses had to ratify the signatories as well. The majority of the issues which the WTO itself concentrates on come from prior trading negotiations, particularly from the lengthy Uruguay Round which went on from the years of 1986 through 1994.

The World Trade Organization has long struggled to finalize negotiations on what is now referred to as the Doha Development Round. They launched this latest endeavor back in 2001 to concentrate on the developing nations of the world. Its future remained uncertain as the 21 subjects whose deadline expired in 2005 continued to stymie participants of the trade regulating organization.

Among the major obstacles were the arguments between free trading of industrial goods and associated services while still keeping farm subsidies for the agricultural sector (which developed nations insisted on), as well as the fleshing out of fair trade rules on agricultural products (insisted on by developing nations). These obstacles ensured that no further negotiations or initiatives could be launched to go beyond the Doha Development Round.

The present day Director General of the World Trade Organization turns out to be Roberto Azevedo. He heads a staff of more than 600 individuals based in Geneva, Switzerland. The first comprehensive arrangement which the member states agreed upon was the Bali Package, a facilitation of trade agreement. They finally signed off on this on December 7th of 2013.

The immediate predecessor to the World Trade Organization was the GATT General Agreement on Tariffs and Trade. The member states of the world established this group following the conclusion of the Second World War. This occurred as part of the marathon cooperation efforts of the victors of the world war. They were dedicated to expanding the cooperation in spheres of international economics to help rebuild the devastated world.

Among these organizations which have stood the test of time are both the International Monetary Fund, or IMF, and the World Bank. The negotiators attempted to set up a similar international group to focus on trade and trading rules called the ITO International Trade Organization at that time. It never got off the ground effectively since the United States and several other signatories never approved it. This left the GATT to gradually evolve into the eventual de facto world trade organization.

By the 1980s, the GATT was struggling to adapt to the increasingly globalizing and expanding world economy. The member states came to the conclusion that the existing system would not suffice to deal with problems of this brave new world order. This was the reason they launched the eighth GATT round of talks which eventually became famous under the name of the Uruguay Round. These were held in Punta del Este, Uruguay.

It represented the largest mandate to negotiate trade in the history of the world (which actually was mutually agreed upon and signed). It covered an expansion of trade system ideals into intellectual property and services trade. The Marrakesh Agreement finally emerged from the last ministerial meeting held in Marrakesh, Morocco. Fully 60 different agreements, decisions, annexes, and understanding became adopted as a result. This led to the eventual creation of the WTO.

XAU Precious Metals Index

The XAU precious metals index proves to be a stock shares index which trades on the United States' based Philadelphia Stock Exchange. This index is comprised of 29 different precious metals mining firms. Though there are 29 participants in the index, the index is heavily dominated by only the three largest of them. These three overwhelming players are mega-gold mining companies Barrack-Placer, Newmont Mining, and Anglo Gold Ashanti. Between the three of them, they represent over half of the entire index.

As of May 5, 2017, the 29 companies comprising the XAU precious metals index were as follows: Agnico Eagle Mines Limited, Anglo Gold Ashanti Limited, Barrick Gold Corporation, Coeur Mining Incorporated, Compania de Minas Buenaventura, El Dorado Gold Corporation, First Majestic Silver Corporation, Freeport-McMoran Incorporated, Gold Fields Limited, Gold Resource Corporation, Goldcorp Incorporated, Harmony Gold Mining Company Limited, Hecla Mining Company, Iamgold Corporation, Kinross Gold Corporation, McEwen Mining, New Gold Incorporated, Newmont Mining Corporation, Nova Gold Resources Incorporated, Pan American Silver Corporation, Primero Mining Corporation, Rand Gold Resources Limited, Royal Gold Incorporated, Sandstorm Gold Limited, Sea Bridge Gold, Silver Standard Resources Incorporated, Silver Wheaton Corporation, Still Water Mining, and Yamana Gold Incorporated.

Back in 2006, the Philadelphia Stock Exchange expanded its XAU precious metals index and grew the exposure beyond the traditional North American, British, South African, and Australian based miners to include significant exposure to Eastern Europe, South America, and Russia. They did this by adding in another four mid cap and small cap companies that had gold mining properties in those three parts of the world. At the same time, Placer Dome was acquired by Barrick Gold and became removed from the index.

The four new companies which they added to this important precious metals index were Royal Gold Incorporated, Rand Gold Resources Limited, Couer D' Alene Mines Corporation, and Bema Gold Corporation. Bema Gold Corporation was later acquired by Kinross Gold Corporation and subsequently became delisted from the XAU precious metals index. It is not terribly surprising that Canadian Bema Gold Corporation was taken over, as even in the heyday of rising gold prices back in 2005, Bema proved to be an anomaly in the gold mining world as it represented one of the only gold companies on earth to lose money in the booming gold price days of the mid 2000's.

The development of adding additional gold mining company exposure to Russia, Eastern Europe, South America, and Australia came about because of geographical leadership changes in both the gold and silver mining industries. The XAU precious metals index has long been the most closely studied and heavily watched bell weather of gold mining company shares. It outperformed the overall stock markets in the first five years of the new millennium, and managed to triple in market cap and overall share pricing from 2001 to 2005.

The Philadelphia Stock Exchange allows trading of the XAU precious metals index every Monday through Friday from 9:30am until 4pm local Philadelphia time. This index has only one serious rival in the world of gold mining companies' indices. This is the HUI Index listed as the AMEX Gold BUGS Index. The two indices represent the world's most closely followed precious metals composites.

There has occasionally been some confusion with the name XAU precious metals index. This is because XAU also denotes a single ounce of gold. Thanks to the ISO 4217 currency standard, the symbol became representative of the yellow metal itself.

Yield to Maturity (YTM)

Yield to Maturity is also widely known in investment and analyst circles by its acronym YTM, as well as by the phrases book yield and redemption yield. This represents the aggregate return which investors can expect to receive for a bond if they keep the security until the end of its actual life. This is why YTM is generally called a longer term bond yield even though it is still expressed as a rate per year. Another way of saying this is that this proves to be the investment's internal rate of return for the bond if the owner keeps it all the way through maturity. This assumes of course that the bond issuer makes all of its payments both on time and in the full amounts contracted.

In order to understand the Yield to Maturity calculations, it is critical to realize that the formula assumes all coupon payments the issuer makes will be exactly reinvested for the rate of the current yield of the bond. The formula similarly considers the bond's par value, current price on the market, term to maturity, and coupon interest rate. All of this makes the YTM a complicated yet good formula for determining the return of a bond. It allows investors to effectively compare and contrast those bonds which possess varying coupon rates and maturity dates.

There are several different ways to figure out the Yield to Maturity. It is a complicated formula so many investors simply fall back on pre-printed and -figured bond yield tables. Determining the exact YTM requires either a software program or the use of a financial or business calculator. This is because the value for a basis point drops as the price for a bond increases in an inverse manner. Many firms actually calculate YTM for six month time frames as well as on an annual basis. They do this because most coupon payments take place twice per year.

A significant difference between Yield to Maturity and the current yield lies in the fact that the YTM takes into account money's time value, while the simplified current yield computations will not. This is why investors often prefer to utilize the YTM instead of the current yield when they are crunching number on bond returns to compare and contrast with other bond issues and different types of investments.

There are a number of similar yet still variations on the classical Yield to Maturity figure. These should never be confused with the true YTM. Among these are the Yield to call (YTC), Yield to put (YTP), and the Yield to worst (YTW). Yields to call go with the assumption that the bond issuer will recall the bond by repurchasing it in advance of it reaching maturity. This assumes that the resulting cash flow period will be shortened. Yield to put is much like the YTC, only the seller is allowed to and may sell the bond back to its issuer on a specific date for a pre-determined price. Finally, Yield to worst means that the bonds in question can be put, called, or even exchanged. This is why YTW bonds usually have the smallest yields from the three variations on YTM and the YTM rate itself.

There are some important limitations to the utility of Yield to Maturity as a measurement for comparing and contrasting various bonds against other bonds and other forms of investment classes as well. With YTM, these calculations never take into account the actual taxes which investors will have to pay on the bonds. This is why YTM is sometimes called the gross redemption yield. These calculations for yield also do not factor in either selling or buying costs for the bonds themselves.

It is also important to keep in mind that YTM is limited by the fact that both it and current yields are estimate calculations. They can not ever be 100 percent accurate or reliable. The true returns will vary with the realized price of a bond when a holder sells it. The prices of such bonds can vary significantly as the market actually determines them (and not the issuer). Such variations in the value of a bond and the price for which it is sold may impact the YTM substantially. They more drastically impact the current yield calculations and measurement in the end.

Zero Balance Account (ZBA)

The zero balance account, also known by its acronym ZBA, refers to the type of checking account which maintains a permanent balance of zero. The account does this through an automatic transfer of funds out of a master account. The amount which transfers over only proves to be sufficient enough to cover any and all checks which other financial institutions present to the bank where the holder's account resides.

Corporations utilize these zero balance accounts in order to draw down excessive balances from separate accounts. It also helps them to keep better and stricter control over amounts they disburse in the ordinary everyday course of business operations.

These accounts will therefore only have a zero balance within them. The only exception to this zero balance account status is when checks are written against them and presented to the bank in question. In this way, companies are able to keep the balances as close to zero for accounts that do not have any reason to hold excessive reserves. The activity in these ZBA's is restricted to only processing payments. This is why they do not maintain any ongoing balances.

Because of this, a larger sum of funds will remain available for the company to deploy. They can instead put them to work in investments and company cash flow purposes rather than keeping low dollar amounts lying idly by in a number of sub-accounts. It does not present a problem when checks must be paid off from these special zero balance accounts, since the electronic clearing system recognizes that these accounts are in fact ZBA's and they will move the necessary funds over from the master account at the financial institution in the precise dollar amount needed to clear the check.

Companies and other organizations can also rely on a zero balance account to fund purchases which employees make with their debit cards. This allows them to carefully monitor all of the financial transactions and any activities which take place on the cards, since the debits must be pre-authorized. This works well for companies and charitable not for profit organizations which are protected by not maintaining any idle funds within the ZBA's.

The debit card transaction will not be approved by the bank which backs them until and unless the requisite funds become available to the account by a transfer from the authorized account representative at the firm or NGO. This means that debit card transactions simply can not be run without prior authorization by the appropriate superior in the organization. Businesses are able to reduce their risks of activities which are not approved of occurring.

This is critically important to especially larger organizations with many employees and numerous sub accounts and associated corporate debit cards. There is no better spending control oversight for these types of situations than the zero balance account. Incidental charges can be monitored throughout the sizeable operations.

Since incidental expenditures are variable in nature, it is harder to fund and control them without such an account. Large companies and not for profits effectively reduce rapid access to the company or charitable funds with these debit cards. In this way, they have put into place the best practices for approval procedures. It ensures that such procedures will be adhered to in advance of a purchase being made by an employee.

As budget monitoring tools, these ZBA's are also ideal. They may be established as one account per department or business operation. This allows the accountants at the company an easy and fast means of monitoring annual, monthly, and even weekly to daily purchases. The company book keepers are also able to effectively track particular shorter term projects and their financial expenditures by utilizing such a ZBA. Projects which are in jeopardy of running significantly and rapidly over budget also benefit from such accounts. The overseers can maintain control of all purchases by requiring proper approval and notification before the charges take place.

The master account of such zero balance accounts is the critical component of this entire concept. As the central operational center for all fund management in the organization, the account will be employed to disperse funds to all ZBA subaccounts as needed. These master accounts typically include other benefits like better interest rates for balances which they hold.

More books by Thomas Herold

www.ingramcontent.com/pod-product-compliance
Lightning Source LLC
Chambersburg PA
CBHW072012230526
45468CB00021B/1206